The Reminiscences

of

ADMIRAL HARRY DONALD FELT

U. S. Navy (Retired)

Volume I

U. S. Naval Institute
Annapolis, Maryland
1974

Preface

Volume I of the reminiscences of Admiral Harry Donald Felt, U. S. Navy (Ret.) covers a series of four interviews with him in the B.O.Q., Makalapa, Pearl Harbor, Hawaii. The interviews were held between 2 March and 7 March 1972 and were conducted by John T. Mason, Jr. for the Oral History Office of the U. S. Naval Institute. They cover the Admiral's career up to the time of his assignment as Commander in Chief, Pacific in 1958.

Volume II will follow and covers the balance of Admiral Felt's naval career to his retirement in 1964.

The Admiral has read the MS for the interviews in this volume and has made some very minor corrections. Otherwise the text stands just as it was transcribed from the tapes.

A subject index has been added for the convenience of the researcher.

ADMIRAL HARRY D. FELT, UNITED STATES NAVY, RETIRED

Admiral Harry Donald Felt was born in Topeka, Kansas but moved to Washington, D. C. when he was ten years old. He entered the U. S. Naval Academy in 1919. Upon graduation, he served five years in battleships and destroyers before reporting for flight training at Pensacola. He was designated a Naval Aviator in 1929 and has been flying naval aircraft regularly ever since. There followed normal tours of aviation duty both aboard ship and ashore.

The beginning of World War II, Pearl Harbor Day, found Lieutenant Commander Felt in command of a carrier-based dive bombing squadron. Shortly thereafter, he was assigned as Carrier Air Group Commander aboard USS SARATOGA. As Air Group Commander he participated in the first offensive action of the war---the occupation of Guadalcanal. During this action he was awarded the Distinguished Flying Cross for heroism and extraordinary achievement in aerial flights against the enemy. A little later, Lieutenant Commander Felt was awarded the Navy Cross for leading an attack by his Air Group on Japanese forces at sea.

There was a break here in his Pacific war service when he went back to the United States in the Operational Training Command for about a year training combat pilots. This was followed by a year in Moscow as a member of the U. S. Military Mission to the Soviet Union, the first naval aviator to serve in this capacity. He then returned to the Pacific in command of the carrier USS CHENANGO, and participated in the Okinawa campaign and the occupation of Japan. For meritorious service in these campaigns, Captain Felt was awarded the Legion of Merit and the Navy Unit Commendation.

After the war, Admiral Felt served in several capacities on the staff of the Chief of Naval Operations. In addition he attended the National War College and served as Chief of Staff of the Naval War College at Newport, Rhode Island. His post war sea duty was both varied and interesting. He commanded the attack carrier USS FRANKLIN D. ROOSEVELT and later served as Commander of the Middle East Force in the Persian Gulf area. As a Flag Officer he commanded an Anti-Submarine Carrier Division and an Attack Carrier Division, and held the post of Vice Chief of Naval Operations.

From April to August 1956 he had command of our mobile and strategically powerful SIXTH FLEET in the Mediterranean, then served for two years as Vice Chief of Naval Operations. On July 31, 1958 he became Commander in Chief, Pacific and "for exceptionally meritorious service..." in that capacity was awarded the Distinguished Service Medal. On July 1, 1964 he was transferred to the Retired List of the U. S. Navy.

Admiral Felt is married to the former Kathryn Cowley of Mobile, Alabama, and they have one son, Lieutenant Commander Donald Linn Felt, USN, also a Naval Aviator.

Navy Office of Information
Internal Relations Division (OI-430)
14 August 1964

ADMIRAL HARRY D. FELT, UNITED STATES NAVY, RETIRED

PERSONAL DATA:

Born: Topeka, Kansas; June 21, 1902
Parents: Harry V. and Grace Johnson Felt (both deceased)
Wife: Kathryn Cowley of Mobile, Alabama
Son: Lieutenant Commander Donald Linn Felt, USN
Education: Public Schools, Goodland, Kansas and Washington, D. C.;
U. S. Naval Academy, BS, 1923; National War College, 1948

PROMOTIONS:

Ensign, June 8, 1923
Lieutenant (jg), June 8, 1926
Lieutenant, May 24, 1931
Lieutenant Commander, June 23, 1938
Commander (T), January 2, 1942
Commander, June 30, 1942
Captain (T), July 15, 1943
Captain to rank from May 1, 1943, August 7, 1947
Rear Admiral (T), January 1, 1951
Rear Admiral to rank from January 1, 1951, May 1, 1953
Vice Admiral to rank from February 7, 1956
Admiral, September 1, 1956
Transferred to the Retired List of USN, July 1, 1964

DECORATION AND MEDALS:

Navy Cross
Distinguished Service Medal
Legion of Merit with Combat "V"
Distinguished Flying Cross
Navy Unit Commendation awarded USS CHENANGO
American Defense Service Medal, Fleet Clasp
American Campaign Medal
Asiatic-Pacific Campaign Medal, four bronze stars
European-African-Middle Eastern Campaign Medal
World War II Victory Medal
Navy Occupation Service Medal, Asia and Europe Clasps
National Defense Service Medal
Korean Service Medal
United Nations Service Medal
Philippine Liberation Ribbon

CITATIONS:

Navy Cross: "For extraordinary heroism and distinguished service as pilot of a plane in action against an enemy surface force northeast of the Solomon Islands on August 24, 1942...Opposed by intense anti-aircraft fire

Adm. H. D. Felt, USN, Ret.

and enemy fighter planes, (he) led an air attack which resulted in the damaging or sinking of an aircraft carrier, the damaging of a heavy enemy cruiser and the sinking of a Japanese destroyer..."

Distinguished Service Medal: "For exceptionally meritorious service ...as Commander in Chief, Pacific, from July 1958 through June 1964. Admiral Felt combined sound judgment and political acumem with an extraordinary ability to command large military forces. During a period of continued turbulence, unrest, and armed conflict in the Pacific Command, marked by a crisis in the Taiwan Straits in 1958, a series of crises in Laos extending from 1960 to the present, and continued turmoil in Vietnam culminating in the current crucial operations against the Viet Cong, he demonstrated exceptional military and deplomatic skill in positioning forces and taking actions to meet the threat of aggression. As United States Military Advisor to the Southeast Asia Treaty Organization (SEATO), Admiral Felt, by his unwavering fairness and objectivity, earned the respect, admiration, and trust of the representatives of all member nations. As the Commander responsible for operations in the largest United States joint military command in the world, he skillfully and impartially used individual service capabilities to maximum advantage, winning the respect and confidence of his Service Component Commanders which has led to the development of balanced forces over ready to thwart threats of aggression..."

Legion of Merit with Combat "V": "For exceptionally meritorious conduct...during operations against enemy Japanese forces near the Ryukyu Islands from May 2 to June 14, 1945. During 36 days of combat air operations conducted under constant threat of hostile air and submarine attack, (he) assisted in the infliction of damage on enemy airfields and defense installations, thereby contributing materially to the conquest of Okinawa...

Distinguished Flying Cross: "For heroism and extraordinary achievement while participating in aerial flight as Air Group Commander during action against enemy ground forces in the Guadalcanal Tulagi Area on August 7-8, 1942..."

Navy Unit Commendation: "...Operating for long periods in the most advanced areas, the USS CHENANGO and her attached air groups penetrated hostile submarine infested waters to seek her targets and to destroy or damage Japanese warships, aircraft, merchant craft and shore facilities ...Attacking boldly by day and night in the face of heavy enemy resistance, the courageous officers and men of the CHENANGO achieved a notable record of service and aggressiveness in combat, thereby upholding the highest traditions of the United States Naval Service."

Adm. H. D. Felt, USN, Ret

CHRONOLOGICAL TRANSCRIPT OF NAVAL SERVICE:

Jul 1923 – May 1925	USS MISSISSIPPI
May 1925 – Aug 1928	USS FARENHOLT
Aug 1928 – Aug 1929	Naval Air Station, Pensacola (instruction)
Aug 1929 – Oct 1931	VS Squadron 3-B, Aircraft Squadrons, Battle Fleet (Changed to VS Squadron 3-B, Carrier Division 2, U. S. Fleet)
Oct 1931 – Jan 1934	Naval Air Station, Pensacola (Flt. Instr., Aide to Comdt.)
Jan 1934 – May 1934	USS MINNEAPOLIS
May 1934 – Jun 1935	VS Squadron 10-S (USS HOUSTON) (changed to VS Squadron 11-S)
Jun 1936 – Jun 1937	VJ Squadron 2-F
Jun 1937 – Jun 1939	Naval Air Station, San Diego, Calif.
Jun 1939 – Dec 1941	Bombing Squadron 2 (USS LEXINGTON) (Commanding Officer)
Dec 1941 – Oct 1942	Air Group (Commander) USS SARATOGA
Oct 1942 – Jan 1943	USS SARATOGA (Air Officer)
Jan 1943 – Feb 1943	Naval Air Station, Daytona Beach, Fla. (CO)
Jul 1943 – Mar 1944	Naval Air Station, Miami, Fla. (CO)
Mar 1944 – Feb 1945	Member, U. S. Naval Mission to USSR, Moscow
Feb 1945 – Jan 1946	USS CHENANGO (CVE-28) (CO)
Jan 1946 – Jul 1947	Office of Chief of Naval Operations, Navy Dept., Washington, D. C.
Jul 1947 – Jun 1948	National War College, Washington, D. C.
Jun 1948 – Jul 1949	USS FRANKLIN D. ROOSEVELT (CO)
Jul 1949 – Apr 1950	Naval War College, Newport, R. I. (Staff)
Apr 1950 – Mar 1951	Naval War College (Chief of Staff and Aide)
Mar 1951 – Oct 1951	Middle East Force (Commander)
Oct 1951 – Jun 1953	Naval Operations, Navy Department
Jun 1953 – Apr 1954	Carrier Division 15 (Commander)
Apr 1954 – Jul 1954	Carrier Division 3 (Commander)
Jul 1954 – Apr 1956	Office of Chief of Naval Operations (Asst. Chief of Naval Operations – Fleet Readiness)
Apr 1956 – Sep 1956	U. S. Sixth Fleet (Commander)
Sep 1956 – Jul 1958	Vice Chief of Naval Operations
31 Jul 1958	Commander in Chief, Pacific
1 Jul 1964	Transferred to Retired List of USN

Navy Office of Information
Internal Relations Division (OI-430)
14 August 1964

DECLARATION OF TRUST

The undersigned does hereby appoint and designate as his (her) Trustee herein, the Secretary-Treasurer and Publisher of the United States Naval Institute to perform and discharge the following duties, powers, and privileges in connection with the possession and use of a certain taped interview between the undersigned and the Oral History Department of the United States Naval Institute.

1. Classification of Transcript.

( )a. If classified OPEN, the transcript(s) may be read or the recording(s) audited by the qualified personnel upon presentation of proper credentials, as determined by the Secretary-Treasurer of the U. S. Naval Institute.

(✓)b. If classified PERMISSION REQUIRED TO CITE OR QUOTE, the user will be required to obtain permission in writing from the interviewee prior to quoting or citing from either the transcript(s) or the recording(s).

( )c. If classified PERMISSION REQUIRED, permission must be obtained in writing from the interviewee before the transcribed interview(s) can be examined or the tape recording(s) audited.

( )d. If classified CLOSED, the transcribed interview(s) and the tape recording(s) will be sealed until a time specified the interviewee. This may be until the death of the interviewee or for any specified number of years.

2. It is expressly understood that in giving this authorization, I am in no way precluded from placing such restrictions as I may desire upon use of the interview at any time during my lifetime, nor does this authorization in any way affect my rights to the copyright of my literary expressions that may be contained in the interview.

Witness my hand and seal this _____ day of ___August___ 1974

_____

I hereby accept and consent to the foregoing Declaration of Trust and the powers therein conferred upon me as Trustee:

Felt #1 - 1

Interview No. 1 with Admiral Harry Donald Felt, U.S. Navy (Retired)
Place: BOQ, Makalapa, Pearl Harbor, Hawaii
Date: Thursday morning, 2 March 1972
Subject: Biography
By: John T. Mason, Jr.

Q: Admiral, it's certainly nice to meet you at last. I've heard so much about you from so many of your friends and men who served under you, and I'm delighted that you're going to do a full-length story of your fabulous - and I use that advisedly - naval career.

Would you begin in the proper manner by giving me the date of your birth, the place of your birth, and saying something about your family background, and then your early education?

Adm. F.: I'll try to do justice to this, Doctor. I'm very pleased to meet you and I think I'm happy at accepting your invitation!

Q: Well, we hope, as we go along, you'll be more so.

Adm. F.: Gee, you want me to start way back to the beginning of Donald Felt.

Q: Back in 1902, wasn't it?

Felt #1 - 2

Adm. F.: Yes, 1902. I'm told I was born in Topeka, Kansas, on the 21st of June 1902, and I suppose my earliest remembrances of life in Goodland, Kansas, way out on the plains of northwestern Kansas -

Q: That's in the wheatfields, isn't it?

Adm. F.: In those days, it was the prairie, now lush with wheat, of course. I started my formal education in Goodland. I suspect they were pretty good at the three Rs. And moved to Washington, D. C., when I was about eleven years old.

Q: How did that happen? Was your father in the military?

Adm. F.: No, my father was a railroad man, but my uncle was elected to the Senate when Wilson was elected to the presidency.

Q: He being Senator - ?

Adm. F.: Senator Thompson. I guess there was a big split in the Republican Party and Senator Thompson, a Democrat, got elected to the Senate and brought my father and family to Washington in a government position there. Anyhow, I went to Washington as a raw, eleven-year-old kid with one suit of clothes, in the middle of Washington summer that suit of clothes being knickerbockers of heavy woolens and a coat, a formal bow tie, dressed up Sunday best as I had been in Goodland.

Felt #1 - 3

Those years in Washington were very wonderful.

Q: Did you go to Central High?

Adm. F.: First I went to what was called John Eaton School for sixth, seventh, and eighth grades, living in a community that was relatively new surrounded by woods and all the beauty of Rock Creek Park, which had not yet been spoiled. You probably remember - or maybe you don't, Doctor - the Wardman Park Hotel?

Q: I do indeed.

Adm. F.: It has some other name now, but it wasn't yet built in those woods. You mentioned Central, yes, I then went to Central High School the first year the new school was opened. It was a pretty wonderful place, in our opinion, in those days. There were two gymnasiums, one for girls and one for boys, stadium, swimming pool - wonderful!
   However, somehow or other I'd made up my mind I wanted to go to the Naval Academy.

Q: Coming from Kansas, now!

Adm. F.: Coming from Kansas. I'd never seen the ocean until I went to Washington, of course. There was no naval background in my family except some fellow in the Revolutionary War had the title "ensign", but I believe that was an Army title.

I believe my Uncle Will, Senator Thompson, may have been frustrated as a boy because I think he was the one who wanted to go to the Naval Academy, but he transmitted this to me apparently.

Q: That probably indicates the fact that you looked up to him?

Adm. F.: Yes. He took me down there a couple of times. So, after two years of high school, the decision was made in the family that I have a try for the Naval Academy.

Q: There were no objections on their part at your going into the military?

Adm. F.: No objections at all. That was fine with them. As a matter of fact, economics being as they were and family income being as it was, education at the Naval Academy was pretty attractive.

So I worked for a couple of summers to make a little money to contribute to my entrance fee at the Naval Academy and went to prep school at a place called Shadman's. I believe it's still in existence under another name.

Q: It was in Washington?

Adm. F.: In Washington. Real tough routine, every Saturday

morning taking entrance exams for the Naval Academy, using old Naval Academy entrance exams.

Q: What kind of a student had you been in high school?

Adm. F.: I was supposed to be a pretty good student. At grammar school I was one, two, or three most of the time. At high school not that good. I would say a fairly good student, but not exclusively dedicated to the academics. As a matter of fact, I loved athletics despite my shortcomings of size and abilities.

Q: That's no handicap in certain areas.

Adm. F.: Well, to get back to this so-called story. I took the entrance exams in the spring, after going to prep school. All this was in lieu of the third year of high school. I passed the entrance exams, and then there was a gap of, oh, I suppose a couple of months between that event and entrance into the Naval Academy, so I went back to high school. I had a wonderful time.

I entered the Naval Academy in the summer of 1919. I would have graduated from high school in 1920.

Q: That was rather unusual, wasn't it?

Adm. F.: I was pretty young. I was just turning seventeen - I had just turned seventeen. I suppose I was pushing the scales at about 120.

Q: You entered on an appointment from Senator Thompson?

Adm. F.: No, from the congressman from my district in Goodland, Kansas.

To jump ahead, there I was having no high-school diploma. These days when people start to reminisce about their schooling they seem to be somewhat shocked when I tell them I never graduated from high school! But I am an honorary graduate of Central High School now.

Q: And I expect you're a part of that active alumni.

Adm. F.: Yes, I'm glad you mentioned that.

Q: Tell me.

Adm. F.: Well, some years later Central was taken over as a black school, and the Alumni Associated decided to transfer all the trophies to Western High School, I believe, temporarily and decided to keep the Alumni Association active. I believe it's the only high school alumni association I've ever heard of.

Q: It's the only one I've ever heard of, too.

Adm. F.: And I believe some of the Eastern High School people have joined it. It's still active and I suspect the key figure is a classmate of mine, Bob Newby, who's kept it together all these years. Anyhow, when I was Vice Chief of Naval Operations and a four-star admiral I was invited to an affair one evening and made an honorary graduate!

Well, let's see, where are we?

Q: You're entering the Academy.

Adm. F.: Do you want me to go on from there?

Q: Yes. Did you find it a handicap to come is so young?

Adm. F.: I didn't think so then, but looking back on it, there are two sides to the coin. In retrospect, I realize I was young and it was a handicap as a midshipman. It wasn't a handicap scholastically, but it was in physical sports and things like that. On the other hand, again in retrospect, having managed to complete the course and get a commission as a relatively young person, it was an advantage. So, I guess the latter is the most important.

Q: Would you give me a picture of the Naval Academy at that time?

Adm. F.: I remember plebe summer somewhat like this. Entering in the latter part of June when most all of the plebe class had already been organized and the company officers were already set up. One of the things that impressed me right off was when I stopped to think, how do they choose these company officers? Most of them were kids who had come in from the enlisted ranks or were sons of naval officers. For example, they never asked me if I had any prior experience at military drill, and I'm glad they didn't because I'd had one year as a cadet, a high-school cadet. Anyhow, I was in the rear rank.

I remember that summer as hot, sticky, muggy as Annapolis can be in the summer time, the emphasis being on shaking us down and disciplining us, close-order drill, and a lot of the kids had never had any. A lot of physical exercise. I believe they started to teach the kids who'd never had language something about language. Some of the things I didn't like at all. They had a bunch of duty officers around there who were graduates of that year's class, I guess, and they seemed to be in competition with each other as to who could put the most midshipmen on the report.

Q: Who could prove how tough he was!

Adm. F.: Yes, which I didn't think was very nice. I got my first impression of the regulation book and I thought a lot of it was pretty ridiculous, which probably set the tone for my accumulation of demerits! And there was one youngster in our class who had busted out of West Point. He was a pretty knowledgeable young fellow and he had a friend who was an officer around there who owned a motorcycle and an officer's cape raincoat, and he used to go out on that officer's motorcycle into town.

There were a lot of contrasts but, all in all -

Q: All in all, you did take to the discipline?

Adm. F.: We seemed to make out all right.

Q: How did you find the course of study?

Adm. F.: Well, plebe year, it was pretty fundamental. I think there were only about four major subjects. Mathematics, of course, was one, marine engineering, English, languages.

Q: What was your language?

Adm. F.: French, and I probably made a mistake in choosing French because I'd had two years in high school and the real good fundamental basics, and the system at the Naval Academy was to start with the lowest denominator, people who'd never had any. I mean you were in a class with people who'd never had any, so it was just a repeat with the result that I didn't work at it. It wasn't any challenge at all. We only had two choices, Spanish and French. I probably should have chosen Spanish.

Felt #1 - 10

Q: What was the background of the majority of the class? Had they completed high school, or were some of them from college, or just what?

Adm. F.: I never examined that precisely. I had some feel for the age bracket. In those days it was minimum 16, maximum 20. There were a few who'd been one year to college, not many. I would say the majority were - on entering, now, I'm talking about - were probably eighteen years or nineteen years.

Q: Had your time at Shadman's been a real help to you in that first year, plebe year, or was it simply just helping you to get in?

Adm. F.: It was just helping me to get in. The discipline of study, of course, is something that's always helpful, but I got that a long time ago from my mother, rather than Shadman's.

Q: Tell me about that.

Adm. F.: What?

Q: About your mother inculcating that into you.

Adm. F.: I don't know how she did it!

Q: She taught you how to study?

Adm. F.: She made me study. I don't know how she taught me. I guess you have to learn that yourself.

I suppose, getting back to that plebe year and the Naval Academy four years as a whole - and you and I talked before we turned this tape recorder on about the changes that have transpired over the many years since I was there - I think I could make a general accusation that we weren't taught. I'm not sure that's the right word to use.

Let me skip way up to the first-class year, for example. They had a thing called Speech Class, where you went to a dinner down in the basement of Bancroft Hall, a little separate room, and there might have been fifteen midshipmen at this dinner, and each would have to get up and make an after-dinner speech, but we were never taught any of the rudiments of speech. We were never told the difference between - I mean what are the different kinds of speeches, how to put a speech together, how to prepare for a speech, what are your points. We weren't taught anything, just told to get up and make a speech.

Q: And just once?

Adm. F.: Once!

Q: It doesn't seem they would have much value.

Adm. F.: No, they didn't, except to embarrass.

The manner of writing, we must have had English three or

three and a half years of the four - maybe four, I don't know - I don't think they called it History either, I think they just called it English, and I suppose we must have written some compositions like we did in grade school, never wrote a thesis. We were never told how to prepare for a thesis. We were introduced to the library but we were never really instructed or taught how to research.

So when a fellow gets out into the fleet and has to write papers, he starts from scratch, really, unless he's learned by osmosis from reading literature.

I don't know whether I've made my point or not.

Q: Yes, I think you have. There was no individual tutoring, so to speak on the part of the instructors there?

Adm. F.: No. Yesterday, at the nineteenth hole, we were reminiscing about - oh, it started by our wondering whether the University of Hawaii basketball team would be invited to the NCAA.

Q: The headlines last night said yes!

Adm. F.: Right. Some of them started to reminisce about the Naval Academy and one fellow was talking about Fred Borries. He was an old friend of mine, he was in my squadron at one time, a great athlete. And finally this fellow said, "You know, when I taught steam engineering - " I said, "Wait a minute, now, did I hear you 'when you taught steam engineering'"?

He said, "Yes, what are you talking about?" I said, "My memory of instructors at the Naval Academy is not as teachers, they were monitors and all they did was draw slips and man the board." Getting back to my point and trying to explain it again.

Q: Yes. Were there civilian instructors there in those days?

Adm. F.: Yes, a few. Wait a minute, there were more than a few. Language were all civilian and they were good. The point I'm making is that - and they changed this, incidentally, before I graduated - instead of setting up classes in what you might call advanced language, where you start reading newspapers and talk and so forth, we all had to start learning how to pronounce the words and put the grammar together.

Q: Irregular verbs!

Adm. F.: Yes. In physics, chemistry, electrical engineering, there were civilian profs, some civilian profs in math, English. I suppose, come to think of it, there were probably more civilians than uniformed profs. The uniformed profs were in ordnance and gunnery, seamanship, and navigation. Some in the others, some in mathematics, as a matter of fact.

But, you know, since you bring up that civilian prof thing,

I only remember being at, maybe the most, three lectures in electrical engineering and they were good. The English Department we thought was sissy and we used to make fun of them.

Q: Inappropriate to a professional school!

Adm. F.: Well, it was a shame because this is where your feeling for - well, for the world -

Q: This is where you get your cultural background!

Adm. F.: That's right, and I wish I could remember the head of the English Department. A wonderful man, and we were exposed once in the auditorium where he taught us, and we just loved that fellow because he was just beautiful on the stage. But we weren't taught how to do it ourselves.

Q: A later superintendent in the early thirties told me that his objective as superintendent of the Academy was to turn out men who were leaders as naval officers and who were gentlemen. Would you say that that rule prevailed when you were there?

Adm. F.: Leadership is a thing that it's hard to get the handle to, of course. There are so many handles to it. I suppose every authority on the subject of leadership has one little aspect of leadership he thinks is more important than another.

I'm sure that the objective of the Naval Academy when I was there was to inculcate leadership into the men. I think it was successful. They didn't teach leadership as a subject. It just sort of came by example, by making you do things and trying to understand the reason for doing things.

For instance, our midshipman cruises is a graduated thing. This was in the coal-burning days. On the first cruise you scrubbed decks half the time and shoveled coal out of the bunkers the other half. The object of the drill was to teach you how an enlisted man has to live and work, and we lived as enlisted men.

The second cruise we were graduated to maybe being a second-class or third-class petty officer type of work and, down in the engineering department, being a water tender - no, no, not a water tender - firing the boilers. I was unfortunate enough to be in the boiler room with two other kids the same size as me and the slice bar being about twice as big as any of us, trying to keep the steam up with, incidentally, one bucket of water to get clean with afterwards!

Q: This was on some old battleship?

Adm. F.: Yes. The first one was the Michigan and the second one was the North Carolina. My last cruise as a midshipman was fantastic. Then you get graduated up to being a sort of chief petty officer type. It was in the Olympia, Admiral Dewey's flagship. Let's see, we went up to Newfoundland and then south. We shot the guns, too. I was scared to death!

Q: You were putting into practice, then, some of the theories you had learned?

Adm. F.: Yes. The question was, I suppose, if I can remember it, "Did you learn anything about being a leader?"

I'm jumping around terribly on this thing. I think you expected it to be chronological. But reading Shipmate just the other day - maybe it was the Annual Meeting of the Alumni Association - the question was asked, "Does the Naval Academy produce young officers capable of being division officers?" and the answer was confused.

Well, when I graduated, no, we weren't capable of being division officers, but it was the system in those days - remember, this was the battleship days and practically all the graduates went to a battleship, not all, but most, which was sort of a postgraduate to the Naval Academy, where you went in as a junior division officer and you were absolutely thoroughly prepared for that. You knew something about handling men. If you didn't there was no hope for you. You were motivated to be a leader. I think that was my biggest motivation. I wanted to lead men.

Yes, you were qualified to do that. You knew something technically about what makes the thing go, and, being motivated, you wanted to learn. So, after a year or so, yes, then you were qualified to be a division officer.

Felt #1 - 17

After two years in a battleship I went to a destroyer.

Q: This desire of yours to be able to lead men is something that was instilled in you in a gradual way during your years at the Academy?

Adm. F.: I suppose so.

Q: Very subtly, I suppose.

Adm. F.: I don't know. As I remember, people used to ask me "Why do you want to go to sea?" Well, I look back on my days as a boy in Goodland, Kansas, and in those days I wanted to be a hardware man and a baseball player. I wanted to be a baseball player because I always had that kind of ambition and followed it as long as I could. And I wanted to be a hardware man because my uncle in eastern Kansas whom I visited every summer owned a hardware store!

But, later, as I remember, I said, "I do not want to be tied to a desk. I want to be outdoors, where men are working and where I can participate." I think that was my general philosophy. Going to sea, I don't know, that was a bias I guess.

Q: Tell me about your athletic participation at the Academy.

Adm. F.: Well, it wasn't very extensive. Plebe summer, as I

say, I got in the latter part of June and immediately went out for the plebe baseball team and made the baseball team. Then, every year thereafter I'd make the varsity squad until the last cut, and I'd be cut and go back to playing class baseball. We had a very fine class baseball team. I was captain of the team, and we won the championship one year. There's a picture of that team in the last copy of Shipmate.

Q: I saw it.

Adm. F.: Did you? I tried basketball but I wasn't any good at that. I was too small.

Q: What about rowing?

Adm. F.: I rowed in those damned boats where they used to take us all the way out to - what's that lighthouse way out there in Annapolis Roads? Do you remember the name of it?

Q: No, I don't.

Adm. F.: We'd row out there on a Saturday morning and then they'd hoist a signal and we'd have to race back. In those cutters, rowing cutters, do they still have them?

Q: No.

Adm. F.: No? Great big heavy things. And, of course, you wanted to get back fast as you could because you had to go down to the tailor's shop and get your clean suit out for Saturday inspection! Time was of the essence.

Q: Did you have any feelings against the regulations which confined you to the Academy to a large extent? I'm thinking of the relaxation of the rules now.

Adm. F.: Oh, sure. They were very strict in those days. Plebe summer we weren't allowed outside of the walls until Labor Day - I believe it was Labor Day. It was some late holiday. And plebe year we weren't allowed to have a date, drag a girl. We could go to the dances and watch from the balcony. Juniors. The dances were over in the Armory, you know the big balcony in there. I don't know how many times we were allowed outside the walls. Perhaps once a month.

If some of your relatives came down and invited you to dinner, you could go out to dinner Sundays on a special pass. Then, the first class had what they called the "first class gate." I believe they were allowed to go out every afternoon.

Q: After classes and before formation?

Adm. F.: Yes.

Q: Did you think this was confining? What is your attitude

toward that kind of discipline at the Academy?

Adm. F.: I don't think we were very resentful of it because there were so many activities inside, if you wanted to participate.

Let me jump to a period that I'm not very familiar with. It was when Bob Pirie was commandant. I don't remember what year that was. Maybe it was when my son was at the Naval Academy. I'd go down on a Saturday to see a football game and I found more midshipmen out in town than at the football game. I think Bob kind of clamped down on the boys on this score. During the fall football season it was mandatory that anybody who wasn't participating in some sort of sports after the drill period would go to watch football practice, and we loved it.

Of course, there was a regulation against smoking and all that sort of thing, which we thought was pretty damned silly and we broke the regulation in as many ways as we could do it.

Q: And against beer drinking?

Adm. F.: Oh, this was prohibition days, of course. I'll get to that later.

I remember as a youngster going to football practice, and I've mentioned this to some of my football playing friends and they didn't know about this. There was a thing called Oil Burners' Row. This was on old Farragut Field, wooden stands, and the top row was Oil Burners' Row, where you chewed tobacco and spit over the back of the stadium! This is silly to talk about the Naval Academy this way.

On the regulation thing, I drew quite a few demerits. I never drew a big one.

Q: Tell me about it.

Adm. F.: One of the big ones was to be caught smoking. As I remember it, that was, oh, about a 25-demerit offense and maybe being sent down to the ship.

Q: To the Mercedes?

Adm. F.: Yes, the Reina Mercedes. I never got caught at that, but I picked up a lot of little ones - sleeping in and all that sort of thing.

I graduated I don't exactly where but about the middle of my class.

Q: How large was that class?

Adm. F.: About 450. I don't know, some place about 150 or 160, somewhere around there. I don't have the record of it, but I used to have it and, as I remember, along about the second-class - or maybe the first-class - year they had a thing on aptitude for the service, and in those days it was based entirely

Felt #1 - 22

on the amount of demerits you picked up. I think I was pretty near the tail end of my class.

Q: Pretty poor aptitude!

Adm. F.: Yes, they didn't have much hope for me!

Q: That's an interesting point.
Did you have any active interest in aviation when you were there?

Adm. F.: I'm told by my mother I did. I'd forgotten it. She told me later that about the end of plebe year I wrote her a letter and told her I was going to be a naval aviator. She must have done a pretty good job of discouraging me because I seem to have forgotten it, and when I graduated I apparently had no desire along those lines.

Q: Was there any introduction to aviation at that time at the Academy?

Adm. F.: No.

Q: The powers that be were not very interested, were they?

Adm. F.: No. In 1923 aviation was just a cub, of course. The battleship was the king of the Navy then, and, as a matter of fact, there was great competition among graduating midshipmen for certain battleships.

Q: Was that based on the modernity of the battleship?

Adm. F.: No, the image, the record. I don't know just what, but anyhow my group and another group decided that the Mississippi was the best in the fleet. There was only room for a certain number of us so we got together and gambled to see who - we had our choice in those days - would ask for the Mississippi and my group won. It turned out to be very wonderful because it was Iron Man ship, the big athletic ship.

Q: Who was skipper of her?

Adm. F.: Brotherton, and Red Reinicke was the gunnery officer and the athletic officer. The first thing that happened to us after we reported aboard in San Francisco, they got all of us young ensigns together and pointed at each of us and said, "Now, what do you play?" and he gave us each an assignment in some sort of athletic endeavor.

Q: How many of the graduates went on board the Mississippi in your group?

Adm. F.: I don't remember exactly. Maybe twelve.

Q: A fairly good contingent.

Adm. F.: Yes, and in those days, of course, there was a JO mess, with two classes in the JO mess. In other words, when I joined the Mississippi the class of 1922 were seniors in the mess.

Q: Tell me about life aboard the Mississippi.

Adm. F.: It was great. I mentioned that the Mississippi was the Iron Man ship, the Number One in athletics, had the red E on the stack for being Number Two in engineering, Es on a lot of the guns. And then came that disastrous experience when we went out to fire a practice and had a gun explosion in one of the turrets, which was the high-scoring E turret in the fleet. I lost a classmate in that turret.

Q: Were you in gunnery?

Adm. F.: I was in gunnery in the 5- and 3-inch business, and learned a lot. I was Number Two JO in joining up and Sokum Soucek was the Number One JO. Conrad was the division officer, class of 1920, class of 1921, class of 1923.

Q: Which Soucek is that?

Adm. F.: This is Apollo. Anyhow, it was a pretty wonderful

life, active, a life where the routine was such that you spent a lot of time with your men - clean up in the morning, of course, quarters in decent uniform, shined up, following which there'd be an instruction period where you got your men around for various types of instruction. General quarters, battle drills. Being an athletically inclined ship, most of the officers were sympathetic to it so that you could get your team off the ship and go ashore and practice.

Q: This was in the Atlantic, was it?

Adm. F.: Pacific. The _Mississippi_ was our home. That's something that you don't see in ships any more. We called it our home, and we spent money to make our home more livable - buying things for the mess. We were closely knit. Prohibition days. Remember, in these days cruises to Panama, enlisted men going ashore having to be back by five o'clock, drinking all the beer they could drink in that short time. Arguments, fights between ships as to who's got the best ship. The same with the officers. Great competition.

I read every once in a while that competition I'm talking about now, in some of the theories of modern education, competition isn't good, you shouldn't give grades to students. Competition is the spice of life, it seems to me.

Q: This attitude is that it's discriminatory?

Adm. F.: Yes, I think so.

Q: To the less favored.

Adm. F.: Yes. Well, anyhow - oh, I said it was a home ship and it was a place to entertain. I've watched my son grow up in the Navy and I've witnessed at least a piece of the Navy as he's grown up, and the business of inviting guests out for dinner seems not to be popular any more. Maybe it's because in my day most young people were not married, they hadn't enough money to get married. I don't think there was a single person in the JO mess who owned a car. Not only having guests for dinner, but dances, dress up. People loved it.

Q: And, of course, the prevailing attitude is somewhat different toward dinner, too, from what it was in those days.

Adm. F.: Oh, sure.

Q: It was a social occasion.

Adm. F.: And in those days there was only one sitting, if you know what I mean by that word. Now, in the big ships like in the carriers they eat all round the clock because of the operating routine that they have to follow these days. We always had to dress up for dinner - by "dress up" I mean that if we were in the tropics white service uniform, otherwise blue service uniform. There wasn't such a thing as a working uniform in those days. By that I mean there wasn't khaki - there was for enlisted men, of course, the dungarees.

I can remember going on midshipman cruises and officers who were with us wearing white service uniforms with oil spots all over them!

I think I'd like to make a comment about the differences I see between the recreational facilities available to Navy personnel now and those available to us in my young days. I think one of the most remarkable things that has happened is the foresight and ability to create these recreational facilities for the young people today. I had occasion to write a letter to a friend of mine who was an enlisted man in one of my aviation units who became an officer and retired, I believe, as a lieutenant commander living down in Florida. He wrote me saying he'd been talking to a lot of his retired friends, including flag officers, who were very concerned about the so-called Zumwalt permissiveness.

I wrote back a long letter and challenged these charges. The main charge being that the new Chief of Naval Operations had destroyed the morale of the Navy. I said I didn't believe that at all, that the morale of the Navy had been destroyed long before his time. He was trying to restore the morale of the Navy, that the morale of the Navy had been destroyed by some very bad personnel decisions, the main one being that, due to the belief that the Vietnam War would only be a short war, it was a very prolonged war, still on the basis of the draft, and the draft is the main reason for all the discontent among our youth today.

On the matter of beards and haircuts, I said, gee, the regulations have always permitted a beard. In fact, I had one at one time. When I got tired of it I shaved it off. I see beards all over the Pearl Harbor area, all over the golf course, but gradually they're coming off, and this is just human.

To get back to my point about recreational facilities, I said one of the finest things that's been done - and there are a lot of reasons why morale is low, the operating tempo is one reason it's low, the fact that people are away from their families so much, and all that sort of thing -

Q: Very important.

Adm. F.: Sure. But on the plus side, look at what they've got these days. My goodness, there wasn't such a thing as a golf course in my young days, for instance. Getting back to Mississippi days, there was one athletic field and it wasn't kept up. It was full of holes and all that sort of thing. Over in San Pedro. Swimming pools, tennis courts, no. Officers' clubs, there weren't any such things as officers clubs. Enlisted men's clubs? No. You had to make your own in those days.

But, here again, we were closely knit because this was our life.

Q: You were a family!

Adm. F.: Yes, we had to make it. All right, I'll leave the <u>Mississippi</u> -

Q: In leaving her, may I ask were there any outstanding experiences while you were on board that you might like to recall?

Adm. F.: Well, I've mentioned the turret explosion.

Q: Yes. Where did she go other than up and down the coast?

Adm. F.: Well, we made the standard fleet cruises. In the summer time it was standard operating procedure in those days for the fleet to go north to Puget Sound and operate in the Puget Sound area. They'd have a thing called Fleet Week up there, and then work back down to San Francisco and back to the Long Beach area. Panama.

Q: Did you get out to Pearl?

Adm. F.: Yes, the second year we came to Pearl, and that's where I was detached.

Q: There was very little here, wasn't there, in the way of naval installations?

Adm. F.: Let me see. Yes, we went alongside the coal pier at the base here and coaled ship. When I mentioned that later on when I was up here at Camp Smith to one of my aides, a full commander, he came back two or three days later and he said, "Admiral, you were pulling my leg. You didn't coal ship!" These kids have never seen anything but an oil-burner and wouldn't believe it. But we coaled ship at that pier and then tried to clean the ship up. We were granted liberty. We got into white uniforms, still all this coal dust all over every place, trying to keep our uniforms kind of clean, walked through the base to the main gate, which is now called Nimitz Gate, where we boarded a train to get into Honolulu. My first act after getting into Honolulu was going to a barber's shop where they had a bath tub back there and took a bath! Better than taking it out of a bucket. Then there was a street car to get you to Waikiki. There was only one big hotel on the beach in those days, that was the Moana. The Royal Hawaiian hadn't yet been built. At the Moana we had a locker room where you could rent a bathing suit, and the bathing suit was the type with the arms down to elbow length and the legs down to almost knee length.

There was a tradition in the _Mississippi_ that when you went on a cruise like that, all the JOs had to have their heads shaved, and if they didn't agree to having it done it was done forcibly. I have a picture of that JO mess with all of our heads shaved, and can't you imagine what we looked like. Wait a minute, am I getting confused? Back up.

Remember I was talking about the coal ship business?

Q: Yes. It's sensible to have a head shaved -

Adm. F.: That (coaling and taking a bath in Honolulu) was as a midshipman, that wasn't as an officer. That was on the first midshipman's cruise.

All right, let's get back to the <u>Mississippi</u>. Can't you imagine what we looked like as we arrived on the beach at Waikiki with these - of course, the bathing suits were standard then, there wasn't anything unusual about them - but all of us with bald heads!

Q: Wasn't it about that time that Nimitz was out here setting up a sub base?

Adm. F.: I don't know. I wasn't very conscious of submarines. I'll get to that a little later. Anyhow, you asked about outstanding things, and I guess that's about it. I had a very beautiful experience when I was detached. There was a dinner party given. Captain Brotherton was the host in Honolulu, and I was asked to make a speech. That's when I think I had occasion to regret the most that I hadn't had any instruction in speechmaking!

Q: You were getting the practical instruction at that moment.

Adm. F.: Yes. When I left the ship, there was the race boat crew alongside the gangway and I was put into the race boat crew and rowed from the Mississippi to my new destroyer.

Q: What was the state of personnel on board at that time? That was in the period when enlistment was difficult, wasn't it?

Adm. F.: No, not that I recall.

Q: The Mississippi had a full complement?

Adm. F.: Oh, sure, and we had on board what they called "plank owners," people who'd been in the ship for years and years and years. There was great continuity. Not very much turnover. It's hard to remember the age brackets, but everything was pure enlistment, of course, and a great pride in belonging and continuing to serve in that ship, and no urge to get ashore instead of serving on board. Some of the chief petty officers had been in that ship for six, seven, eight years.

Q: Without family connections?

Adm. F.: They must have had families, but the family problem didn't seem to be an urgent, pressing one. Most of the people were not married, at least the youngsters.

Felt #1 - 33

Q: How do you analyze the difference between that time and now in terms of family problems?

Adm. F.: Let me go to my destroyer, and I'll try to pick that up.

Q: All right, fine. Was this a selection that you desired, to go to this destroyer?

Adm. F.: Yes. The crew in that destroyer were, well, I suppose in those days they called the destroyers the "dungaree Navy," and that was good, that's the Farenholt. It didn't mean that they were dirty, but it meant that they were working people. Now, I would say they were more mature. A lot of them married, but the operating routine was such that they saw their families.

I joined the Farenholt in Pearl Harbor in 1925 and then we made the Australian cruise in 1925. That was a pretty long cruise. Then we operated out of San Diego. Unless you were in upkeep, alongside a tender or something like that, you usually went out on a Monday and came back on a Friday. That may sound like it's tough from the point of view of family life, but it can't hold a candle to what the kids are doing now.

Q: You at least had your weekends.

Adm. F.: That's right. There were no discipline problems at all. I inherited a competitive spirit. I say "I did," I was just a youngster.

Q: What was your job?

Adm. F.: Well, I became a gunnery officer and the communications officer, and this, that, and the other - a sort of deck hand. Incidentally, having been brought up in the Mississippi and broadsides, I knew something about gunnery, and one of the shocks I had was to learn when I came aboard the destroyer that there was nobody in the destroyers, any of them apparently, capable of lining up the batteries for a long-range battle practice. It had to be done by tender personnel. A year later they organized what they called a Destroyer Gunnery School. This was unbelievable to me because that's what we did all the time in the battleship with our broadsides.

But, to get back to the personnel business, I found a very high competitive spirit between the Farenholt and the flagship of the other squadron in communications, signals - one-two, one-two, like that, back and forth. The only athletic undertaking was the whale-boat crew thing, which the Farenholt had won, and I organized what I called the Engineers' Crew. There'd never been one of those. I didn't know a damned thing about rowing, but I knew that in order to row you had to be in good physical condition, so I'd get these guys up if we were in port, take them ashore and cross-country them, and when at sea we'd medicine-ball each other. We won that.

I wrote some years after I retired and asked the chief

of the Bureau of Personnel if I could have a copy of my fitness reports. I hadn't seen many of them and sure enough they gave me a copy of all of them, and one I just loved. This was when I joined the <u>Farenholt</u>. I had four different skippers and one of them wrote, "This young officer has a flair for leadership." I thought that was great. Remember, you talked about leadership?

Q: Yes.

Adm. F.: A flair for it, but I had some kind of embarrassing experiences.

Q: It implied imagination, too, in developing all these different facets?

Adm. F.: The most embarrassing experience I had, we were in Newport Harbor in a fleet cruise around there, anchored in Newport Harbor, and there was to be a boat race, motor boat race. No, I take it back, it was to be a sailing race. I thought I had the date all straightened out and we'd allowed our bo's'un's mate, who was the coxswain, to go on leave and I told him to be back from leave on a certain date when we were going to race.

The day before the race I told the skipper - asked the skipper if I could have his boat and go out and cruise around the course, and he said, "Sure, that's a good idea." When I got there I found the race was under way! I'd missed it by one day, and had to come back and confess! I was very fortunate in having good skippers.

Q: You said before that you were appalled at the state of gunnery on board the destroyer when you came on duty. How can a situation like that develop when there was more or less a feed-in from the battleship trained men to destroyers?

Adm. F.: I couldn't figure it out. This was true in that group in San Diego. Now, whether it was true in the Atlantic I wouldn't know. Maybe the feed-in was of people who hadn't had gunnery in the big ships. I don't know. I just couldn't understand it.

Q: Tell me about that Australian cruise aboard the Farenholt.

Adm. F.: Well, the small ships went to Melbourne and the big ships went to Sydney.

Q: What was the objective of it?

Adm. F.: Just a goodwill cruise.

Q: Showing the flag?

Adm. F.: Yes. The people of Australia just turned themselves inside out to be gracious hosts. We were numb. There were invitations to a party every night, and the uniform was tails, boiled shirt, full evening dress, boat cloaks and the works. The racing season was on and you know Australians are nuts about racing. We were invited to the Jockey Club, always given tips on the horses, we had free transportation on all the public transportation facilities, a trip up into the mountains by train. It got to the point where there was a little bit too much entertainment. The invitations just came from all sides and the Admiral had to try to fill the invitations. So, unless you had the duty, you were out every night.

Q: This made it hard on morale, didn't it?

Adm. F.: Well, we were young and could take it. I remember the theatre. Remember now, the heating systems in those days were nothing but fireplaces, I guess, in the houses and in the theatre there was no heating system at all apparently, because when the curtain went up this blast of cold air came off the curtain and everybody in the audience got up and put on their overcoats!

Then we went to New Zealand and the situation there was a bit different. Pretty grim the first day because the authorities had asked for us to parade, and then there was some violent objection to this parade business and they said that there was going to be a riot of some sort. It all stemmed, apparently, from the experience of New Zealanders vis-a-vis Americans in America after World War I. I never knew anything about this, but the story I got was when the New Zealanders came back from Europe to New Zealand via America, they just raised hell, or the Americans raised hell with them. I don't know. I think it was a lot of labor-instigated thing.

Q: It really was a wave of anti-Americanism.

Adm. F.: Yes, that's what it was. So the parade was canceled and we were restricted to the ship until this was all straightened out, the first day. It got straightened out and then it was all right. A little bit different attitude on the part of the people. They were not quite as open and gracious as the Australians had been. I believe we were in a Scottish area.

Q: The dour Scots!

Adm. F.: Yes. But that was a very interesting cruise. Where shall we go now?

Q: When you reflect on your period of service in a destroyer, what could you say it contributed to your knowledge?

Adm. F.: First of all, responsibility being given to young officers. You see, I went there as an ensign and before long

I was a responsible head of department, you might say, gunnery officer, a first lieutenant.

Q: Advancement was more rapid.

Adm. F.: Sure, and from a tactical point of view, handling the ship. For some reason or other, I was always called to the bridge to take the con when we were doing maneuvers. I had one skipper, M. S. Tisdale, who rewrote the tactical instructions and I helped him with that. So it was a growing-up experience.

When charges are made by some people that in the Navy you're not given any responsibility, all you do is take orders, that's a false accusation.

Q: If you have imagination, you can use it, can't you?

Adm. F.: Why, sure. It's given to you and you either carry it or you don't. I suppose that's the best answer I can give to your question. I spent three years in this destroyer and that was enough.

Q: And during that time, apparently, you must have been generating some enthusiasm for naval aviation. How did this happen?

Adm. F.: Well, classmates of mine had gone to Pensacola for

training after two years. That was the rule then, that you couldn't take aviation training until you'd done two years in the fleet. Of course, I'd done two plus some more in the destroyer. I got interested again. Remember, Lindberg flew to Paris —

Q: In 1926, wasn't it?

Adm. F.: 1926 or 1927, along in there. So I got the bug and I'd had enough of the destroyer business. Before I got the bug I applied for duty in that outfit down in the Panama Canal area. That didn't pan out and I applied for duty in the Asiatic Fleet and, fortunately, that didn't pan out. So I got the aviation bug.

Q: Were you discouraged by your senior officers?

Adm. F.: Yes.

Q: On what basis?

Adm. F.: Well, the senior officers didn't really believe in aviation. As a matter of fact, it took many, many years before they did believe in it. They tried to discourage me, but as I remember the endorsement on my request forwarded recommending approval but "with regret" or something like that.

Q: Was this Captain Tisdale?

Adm. F.: Probably was. I've forgotten just how it was worded. There may have been something about that time about physical exams. I've forgotten exactly how it worked. Perhaps it was something from Washington saying, "Everybody who passes successfully their annual physical exam should take the aviation exam," which I did and passed. Or a combination of these things, I suppose. Anyhow, I got my orders to Pensacola and did not go through the normal routine.

The normal routine was for a fellow to take some pre-flight instruction either in Norfolk or San Diego, I believe, and then if you got through that, you'd go to Pensacola. They sent me directly to Pensacola -

Q: In 1928?

Adm. F.: In 1928. An instructor got hold of me and the first thing he asked was if I'd ever been in an airplane before, and I said no. He said, that's fine. I said, "What do you mean?" and he said, "You haven't learned any bad habits."

I want to go back to something. We were talking about submarines a while ago. Remember you asked me if I knew -

Q: - whether Nimitz was setting up the base here at Pearl.

Adm. F.: Correct. This was while I was in the Mississippi

that an order came out, everybody who passes the annual physical exam is subject to being ordered to submarines. I didn't want to go to a submarine. I'd seen a little bit of it. These were in the days when the boys went out cruising and came back and got their bath at the YMCA ashore and all that sort of thing. So I asked if I could be sent over to the hospital ship and be given a physical examination, and they said all right. I told the doctor he'd better look for that heart murmur which I'd had as a kid, and sure enough, he found it and disqualified me for submarines!

Q: But not for aviation?

Adm. F.: No!

Q: Tell me about Pensacola in 1928.

Adm. F.: You started out in what they called Squadron 1 in little yellow seaplanes, float planes, where you learned to solo and make landings and handle emergencies when the instructor would chop off your power and you'd have to pick out a place to land safely. Then you went to a land plane - same type of plane but with wheels - for small-field work. I don't know whether they had formation there or not.

Then to a third squadron, which was a service-type airplane. I believe this was the first time you got in an airplane that had brakes. You operated from a very small field.

And then to another seaplane outfit. This was the big boat type. And finally to a fighter outfit, and the determination was made finally as to what type combat you'd be ordered to.

Q: How much attrition was there in this whole process?

Adm. F.: Oh, gee, I would say about 40 percent. It took about a year to get through the course.

I met a girl during this time - let me go back a little bit. I started out living at BOQ and finally some friends of mine moved to quarters in the country club.

Q: A little more plush!

Adm. F.: A little plush, and I finally joined them there. The Country Club is the place where all the Saturday night dances were held and all that sort of thing, and during this period a couple of ladies, one in Pensacola and the other in Mobile, decided to throw a party at the Country Club - a dinner dance type of party, and invited us four bachelors. Apparently, we took dim view of this. Two of the bachelors found reasons to leave town, they had something more pressing -

Q: They didn't like this matching process!

Adm. F.: Yes, but Red and I decided we'd go to the party and I met this girl from Mobile, and every weekend thereafter went over to see her. We finally decided we'd better get married. Bad weather set in at the tail end of my flight training and things were kind of drug out, but we got married before I finished flight training, so I took her to Pensacola for the last couple of weeks there.

Q: She obviously didn't object to a pilot!

Adm. F.: No, but it was many, many years before she'd fly.

Q: Really?

Adm. F.: Yes. I'm talking now about getting out of Pensacola and getting their wings, but there was a new rule or authority for a naval aviator to take his parents or his wife on a flight, local flight, once a quarter or once every six months. She wasn't enthusiastic about that at all until many years later.

Q: How large a class entered with you at Pensacola?

Adm. F.: I believe there was a new class brought in every month, and I have a picture of my flight class. I'm not sure that everyone who entered in that flight class is in the picture. It was taken some place along the course of the flight-training period, and I would say there were about ten or twelve. Very interesting.

Q: Were there casualties among them?

Felt #1 - 45

Adm. F.: Yes, later. One of them became commandant of the Marine Corps.

Q: Who was that?

Adm. F.: Dave Shoup. Fitzhue Lee, P.D. Stroop. It was quite a distinguished group of young people.

Q: Did you have any experience with gliders?

Adm. F.: No. The gliding business didn't start until I was an instructor later on at Pensacola. I've forgotten the name of the little fellow - I couldn't possibly recall it now - he was an AEDO. Maybe you have his name?

Q: No.

Adm. F.: We both can visualize him, we both know him, but we can't at this moment recall his name. He came from the aircraft factory, I believe, and brought his glider down there to Corry Field. That's Squadron 2. And they fooled around with that for quite a long while. Some instructors thought it was a very good thing, but apparently it didn't really take.

Q: Ralph Barnaby.

Felt #1 - 46

Adm. F.: Sure, Ralph Barnaby.

Q: His theory, I believe, was that it would be a way of testing aptitudes for prospective pilots. If they survived the glider treatment, so to speak, they had an aptitude for flying.

Adm. F.: I didn't participate in it. As I remember, at that time I was - well, I was either instructing in another sqadron or was aide to the commandant. I can't remember which. But my impression of it was that it was the instructors who were getting this training with a view to instructing students, but what the main objective was I really can't recall.

Q: Well, this certainly changed the course of your naval career, didn't it, this experience at Pensacola?

Adm. F.: I went from Pensacola to Scouting Squadron 3, which was based in the Lexington. These were exciting days for me.

Q: This was with the Pacific Fleet?

Adm. F.: Yes. The main mission of the scouting squadron, of course, was to take off from the carrier and go out and find the enemy, and the way they set up the problems in those days was to pit one carrier against the other carrier - the Saratoga and the Lexington. Whoever found the other one first usually got attacked first and that was the end of the drill. On the other hand, the philosophy of use of naval aviation was to support the battle line. In other words, two battle lines with a carrier behind each battle line to support, so whichever knocked off the other carrier first would win that part of the battle.

The facilities in those days were practically zero insofar as navigation and safety of life from that point of view is concerned. Trailing wire antenna and di da da ley. No such thing as radar, of course. No way to home on a ship. Navigation done by the seat of your pants on a little boards, guessing on the wind -

Q: What about weather reports?

Adm. F.: We had a weather forecast man aboard, but the object of the drill was to go out in a sort of a triangular thing and search a sector and come back, hoping you'd find the ship when you got back.

Q: What about landing gear, arresting gear, and that sort of thing?

Adm. F.: The same old thing, except that it was a straight deck, of course, with a barrier up in front of you. Planes parked up in front of the barrier. A landing signal officer. No mirrors or any of this modern stuff.

In those days the <u>Lexington</u> had arresting gear bow and stern. One trip - it may have been later on in another tour of duty - anyhow, we cruised from Hawaii back to the West Coast going backward, so to speak, and landing over the bow instead of over the stern! But they finally took that away.

Q: Admiral Reeves was in command of the fleet, was he?

Adm. F.: I've just been reading the last article in the War College thing written about Admiral Reeves. Yes, he was in and out there as Commander, Aircraft Battle Force. He had his headquarters at North Island.

I suppose this was in the early formative stage of dive-bombing. These were biplanes we were flying, stick and wire and canvas. Very crude, not for high altitude, of course. There wasn't any such thing as oxygen. No way of communicating pilot to pilot, except by hand signals. Push over from pretty low altitude and try to find a target quick and drop a bomb.

Q: How did this technique of dive-bombing come into being?

Adm. F.: I used to know the story of this. The Marines claim to be the father of dive-bombing, and I think this is probably true. I think it was in Nicaragua, but I'm not quite sure.

Q: Did you get involved in any exercise for the defense of

the Panama Canal?

Adm. F.: Not in defense of. We used to attack the Panama Canal on fleet cruises. It didn't apply to us in the Scouting Squadron, but there was always great competition between the Air Corps and naval aviation fighter squadron boys. I think the outcome usually depended on procurement policies - who had the latest type airplane. But they always tangled over the Panama Canal.

Q: Did you have any close calls during this time on the Lexington? It sounds very hazardous.

Adm. F.: No, I don't think so. I can't remember cracking up an airplane on this tour! I managed to find my way back to the ship all the time.

Q: Was there any attempt at night flying?

Adm. F.: I don't believe we did night flying then. I'm having a little trouble because I'm trying to push myself all the way back to 1929, 1930, and 1931. I want to try to get my memory straightened out.

You asked me if I had any hazardous or outstanding experiences. Ernie King was the skipper, a great guy but I learned a lot about Ernie as a young man in that Scouting Squadron. A guy who demanded an awful lot of somebody and who would really pour it on if he found he could whip you.

Q: Sound like the characteristics of a bully!

Adm. F.: Well, I don't know whether you'd call him a bully or not. But if you stood up to him, he liked that. Let me go back just a minute.

I said before that we went out and searched a sector and it was, in those days, two planes together so one could check the other. If one went down he could radio back with his key that there was one down in the water. Ernie started a thing of drafting up a coded message, up there on the navigating bridge, and sending it down to the ready room to the leader of the two-plane sections, which gave the fellow his orders as to where to go and so on and so forth. OK. You had to decode it and then work out the first leg of your navigation, but before you got it fully decoded the word would come "man your planes," and this is when I first became somewhat entangled, because I refused to man my plane until I had that first leg worked out. I wasn't going to take off that ship not knowing where I was going or where the ship was going to go. You had a problem of navigation going to a certain place, while the ship was going to some other place. It's a relative motion sort of thing.

I had a little trouble with my executive officer on that. The word having come down "man your planes" meant just that to him, regardless. You know, I never heard one word of criticism from Captain Ernie King because I wouldn't man my plane until I was ready.

Q: There's a sensible man!

Adm. F.: He knew what the problem was. Sure he did. Now, what I'm leading up to is we were way down off Panama some place and we were all sent out, fighters, everybody else was sent out, and somehow or other I stumbled back onto the ship after I'd made a very radical change of course. In other words, I got back where I thought I was going to find the ship and she wasn't there. Just by luck I got back to the ship and I went up to the bridge and saw the navigator and said, "What are you doing? Where are you going?" He showed me, and I said, "This isn't what we expected you to do, and you've got a whole fighter squadron out there expecting to come back and find you here, where I expected to find you, instead of here." Well, he went to Ernie and Ernie understood right away and he turned around, started to make smoke, turned on all the searchlights, and they got that fighter squadron back, just before they gave out of gas. They were all ready to plunk in the water.

I never knew exactly why this happened, but I think it was because they were using a plotting sheet instead of a chart, and there happened to be an island there that didn't show on the plotting sheet, and they'd gone some place else to avoid the island.

But working under Ernie King was quite an experience. As I remember Hoover was the exec.

Q: Genial John?

Adm. F.: Genial John.

Q: It must have added to your knowledge of leadership - I mean your understanding of leadership?

Adm. F.: Of people, anyhow!

Q: What kind of a pilot was King? I know he had his wings.

Adm. F.: I never flew with him, but while I was at Pensacola as a student - this wasn't the first, but I believe the second, wave of sending senior officers down there. They soloed and were given their wings, but they didn't go through the full course. What it was all about, as I understood it, was to give some seniority to naval aviation. You see, naval aviation didn't have any seniority.

Q: An obvious attempt to catch up!

Adm. F.: Yes, so there was a whole group of them who came down and I think Ernie was probably ahead of me. One of them was Ted Sherman.

Q: Was Towers one of them?

Adm. F.: No, he, of course, was one of the original naval aviators. He was a full-fledged aviator. This was a very wise move. Otherwise, I don't think naval aviation would have survived.

Q: Who was responsible for that idea? Was that Admiral Moffett?

Adm. F.: I don't know. I say that truthfully. I don't know. If you ask me to make a guess, I would say probably Jack Towers, but I'm not sure.

There's one little thing I want to add to the time of my life that I was in VS-3. This has to do with people. I'll just pick out one person, Dixie Keefer, who was really a guy. He came as exec with years of experience under his belt. He decided that he'd ride in the rear seat when we were doing gunnery, and we used to go up to Oceanside or some other place and fly from an old creek bottom - go out and do our gunnery off the coast there. I had Dixie in my back seat as I was making runs on the sleeve, and all of a sudden the motor got rough and it looked as if possibly we were going to have to make a forced landing. I looked back and couldn't find Dixie, he wasn't there! But the motor caught and we came in and landed all right, and, sure enough, Dixie was there.

I said, "Dixie, what in the hell were you doing?" Where were you?" He said, "I was taking off my shoes. You know, I can't swim."

Q: Did you run into Ken Whiting in that period?

Adm. F.: Not in that period, a little bit later.

Q: Since you were a gunner on board the Mississippi, what about the improvement in gunnery practice due to using planes as spotters and so on?

Adm. F.: That was a big improvement, of course, having an airplane go up there and spot. I didn't do any of it until later, when I was in a cruiser. When I was in the Mississippi this was relatively early in the days of airplanes aboard -

Q: Did they have a catapult?

Adm. F.: Yes. We had two catapults, one on top of a turret, and one on the stern. These guys were fantastic, as far as I was concerned.

Q: Did you want to go and do likewise?

Adm. F.: Apparently not. I think one of the airplanes had a seatwhere you could bum a ride, but apparently I never got the urge to do so.

But aviation was the eyes of the fleet at that time.

Q: After that tour of duty, you went back to Pensacola?

Adm. F.: Yes.

Q: This was a signal honor, wasn't it, to go back as an instructor?

Adm. F.: I'm not sure. I had orders to come out here to Pearl to a patrol squadron after two years in VS-3. Kathryn was pregnant at that time and the doctor told her that she should not come to the tropics, something about metabolism or something like that. So the Bureau said, "Carry out your orders unless you can find somebody who will agree to take your orders, and one of the boys, Red Scoles, said he'd like to come. So he took my orders.

Then about three or four months later I got orders to Pensacola, than which there's no more tropical place! By that time Linn was born. I went there as an instructor in that Squadron One seaplane outfit and learned how to be an instructor. Then, instead of being given some students, I was transferred to another squadron where they had the combat-type airplanes and became an instructor there.

Q: What about the process of learning to be an instructor?

Adm. F.: Learning how to do things the wrong way so that you can recognize them when a student does them the wrong way. I guess that's the basis of it.

Q: Who was in charge of the program?

Adm. F.: Gerry Bogan was the skipper of Squadron One. And, incidentally, Gerry gave me my final check when I was a student. I think Gerry was still there, but I may be getting confused with my student days and my instructor days. I probably am.

After a while in this squadron I was detailed as the aide to the commandant - That was Frank McCrary. I got a very fine understanding of how to handle administrative affairs. The chief clerk, whose name I can't remember, was wonderful. He took me under his wing and we developed a system as to how to present the problems to the commandant, the correspondence, and all this sort of thing, make life easier on him.

Q: Pensacola was growing up then, wasn't it?

Adm. F.: Yes, expanding. As a matter of fact, the first enlisted men came down for flight instruction. That was the beginning of the Avcad program I guess.

Q: What were some of the innovations then employed in contrast with 1928?

Adm. F.: It wasn't much different. Same type airplanes. Same routine of five squadrons.

Q: Was there any feed-in for naval aviation from other countries? From the Royal Navy, for instance?

Adm. F.: In those days, no. That came later.

Q: Did we have any concern for a knowledge of Japanese naval aviation in the early 1930s?

Adm. F.: Not particularly. Of course, we were conscious of the agreement on limitations and of course the Lexington and Saratoga were converted from battle cruisers to carriers as a result of that.

Q: They were a gift as a result of that!

Adm. F.: Yes.
By the way, back in the VS-3 days I flew from the old Langley every once in a while, too. That was an experience.

Q: In what sense?

Adm. F.: Trying to land on that damned thing with that stern

Felt #1 - 58

waving around in a semicircle!

You mentioned did we do any night flying and my answer was I can't remember that we did, but there was one thing happening back in those days which I think was remarkable.

Frank Akers, who, incidentally, was my first instructor when I went down as a student, was making blind landings on the Langley in those days, and it took an awfully long while for that technique to be developed to what it is now. As I remember, he was doing that with the Langley secured alongside the dock at North Island.

Q: Here's an example of individual initiative, isn't it, working within Navy Regs?

Adm. F.: Yes.

Q: In these Pensacola days did you have any personal contact with BuAer? Were you cognizant of what was developing there and the general philosophy prevailing?

Adm. F.: In regard to the development of airplane, probably no. The thing that I do recall, however, is that the admiral then in charge of communications came down to Pensacola and got all the instructors together and told us somewhat of the development in communications, and then asked for ideas and stated that the art was such that all you needed was an idea. Technology could pick up an idea and solve the problem. What was needed was ideas. But it sure took an awfully long while for improvement to be made in communications.

Q: Can you give me any idea of what it cost to train a pilot in the early 1930s? I know it's exorbitant now, but I was thinking in contrast what was it then.

Adm. F.: No, I can't. I remember seeing signs later on - this was during World War II, I believe - something like $60,000. Maybe I've got the figure completely wrong, but I don't remember reading or having exposed to me any estimate of the cost of aviation training in those days.

Q: Were the Sea Hawks in being when you were there?

Adm. F.: Sea Hawks?

Q: The forerunners of the Blue Angels?

Adm. F.: Oh, I'm glad you brought that up. The Sea Hawks didn't ring a bell, but while I was at Pensacola John Crommelin organized his precision team. Let me see, Little Bill Davis was on one wing and class of 1925. Then there was another team organized which flew with ropes attached to the planes, and they'd go through loops and things, not the spectacular stuff that John Crommelin did. I remember going with him up to Birmingham to an air show when both teams performed, and I had my first experience as a radio announcer describing the maneuvers and I failed miserably because, like most radio announcers, I thought I had to talk all the time!

Q: How extensively did the Navy participate in those days in these air meets?

Adm. F.: They always participated. That was the only one I ever went to, but the Los Angeles meet I remember the Navy participated in, Chicago I believe it was, and then, of course, sea plane racing was - that's where Tomlinson comes into the picture, with seaplanes. Remember - I can't remember what they called them - but there were races in the Washington-Potomac Area, and I think the Navy had the record at one time.

When was it that Sokem Soucek broke the altitude record, flying out of Anacostia?

Q: What specifically did you duties as aide to the commandant at Pensacola entail, other than easing his way, as you said, and acquiring new techniques?

Adm. F.: Well, I mentioned that. The conception of an aide's job, at least as agreed by Captain McCrary and me, was quite different than some people conceive the job now. Sure, if he had a reception I was on hand to help a little bit, but I was

Felt #1 - 61

not - this may be a crude way of putting it - a servant in any respect.

Q: You didn't have to carry his bag?

Adm. F.: No, I had my own integrity. There are all kinds of different ways of handling an aide and being an aide, and I don't know quite how to describe this other than to say that we respected each other. My job was to help him in any way I could, but I didn't handle his check book or set the table for him or anything like that.

Q: I suppose it's a great help to be in agreement with the general philosophy of the commanding officer whom you serve, too?

Adm. F.: Oh, sure. You have to be to be an aide.

Q: Then this puts a great deal of weight on the selection of the aide?

Adm. F.: Well, I've had some experience of that. I've had lots of aides.

Q: How do you go about selecting an aide?

Adm. F.: The bad experience I've had is allowing someone

else to send me an aide. I think you have to know the fellow or know of him pretty well. I've been very successful in having wonderful aides, and sometimes they've been flops. In this aviation business I've stuck to a rule that an aviator is supposed to be an operator and if he's out of the operating regime too long he loses his efficiency. Therefore, I don't think an aide should serve as an aide overly long. On the other hand, in the non-aviation field the job of an aide is sought, whereas I've had the experience of one time when I was getting ready to deploy to WesPac I inherited an aide who was due to be transferred and I needed a replacement, so I asked ComAirPac to send me candidates. The first question I would ask was, do you wish to be an aide, and the answer was invariably no. And I understood why they said that.

It is a broadening experience, however, being an aide. I've only been an aide once. No, I take that back. I was called an aide when I was Chief of Staff at the Naval War College.

Q: Well, it automatically elevates you to a different level -

Adm. F.: What I'm thinking of particularly is being an aide to CinCPac. There again, it depends on how you handle it, but the way I handled it - of course, he traveled with me all the time - I insisted that he at least try to know as much about the problems as I knew. He was always present at conferences of my staff.

Another way of handling it, of course, is just to let him sit in the outer office and take care of dinner parties.

Q: It's a help but it doesn't help you in the vital things, does it?

Adm. F.: No. The feedback I get from fellows who served as aides to me when I was CinCPac and when I was Vice Chief is that it really gave them the big picture, which is important in the matter of growth. It's a privilege, actually.

Interview No. 2 with Admiral Harry Donald Felt, U.S. Navy
(Retired)

Place: BOQ, Makalapa, Pearl Harbor

Date: 3 March 1972

Subject: Biography

By: John T. Mason, Jr.

Q: It's good to see you again this morning, Admiral. You say you want to go back for a brief time over some of the material yesterday?

Adm. F.: Yes, Doctor, if I may. After meeting with you yesterday and trying to analyze what has transpired so far or what I've said so far I realized I made a couple of errors.

One question you asked me - this is back in the VS-3 days - was whether or not we did any night flying. I stumbled around in my bad memory and answered, no, I didn't think so. After getting home I went to my flight logs and I found the answer was yes, including night carrier operations.

Q: Very interesting. Can you elaborate on that now?

Adm. F.: Not particularly. I just wanted to get the record straight on that.

Q: All right, Sir.

Adm. F.: Then there was another thing about the senior officers who came down to Pensacola and got flight training.

Q: The older men?

Adm. F.: The older men. Again checking my flight log, I found that I had Captain Blakely and Captain Alfie Johnson as my students at one time.

Q: Alfie Johnson certainly was quite senior, wasn't he?

Adm. F.: Yes.

There's another item I should correct. You asked me, referring back to the VS-3 days, whether I ever had an aircraft accident, or words to that effect, and I answered no, I hadn't cracked up a plane. Again I remember yes, I did.

We used to think we were awfully good at making precision landings with no power and all that sort of thing. On this particular occasion I made a beautiful landing in a river bed, right on the edge, but I dug in real deep and flopped over on my back. So, I don't want to take that credit that I gave myself yesterday!

Q: Was the plane salvageable?

Adm. F.: Yes.

Felt #2 - 66

Q: Well, shall we go on to the next assignment?

Adm. F.: Yes. Where do we go now?

Q: To the Minneapolis, in January of 1934.

Adm. F.: Yes. I got orders in December of 1933 to go to Philadelphia and, as I had understood it, to be the senior aviator of the aviation group for the USS Minneapolis, which was commissioning. We packed up during that Christmas season and shortly after the first of the year 1934 got under way for Philadelphia, via Washington.

I stopped in to the detail office on the way and was told, gee, there's no hurry, what are you doing here? I showed them my orders and said, "How come no hurry? I've got orders to get." Then, much to my surprise, I found that I was not to be the senior aviator, I was to be Number Two. Anyhow I went on up to Philadelphia and reported, and the way it worked out Ward Harrigan came as the senior aviator and he spent all of his time in the offices with the captain and the exec and other officers of the ship, preparing all the manuals that have to be worked up when you're putting a ship into commision. I went down to the field and had the enjoyable time of organizing the little air group, the little air unit.

That went on for several months during that winter and just as the Minneapolis was being commissioned - I think the day before the Minneapolis was being commissioned - I received a new set of orders to go to the Houston as the senior aviator. I joined the Houston in Brooklyn Navy Yard.

The Houston had returned from China, from the Asiatic Fleet. The senior aviator was waiting for me at the gangway, very anxious to be relieved. I was anxious to be relieved. I was anxious to relieve him and did so promptly, and then gathered everybody together to see what I had. It turned out that I had four old broken-down airplanes, which hadn't been replaced since serving in the Asiatic Fleet, and about seven aviators, some of them APs - aviation pilots, enlisted pilots - and some officers, seven or eight of them.

I found out also the ship was preparing itself to take President Roosevelt on one of his fishing trips, with ramps and all that.

Q: In southern waters?

Adm. F.: Yes. So I said, now what do we do about flying, and the answer was, "well, we don't do anything here. We're tied up in the Brooklyn Navy Yard. Perhaps we'll spend a day or two in Maine before going south, then perhaps we'll be able to fly."

I said, "That doesn't sound very good to me. Let's fly tomorrow," so we did. I hadn't been in a seaplane for a long, long, time, since Pensacola days, but we hoisted out and taxied out into the North River and had a very interesting time taking off, dodging barges under the Brooklyn Bridge.

We managed to have a little fun at that.

All this time the skipper was watching this with great interest. Every time we'd come back to be hoisted in, the skipper would be up there watching us. This impressed him, apparently, very much, so our reputation with the skipper was established immediately.

Q: What was your idea? To have a little spit and polish for the Commander-in-Chief?

Adm. F.: No, no. The President wasn't on board.

Q: No, but I mean when he got on board.

Adm. F.: No. We were sort of alerted we wouldn't do much flying when the President was on board. I think what keyed this off more than anything else was that, in those days, aviation wasn't really established as part of the fleet and I'd been alerted that when I went aboard I should be very quiet, never assert myself, aviators should stay in the background -

Q: Frustrating, wasn't it?

Adm. F.: It didn't sound well, and I decided that that wasn't the way to go about it. So I think the idea was, not only did I want to fly and see that the other pilots had an opportunity to keep up their proficiency, but to establish ourselves as part of the organization.

Q: Did you get newer planes?

Adm. F.: Eventually.

Q: Tell me about that cruise with the President on board.

Adm. F.: Before I get into that, there was another interesting little development.

Somebody had an idea of a new way of retrieving airplanes landing at sea and being retrieved by the parent ship, which was called the "sled" recovery system and we got the first one and laid it out on the dock at Brooklyn Navy Yard and tried to figure it all out. That was just the beginning of it. I'll get to that sometime later.

Anyhow, we took off on this fishing trip and went down into the Caribbean area. I did not go fishing with the President or his party because every time he was out fishing that gave us an opportunity to fly, which we did all around the Caribbean islands.

Q: Why were you not flying when he was on board?

Adm. F.: That's a question it's difficult to answer. I suspect it wasn't because of the President's desires one way or the other. I suspect it was because of the executive officer, who really didn't want us to fly at all. He just didn't want the noise and the disturbance that flying made.

I don't think there was anything particularly outstanding in that cruise, except watching the President and his party fish and seeing some people who had never caught a fish in their lives coming back with great big sailfish.

Q: Did he have a big party?

Adm. F.: Not too large. I can't remember - you see, there was another cruise too with the President later on and the composition of the parties is confused in my mind. Harry Hopkins was one. Ickes was one, but which one of these trips I can't remember. I do recall the President visiting the White Indians down in the Panama area - They went ashore and visited the White Indians.

There was a certain amount of protocol. The President would go ashore and visit and that sort of thing. We disembarked him in Charleston, South Carolina, and then we took off and went to the Pacific.

Q: To join the Pacific Fleet?

Adm. F.: Uh huh. After we got to the Pacific - I can't tell you the dates exactly - the President came aboard again for another fishing trip.

Q: He liked the Houston!

Adm. F.: Yes. He must have embarked in San Diego. I know he disembarked there. We came out to Honolulu. I don't remember the locale of all of the fishing. I may be wrong in the place of embarkation.

During this time, that sled recovery system - we developed it and demonstrated it to other aviation units.

Q: Tell me about that in detail, will you?

Adm. F.: Well, the normal system was for the cruiser to turn and make a slick for you to land in. That part of it was retained, of course. It made a high-speed turn to smooth the water down, and then taxi up and try to catch this hook of the crane and be hoisted on board. It was pretty hairy because usually you got a cross wing on the thing and everybody would try to fend a plane off from hitting the side, wing tips got crushed, and all that sort of thing.

This was a system whereby they put out a boom with a net, and there'd be a signalman, one of our chief petty officers, up on this boom giving you a signal, just like you're coming aboard a carrier, right, left, and you had a hook on the bottom of your pontoon and you'd just land at pretty high speed, just keep coming, and hook onto this net. That held you off from the side of the ship, so that you didn't bump, hook onto the crane and come aboard.

Q: It must have been quite a jolt, though, when you hit the net?

Adm. F.: No, it just stopped you right there. It was a very good system.

Q: Who devised that?

Adm. F.: I don't know. We happened to get the first set of gear, that's all.

Q: And then you were catapulted off?

Adm. F.: Yes, right.

Q: How did you keep a surplus of pilots busy when you had only four planes?

Adm. F.: We didn't retain those pilots very long. They were transferred very shortly, and I got a new deal and we only had one pilot per plane in the regular organization.

It so happened these fellows who came to me had been students while I was an instructor at Pensacola. It was a very fine little outfit, great morale, a great bunch of enlisted men. I keep in touch with some of them now. Some of them went up and made commander.

Q: And how were you employed while you were with the Houston?

Adm. F.: Doing the same old thing, scouting and spotting. Then, of course, we had our own exercises, gunnery and bombing and things like that.

Q: What kind of a radius did you have for scouting?

Adm. F.: Oh, no more than 100 miles, probably. This was a Vought biplane.

During that period the airplanes were replaced with a Curtiss airplane, what they called the SOC, which was a very fine airplane for that kind of work.

Q: Was it a new plane out?

Adm. F.: Yes. I spent two years in the Houston. As I say, the morale of our aviation in it was just superb, our reputation was high. We always got complimented on inspections. I think this might be an interesting thing to stick in here.

We were on a fleet exercise one time and, as aviators charged with scouting and that sort of thing, we had all the op orders and knew what was going on. The crew didn't know what was going on at all. They'd go to general quarters and stand this watch-and-watch business - condition 2 watch - but they didn't know why they were doing it, so I requested permission to explain the operation to the crew at night movie. I think that was well received, but it just amazed me the lack of knowledge on the part of the crew and a lot of the officers. They didn't know why they were doing something.

I guess the point of my story is that people work better when they know why they're doing it than when they haven't any idea.

Q: That's the old problem of communication!

Adm. F.: Why, sure.

Q: In retrospect, what would you say that experience contributed to the development of your own career?

Adm. F.: In the first place, responsibility of being a senior aviator, and also ship experience. I was senior watch officer.

Oh, one other thing I think might be of interest. It certainly was a pleasant thing for me to hear.

One day when I was up on the bridge on watch the captain said to me, "You know, I certainly think your aviators are the best watch officers I've got." I said, "That's interesting, Captain. Why do you say that?"

He said, "Well, because they take responsibility." Now, there's a cut-off point when you're an officer of the deck on this sort of thing. I think what he was talking about was that some officers can't make a decision so they call the captain all the time to make all the decisions, whereas there are a lot of decisions an experienced watch officer should make himself, and my boys would do it.

Q: By virtue of being a pilot, some of this is necessary, isn't it?

Adm. F.: I suppose. And another thing, we had an admiral's inspection and this was at sea. He called each watch officer individually to come up to the bridge and then handed him a little problem which had to do with relative motion and interception and things like that. My boys all went up with their little aviation chart boards, whereas the non-aviators would go up and they'd get a - what do you call it, a plotting sheet out, parallel rulers, and so on and so forth. My boys would turn their plotting sheet once or twice and have the answer just like that. That made an impression.

Q: This is all interesting because wasn't there a period when aviators didn't stand watch?

Adm. F.: Yes. I think it was overdone in times and places. Aviators would claim that, gee, we can't stand watch because we have to fly. I made a compromise on that. I said my aviators will have eight hours of no watch before flying, otherwise they'd take their regular turn. Eight hours was the rule I made.

Incidentally, those three aviators I spoke of all made

Felt #2 - 76

flag rank.

Q: Who was the skipper of the Houston?

Adm. F.: Woodson was the first skipper.

Q: He certainly had a sympathetic attitude toward aviators, didn't he? That was not always characteristic.

Adm. F.: Yes. There was another development that came about during that period. They decided to have officers ride the back seats as aviation observers, I guess they called them, the idea being that the officer in the back seat would do the spotting for gunfire, rather than the pilot sitting up in front who had other things to handle - flying the airplane and staying out of trouble. They appointed four of the ship's officers to be aviation observers.

That tour lasted two years. I then received orders to go as executive officer to a utility squadron, I guess is the best way to describe it. This was a squadron based at North Island, in the San Diego area, with big boats, seaplanes, and a couple of amphibian-type airplanes. The mission of the squadron was to provide utility services, particularly to provide towing service, towing sleeves for the ships to shoot anti-aircraft at, the battleships, cruisers, and destroyers. These were open-cockpit patrol planes. We'd go to an altitude where it would be freezing, so we were all dressed up in those old-fashioned bearskin flying suits and boots. That was quite interesting.

This was in the days when the PBY was just coming into the Navy. Right next door was a patrol squadron and I recall standing on the ramp and watching PBYs take off for the first flight to Honolulu. Our planes were old Martin airplanes.

Q: That was Captain McGinnis's flight, wasn't it?

Adm. F.: I don't recall.

That tour lasted just one year and I don't think there was anything particularly outstanding about it, except the fog and the weather. One landing was quite a thrill I thought. Returning from a towing mission, over the fog bank, and all we could see was mountain peaks in the back of the San Diego area, which were sort of our navigation beacons, and when we arrived in the San Diego area there was nothing but fog bank. Something had to be done. I didn't want to go back and land in the mountains, so I decided I'd go on down. I thought I knew where I was but couldn't be sure. I was very fortunate. I glided down over San Deigo and broke out about 75 feet, maybe, and there was the water, so it was OK.

Q: What sort of instruments did you have at that time?

Adm. F.: Nothing except the old standard turn-and-bank instrument.

Felt #2 - 78

After that tour I got ordered to the Naval Air Station, San Diego - North Island, and went into engine overhaul as the Number Two. The second year I fleeted up to be the officer in charge of engine overhaul.

Q: You really were getting a thorough grounding, weren't you, in all phases of aviation?

Adm. F.: This was something new. I'm sure I didn't have any particular qualifications for it. Incidentally, I had a long time ago decided not to go for a postgraduate course because I wanted to stay operational, but this was very instructive. We built and fitted out a new engine overhaul plant during that time. We were very active. Airplane engines were having their problems in those days and from time to time we'd have to replace all the engines in the fleet.

Q: When you say they "were having their problems" what were they?

Adm. F.: Main bearings burning out and things like that.
The organization of the plant was interesting. It was half civilian and half enlisted.

Q: Civilian civil service?

Adm. F.: Civil Service, expert people in that field and

enlisted who came in for a couple of years just to round out their experience, and it was gratifying to see how well they worked together. One might expect that there'd be abrasions - a different outlook, you know, different pay scale, and all that. But in many of these shops our enlisted men would be the foreman of the shop, and in some of these there were enlisted men I had served with before. It was a very pleasant and interesting experience.

Q: You say you fitted out this plant. This involved - ?

Adm. F.: A new building, putting new equipment in and all that sort of thing. In other words, making it an industrial shop, rather than just a sort of a hodge podge, which we'd had.

Q: Did it involve going to the plants where the machinery was made and that kind of thing?

Adm. F.: Oh, no. I didn't have anything to do with the procurement of it.

Q: That was done through the Bureau of Aeronautics?

Adm. F.: I suppose so, yes.

Q: When you were overhauling, say, a Curtiss plane, was there a Curtiss - ?

Adm. F.: I didn't have anything to do with the airplane. There were several different departments, you might say. One department would overhaul the airplane's frame. I just had the engines.

You'd bring them in, clean them up, tear them down, inspect, replace, put them back together again, and then put them on the test stand, and, if satisfactory, turn them over to the supply department.

Q: When you were working on, say, Curtiss planes, was there any contact with a Curtiss man representing the aircraft industry?

Adm. F.: There was contact with the engine manufacturers' representatives there. The two main engine manufacturers had a representative there all the time - Wright and Pratt and Whitney. All the time they were working right with us and were very helpful. In those days, these kind of people, the engine representatives and the airplane representatives, went to sea with the squadrons.

Q: They did?

Adm. F.: Yes. They were very good and very helpful.

Q: This was not only to help you but also to help them with future models?

Adm. F.: Well, yes, pick up bugs and send reports back to their companies to correct discrepancies.

Q: You say this was a new enterprise on the part of naval aviation. How did this happen?

Adm. F.: What do you mean?

Q: I mean the overhauling of your own engines.

Adm. F.: No, that wasn't a new enterprise. I'm sorry if I haven't made it clear. When I went to the Air Station as Number Two in engine overhaul, it was a plant that was in a bunch of sheds. You see, Naval Air Station, North Island, going way back, just grew like Topsy and, like so many things in naval aviation, people who started something didn't have the vision to look far enough ahead, and it was just a bunch of old buildings and fit it in as best you can - a production line of sorts, whereas what I was talking about was we built a new building and we put in a real modern production line.

Q: I suppose it was difficult to anticipate in terms of maintenance planes that weren't yet available?

Adm. F.: Yes. Of course, even though naval aviation - I can't quite remember accurately my history, whether it started in Annapolis or whether it started at North Island - but, regardless, the first aviation installation at North Island were a couple of tents. I believe Jack Tower set that up, if I'm not mistaken.

Something else occurs to me just to throw in the pot here. During the period we've been talking about - and I'm not going to try to identify dates - maybe Houston, sometimes when the Houston would go to the Navy Yard we'd all go down to North Island and put our planes - some of them were on wheels at that time, anyhow during this period we had the opportunity every once in a while to ferry airplanes back and forth across the United States. It was a system whereby you applied, got on the list, and if you were lucky you were chosen to take an airplane over to Norfolk. The system then apparently was that certain type airplanes were overhauled in Norfolk and certain other types were overhauled in San Diego. So there was a lot of shuttling back and forth.

Yesterday, while looking at my flight logs and being concerned about the errors I made yesterday morning, I noted some of these records of ferry flights. The rule was that you had to fly in good weather, what they called visual flight rules, daytime only. So it was a series of short jumps, and I added up some of the flight times. For instance, from Norfolk to San Diego took a total of about 23 hours.

Felt #2 - 83

Q: Really! Well, this all helped you to keep up your flight requirements, too, didn't it?

Adm. F.: That's correct. Cross country was part of the training program, of course. Cross country in those days was complicated in that you didn't have all the electronic devices you have now.

Q: You were pretty much on your own from airport to airport, weren't you?

Adm. F.: Reading maps, of course, was essential. There were radio beacons. If you made a trip like this, you'd put a little gadget in so you could receive a radio beacon.

Well, that's the San Diego part. Let me see if I can throw anything of family interest in this. It might be interesting to throw this in. In these days there was no such thing as government housing for the majority of people. Only those who were in command or principal officers at an Air Station had quarters on an air station, so you lived on the community. And this was fine. The community relied on this inflow and outflow of military people and, of course, Coronado was basically a Navy town.

My son was growing up at this time. He'd get a bloody nose every once in a while.

Q: Was a young officer's income adequate to this kind of

living?

Adm. F.: Oh, yes. Rents were reasonable. Facilities- yes, there was one commissary over in San Diego, very difficult to reach, and, as I remember, my manager she used the commisary very, very rarely. She used the local markets, called everybody by their first name. It was a real family community.

Q: Actually, you've been describing a period when aviation was growing up. The record of your services -

Adm. F.: Yes. I think what I'm coming into - I'm glad you gave me that thought. What I'm working up to, I believe, is - I hadn't thought of demonstrating this, but to say that we were a professional outfit, a small outfit, naval aviation, but absolutely pro, which had a lot to do with World War II. So let's work up to that now.

Q: All right.

Adm. F.: I received orders after two years at the Air Station at San Diego to take command of Bombing Squadron 2. This was a dive-bombing squadron. The fleet had just returned from a cruise to the East Coast and this squadron had a new airplane, or was fitted out with a new airplane, just prior to going off on this cruise, and it was a pretty long cruise. They found some bugs in the airplane which restricted it to level flight.

Q: What plane was this?

Adm. F.: This was the O2-U low-wing monoplane - Vought airplane. This had been a very frustrating cruise for the pilots in this squadron. They were supposed to be dive bombers and all the time they were following along behind torpedo planes, dropping their bombs in level flight on hand signals from the leader of the torpedo planes.

Q: Had they cracked up or something several times?

Adm. F.: I don't know. I don't know the genesis of all this, except that they had been restricted to level flight. So when I went down to take over, the skipper had already been detached. So I just took over, looked around, and -

Q: He didn't leave any memos for you?

Adm. F.: No. Much to my pleasure, the restrictions had just been lifted, so we were back in business to dive, and I said, OK, let's go. I was very fortunate. I went out on the first flight, dropped my first bomb, and hit the target! So, in some respects, you see, I was made as the skipper.

Well, I looked this outfit over and it was the shaggiest, crumbiest looking outfit I've ever seen. I'm speaking of the pilots, not the enlisted men. I don't know how many AvCads we had, quite a bunch of them, sloppy - however, they could fly airplanes. I found that out. I asked what had been going on and they said, "We don't have anything to do except fly airplanes." They hadn't been given any jobs. I corrected that immediately and made them ordnance assistant this and assistant that. I gave them something to do and they picked up immediately.

The sequel of all of this, the AvCad thing, is that finally after about a year opportunity was opened to these young men to apply for the regular Navy. Meanwhile, they'd been promoted from AvCad to ensign, USNR. Six of those boys made regular Navy, and all of them went on into World War II, had fine combat records, and - I'm not sure whether all of them did, but the ones that come to my mind immediately - made captain. I'm very proud of those boys.

Anyhow, going back to the beginning, there we were in business again as dive bombers. Excellent crew of enlisted men. So I throw in this thought, that sometimes people when they talk about morale, bringing this thought back to me, I had, as every skipper has, a report book, a mast book. After two and a half years of command of VB-2 there was not one entry in that mast book - not one. Chief petty officers took care of things pretty well, I guess.

But there was another aspect of this. We had young seamen - there wasn't such a thing as an airman yet, they hadn't created that name - in the squadron and we had the cooperation and sympathy of the carriers, who provided us with these youngsters. So they were very carefully screened and we only got good boys. We didn't have any problems at all. Well, with that kind of a set-up and start, we then went out to do the best.

Q: You made this your objective!

Adm. F.: Yes, and we thought we had accomplished that objective, but unfortunately one of our competitors was sent to the Bureau and was put in charge of whatever they called it back there, where they totaled up the scores and divided them by six and came up with who wins. This explains why we were Number Two!

But we had a fine time. We came out here to Honolulu twice in what they called a Hawaiian Detachment. This, I think, was anticipating war with Japan -

Q: This was still in Admiral Richardson's day, was it?

Adm. F.: Before that. It started in 1940. I took over in December of 1939. What had happened here - I think the Enterprise group were the first to inaugurate this Haw Det business, but the Army Air Corps had the land plane facilities at Ford Island here in Pearl Harbor. The Navy facilities were all the big seaplane facilities down on the beach there. Well, the Army Air Corps moved out and we moved in and found nothing but the shells of a couple of hangars and an awful field, coral dust and all that, and over a period of a couple of years developed that. They finally paved the field, improved the hangars, built another hangar. I think that tour of duty at Haw Det might have been three or four months, or something like that.

The first time we all came out as bachelors and lived in BOQ, which subsequently burned down, and the second time most of us brought our families over. I'll come to that later.

During that period my squadron was detailed to go down and participate in the Army maneuvers in Louisiana. I don't know how come we were picked to do it, but it was a very revealing experience. We were based at Lake Charles and had compact oyster-shell runways, operation tents, lived in tents on the high-school grounds, and got our shave and our shower in the high-school gymnasium locker room.

I think the outstanding thing that came about was - again I come back to communications. We were told that we should comply with the Army system, which was to transmit on one frequency and receive on another. By that time, incidentally, we had voice radio, just to come in, now, during this tour in 1941. The microphone wasn't very satisfactory but it was a beginning. Anyhow, we were told to follow the Army system, so I said, "All right, I'll try it." We took off the first morning and our objective was to attack some city up there under a pretty low overcast, and fighters swarmed all over us and kind of split us up. I couldn't talk to my boys. I had the heck of a time getting them back together, but they finally got back together and came back and landed all right.

I went into the General's headquarters and said, "That's the end of that." You see our system was to talk and receive all on the same frequency.

Q: Which is kind of instantaneous, isn't it?

Adm. F.: Well, yes, but they said, no, it won't work because you'll flood the circuit, everybody will be talking at the same time. I said, "All you need is discipline. Anyhow that's the end of that." Then, I found out later that the Army Tank Corps did it the same way we did it, so that kind of helped me with my argument.

Q: You had the evidence to present, too, didn't you?

Adm. F.: Yes, and another feature of it was that their system in those days was to send a plane out, like we did at sea, to scout, let's call it, and it was the enemy's tanks we were after. "Find the enemy tanks, report back, then send somebody out to attack them." Well, the enemy was long gone by the time the attack plane got out there. Of course, our system was to find and attack, right then, so we went for this principle. But, working with the Army on this, it turned out real well. We had a liaison officer on the general staff, a classmate of mine, Binny Williamson. I'll get to Binny after a while, too, who did a fine job keeping this whole thing together.

Then there was a recess, you might call it, a phase, a gap between Phase I and Phase II of the exercises, and we thought we'd done pretty daggone well. We had. We hadn't lost an airplane, nobody was hurt. We put our points across on tactics. So we decided to throw a big squadron beer party, and this turned out fine - lots of beer, everybody having a lot of fun - and all of a sudden some guy showed up and he said, "A hurricane is coming in. You have to evacuate"! So we gathered ourselves together, got out to the field, took off just as it was turning dark for Jackson, Mississippi, where we were told to go and sit out the hurricane.

I didn't know what was the trouble with me, but I was having an awful time seeing properly.

Q: The beer party!

Adm. F.: I thought it was the beer, but it turned out later that one of my cylinder's hold-down bolts had broken and there was oil all over my windshield. It wasn't the beer fuzz at all! I almost lost a cylinder. Fortunately, it stayed with me until I got there, but when we got there we were confused about the lighting and all that sort of thing and it turned out we were landing in all directions, but none of us cracked up. We sat there, checking the weather, and finally I got kind of a directive - it wasn't a real, strict, direct order - to come on back to Lake Charles. I consulted with the weatherman, and, gee, that hurricane is going to hit Lake Charles, so I dragged my feet as long as I could without actually disobeying orders, and finally I said all right, let's go, and we went back. We knew the hurricane was going to hit, so we did everything we could think of to protect our planes. We pulled them out in the mud and buried them in the mud, and turned them into what we thought was the correct direction, you know, tied them down securely, and went to our tents.

The hurricane hit. It didn't damage the airplanes. They were sunk in the mud. It didn't bother us. We all slept through it in our tents, although the water was coming up and everything, and next morning we went down to the high school locker room, and there were all the Army guys who'd spent the night in the locker room. I said, "What the hell are you fellows doing. We slept"!

Q: In tents!

Adm. F.: Yes.

Q: Why did they order you to come back, having ordered you away?

Adm. F.: I didn't debate it when we got back. I don't know.

They wanted to get the exercise started on time, I guess.

Well, we finished that one up and there was only one problem. We had to change one engine. We didn't have a spare engine with us, but they sent us an engine. I left a small crew and one airplane and officer back to change the engine.

On the way back - I've forgotten whether it was that airplane whose engine had been changed or whether it was one of the group, we didn't fly back as a whole group, we split it up to give pilots experience going back -- one fellow lost his man in his rear seat. He doesn't know how. There wasn't any particular trouble. He just found the seat empty and a pair of shoes sitting on the deck in the rear seat. He was in some turbulent weather. Maybe the guy had been bounced out. We don't know. That was our casualty.

So, another tour at this Haw Det business and I brought my family out in May of 1941. We suffered a casualty about the second or third day they were here. Again, a beer party of a Saturday on the beach at Kaneohe. My young son, arriving with an arm in a cast, he'd fallen out of a tree, I asked and got permission from Kathryn to let Linn go with me, providing we'd be careful and not break his arm again. We got in a ball game on the beach and I think the score was tied in the ninth inning, and I hit one, I really hit one, and tried to stretch it to three and slid in on my elbow and dislocated my elbow!

So, instead of taking her dancing at the Royal Hawaiian

that night, I went to the hospital to get my arm fixed up.

While I'm on the subject of accidents. I have to walk back a bit - I guess it was the first tour out here in Honolulu - I spun in off the bow of the carrier - might as well admit it; I spun in, this was in the days of free takeoffs, not catapults - a low-wing monoplane which spun very easily if you just started to stall it. And the technique of takeoff was to pull up as you reached the end of the deck and then go into a turn, the object being to clear the deck of all the turbulence for the next guy, and we tried to take off at some seconds intervals. Well, I made my turn a little bit too sharp, and there I was. I could see myself going in.

I remember reading a book written by a barnstormer who had flown in World War I in the Lafayette Escadrille telling fabulous stories about those early aviation days. And one of these stories was about a fellow who saved himself when he knew he was going to crash by throwing the thing in on its wing, on his wing tips. Well, I remember that flash, and apparently I had just enough control to get it over and, bang, she went in on the wing tips. The plane and I went under water, but we popped up, and that was all right. I had water on the knee on one leg and a sprained ankle on the other.

I was very fortunate because two other people who'd crashed in that same type of airplane earlier and mashed themselves up pretty badly.

By the way, this was before the days of shoulder harness.

Let's slip back a minute.

The lack of vision was appalling sometimes. Shoulder harness seems such a natural thing to have, right?

Q: Yes, a common sense improvement.

Adm. F.: We didn't have it! It came along eventually. We had an airplane in the air group, a fighter - I can't remember the type, F-4 something or other - which was a horrible thing to control on takeoff. It just wanted to take off in a round turn. The pilot had to be awfully good with his tabs and his rudder to keep it straight. I've seen two or three of them crash right into the water and bump alongside of the ship as it went by. The pilot with a shoulder harness would have been saved, but we didn't have them.

Well, let's see, where are we?

Q: Since you were in Pearl at that time and it was so near to big events, tell me about the feeling in Pearl and about reconnaissance flights, if there were any, and that sort of thing.

Adm. F.: Yes - well, let's talk about ourselves first. We were training to fight. We were going out and doing night bombing, for example, on the Utah, developing night bombing techniques. We were using live bombs on target practice for the first time ever. Always before, they'd just been sand-filled or water-filled. I can't remember when this started, but sometime along in the early fall, perhaps, of 1941. My airplanes were always loaded with ammunition, always.

Now, as to the situation here, it's very interesting. There was full 360-degree coverage of this island in the summer of 1941. I'm just trying to get these times approximately correct. In the summer of 1941 this coverage was provided by the Navy patrol squadrons, there were two of them here, I believe, and by the Army Air Corps, even though the Army Air Corps - I say this advisedly - did it reluctantly because they had no heart for flying over water in land planes. Nevertheless, they were part of this coverage. That was in the summer.

As I told you, I went back to the Louisiana maneuvers in the fall, September. When I came back I was all involved in my own business but I gradually realized that something had changed. I didn't quite know what it was. But I'd bump into a group of the VP pilots grousing a little bit and ask them what gives, and they'd say, well, we're working too hard. "What do you mean by that?" "Well, we've slacked off." I didn't pursue it; I just realized something was happening.

All right, we get into the war - I'm jumping ahead now. I've been detached from my command of VB-2. I had it for two and a half years, which was right nice. No, wait a minute, I'm getting ahead of my story. I'm still in the Lexington. I still have VB-2. We have gone to sea two or three days before 7 December with a Marine squadron on board to deliver this Marine squadron to Wake or Midway, I've forgotten which - Midway probably. The news comes that Pearl Harbor has been attacked, so that Sunday morning we put the Marines back down in the hangar - they were just about to take off - and started looking for the Japanese. We were on the south side of the island chain and the Japanese were on the north side.

We didn't find the Japanese.

We finally need fuel, and the system in those days was that a tanker would come alongside the carrier, instead of the other way around, as it is now. It was rough weather, and after several attempts the tanker's skipper decided he couldn't make it, so the Lexington came into Pearl Harbor. Just what that date was I'd have to check my flight log. We disembarked and landed at Ford Island. During that night the Lexington fueled. There were still depth charges being dropped around the harbor because they thought one of the little midget submarines was still in the harbor. We made out the best we could, but during this period I had a chance to talk to some people and found out that on Pearl Harbor Day there was no coverage to the north, and this thing that I sensed earlier was a decision to give coverage to the fleet only while it was in what they called the drill grounds down south.

I say down at a table at BOQ with a bunch of the battleship officers and asked them what happened. One of the things which was told me was that no officer in the fleet could ever conceive of the ships being attacked while in Pearl Harbor. Yes, out in the drill grounds, but not in Pearl Harbor.

Now, let me go back.

Every time the battleships were in port they asked for

aviation service to fly across, down, or what to give the gun crews practice, but that didn't apparently convey the idea that they might be attacked while in Pearl Harbor.

Let me go back still further.

The date, again, is vague to me but I would say about the spring of 1940 a fleet cruise came out this way and we attacked Pearl Harbor, on a Sunday morning, from exactly the same place as the Japanese attacked on 7 December, catching everybody just like the Japanese caught us on 7 December. We attacked Pearl Harbor and the military installations around here. At that time the Japanese consul or consul general lived over here at Pearl something or other, just across from Ford Island, noting this attack among other things. And it's quite interesting now, reading the Japanese stories of the attack on Pearl Harbor, to see that they attacked from the same place we attacked from a year or a year and a half earlier. They learned a lesson, but we didn't.

Q: And is there tangible evidence that the consul general or whoever it was there did report this exercise?

Adm. F.: There's evidence that he reported everything that went in and out of Pearl Harbor and charted the berths. And, incidentally, it was reported on Pearl Harbor Day that the Lexington had been sunk. Kathryn, hearing this - thought we'd been sunk at sea. The fact was that it was the Utah that was sunk, tied up where the Lexington normally tied up when she was in port.

Yes, there's hard evidence that he reported everything he

saw. Now, as to whether he reported that attack, I haven't hard evidence on it, but I think it's a fair conclusion that he did.

Q: May I go back to one remark you made and ask you to elaborate on it in the light of future knowledge? When you were talking with the pilots and this was well before Pearl Harbor Day and they said, "They say we're being overworked," what does this mean?

Adm. F.: Well, it was very vague. The word had gone out that they shouldn't fly as much as they had. There's always been some concern about overflying a pilot. At one time - I don't know what it's like now - a magic number, more than 80, 90, or 100 hours a month is just more than a pilot can take.

Q: Does he get surfeited then?

Adm. F.: I don't know just what happens. I guess he gets over-tired. So, as I gathered it, it was just a relaxation to cut down on flying hours, or expense might have had something to do with it, too. But that's apparently what happened. They just relaxed the whole thing under a crazy concept that being inside this harbor was enough to protect them. Of course, the anti-aircraft defense out here was practically nil.

Q: The reason I asked you about the pilots being overworked is because I understood that when Admiral Richardson was still in command he insisted upon daily reconnaissance flights some distance out, and then when he was relieved of his command there was a change in policy, and it had something to do with expense and the few planes, and what have you.

Adm. F.: It might have had something to do with expense. It might have had something to do with pilot fatigue. I don't know. This is all I know about Admiral Richardson, and I know this only from reading, that he sent back to Washington and said something to the effect "if I am not given adequate protection for my fleet out here, I will take the fleet back to the West Coast." Now, that might not be an accurate reflection of what he said, but basically I think that's what he said, with the result he was relieved, this was by Admiral Kimmel?

Q: Who took over? Yes.

Adm. F.: I attended a meeting at the old Officers' Club here at the Naval Base. It was a building where the center dance floor was large and open, and it was used for critiques, sort of like the war game thing at the Naval War College, and he held forth at this meeting with his whole attention on small-ship operations. He was fundamentally a destroyer man, I suppose. Packets of small ships. Not one word was said, as I recall it, about aviation at that meeting.

Now, we used the word "concept" and I guess you could take it from there.

Q: That says a great deal!

Felt #2 - 100

Shall we go back to the Lexington?

Adm. F.: We've pretty well covered the Lexington. We got into the beginning of the war, coming in that night and re-fueling, and within days - toward the latter part of December, anyhow, I received two sets of orders. One was from Washington to go back to the West Coast and assist a friend of mine in training pilots in airplanes that were coming out then. Remember now, I mentioned this professional outfit we had, but it was an outfit of one pilot per plane, that's all we had. There was no back-up. The idea of this training program was to start providing a back-up.

I received that set of orders and, at the same time, received a set of orders from Admiral Nimitz to take the air group in the Saratoga.

Q: He was already here?

Adm. F.: Yes, he'd come and taken over. Well, it was obvious which set I carried out, and reported aboard the Saratoga when she came in.

Q: Tell me, in a situation like that how do you go about canceling the other set of orders?

Adm. F.: I don't know, I just ignored them! I really don't know what happened to them. Anyhow, Admiral Nimitz' orders were carried out. Yes, there was a question about it. I reported aboard and the skipper and the fellow I relieved were very upset about this. The fellow I relieved was ordered ashore to organize the first CASU - Carrier Air Support Unit, or something like that. This was the beginning of a system set up ashore to support the carriers in upkeep and the carriers' air groups' upkeep.

He was very upset. He went to the skipper immediately, and the skipper said, "I won't stand for this," because he didn't want to lose this boy. He didn't know me. The skipper immediately got his gig and rushed over to see Admiral Nimitz, and Admiral Nimitz told him "the orders will stand," so we carried them out.

Q: A difficult circumstance.

Adm. F.: That posed quite a problem for Felt because the air group commander and the skipper have to work as a team. First of all, I knew all the boys in the Saratoga air group. We were closely associated. The Lexington and Saratoga air groups would fly from each other's ships -

Q: Interchangeable!

Adm. F.: Yes, so there was no problem there. I decided I'd fly every day.

Q: Who was the skipper?

Adm. F.: Douglas. And when I'd come back I'd immediately go to the bridge and report to the captain. It took a little time to kind of break this barrier down, but gradually it broke down, and it finally wound up where I would take him out for his flight time. It worked out all right.

Q: Had you had some connection with Admiral Nimitz before? How did he happen to know about you?

Adm. F.: No, I haven't any idea. I'd never met the man.

Q: I wonder, Sir, if you'd lap back for a moment and talk about the situation at Pearl Harbor immediately after the Japanese attack on that Sunday morning? You said the Lexington came in a short time thereafter for re-fueling purposes.

Adm. F.: Well, let's go back just a minute. You remember I said that we were at sea preparing to launch Marines and, on learning about the attack on Pearl Harbor, we then tried to find the Japanese. It would have been interesting if we had - one carrier air group against the Japanese force, wouldn't it? And, finally, because of being unable to fuel at sea, the Lexington came in to Pearl.

I'm now looking at my old flight log, and we flew in from the Lexington to Ford Island on the 13th of December. Now, you're asking what were my impressions?

Q: Yes.

Adm. F.: First of all, you were impressed, even while flying in to make an approach to land, with the dead odor of the place. That's probably not a very profound way of describing it, but the smell as a result of the burning and everything was permeating the place. It made me pretty sick to see what had happened.

As I say, we landed and we went over to BOQ, all darkened, and found people milling around, and I had the opportunity to talk to some people, particularly to get the slant of the battleship people. During that night, as I've already mentioned, while the Lexington was fueling, there was all sorts of scurrying around the harbor, depth bombs being dropped, ships picking up anchor and moving because it was thought that there were still submarines in the harbor. So it was a pretty ticklish night for everybody. However, the fueling was completed and the ship left the next day and we went back on board.

Q: Itching to get at the Japs!

Adm. F.: Sure. I think it's understandable. A great hate was generated, of course. Dirty Japs.

Q: Betrayal!

Adm. F.: Let's get 'em. Does that some what answer your question?

Q: Yes.

Adm. F.: Let's go on with the Lexington because this was probably the most frustrating period of my then flying career.

After this re-fueling, an operation was set up to make the first strike of the war on one of the islands, or a group of islands. I can't remember the names of the islands we were supposed to hit, but a plan was laid out for us to take off and attack these islands.

Adm. F.: As we were preparing and ready to do this, word would come back "extend the range." OK, we'd extend it up to our maximum, and then word would come down, "no, we won't do it in the daytime, we'll do it at night," with the result that the requirements, as they gradually built up, got way beyond the airplanes' capability, so it was determined that the operation was not feasible and the whole thing was called off. Very frustrating.

Q: Why this straining at the limitations of the planes? Were these orders being given by somebody who was not an aviator and didn't know the - ?

Adm. F.: I imagine that they generated with the Task Force Commander. The impression we pilots got was that he was trying to reduce the risk of the ship getting hit to the point that he put all the risk on losing all the pilots in the water.

Q: It was certainly true that the carrier was a very precious commodity at that time, wasn't it?

Adm. F.: Yes, that's true. Well, after that little experience was when I got my orders to the Saratoga, the air group of the Saratoga.

So, here's the Saratoga ready to go out and train, and we went out here south of Oahu and milled around training, and, sure enough, I believe it was on the 12th of January, we got torpedoed.

Q: What kind of an escort did you have when you were out?

Adm. F.: A couple of destroyers, plane guards, no screen. One of the submarines that had been over here for Pearl Harbor Day just lingered around waiting. I guess we must have crossed through this point enough times for it to get the bead. We were torpedoed. I happened to be in the air at the time and we searched for the submarine. The ship was dead in the water, so we came in here and landed. The ship finally made it in, then was sent to Bremerton for repair.

I think I'm getting this chronologically correct.

I went back with the ship with just part of my air group, enough of my air group to help this fellow who was training back-up pilots, and left part of the air group here. When the ship went in to Bremerton, we flew down to San Diego and joined in this training.

Q: What sort of speed could she make on the way back to Bremerton?

Adm. F.: Well, she had a big patch on her and it was all right. Not high speed. When she got hit with the torpedo she got hit in the engineroom-control area and, as I remember it, it was all electric control and all the switchboards and everything went out.

As I say, we left part of the air group here. It took maybe

three months to get this repair made, and meantime I think they put on an additional blister to give it antitorpedo protection. She got out of the yard and we flew back up to the Puget Sound area and landed on board. Then she came down to San Diego, I guess to get proper supplies and so on and so forth, and headed for Pearl. She was in here for a day, maybe, and then headed out for Midway and we missed Midway by one day, but the part of my air group I'd left here was in it, flying I believe from the Enterprise. Anyhow, we missed and were the butt of a lot of jokes for a long while.

Oh, and we missed Coral Sea, because Coral Sea had taken place meanwhile, too.

Then, as events unraveled, we prepared for the Guadalcanal operation. There might have been some island stuff meanwhile. In the Guadalcanal, here again it was Frank Jack Fletcher - let me see, I think they had three carriers - and as I understood it later, the admiral had some kind of directive not to lose one of those very valuable carriers because the build-up hadn't taken place yet, with the result that we operated in an area south of Guadalcanal.

We took off the morning of the landings and I had the job of controlling the air over Guadalcanal that day. I spent practically the whole day landing aboard to re-fuel and doing this. At the end of that day I found up in a little river a bunch of what looked like landing craft, Japanese landing craft, meanwhile I directed fire here, there, and other places, and I reported this to the amphibious commander, Kelly Turner, and got an acknowledgment from whoever was on the other end of the phone and persisted. I said, "We ought to get these fellows." Well, it was too late in the day and so forth, so he said, "I'd like to have you back tomorrow," and I said, "All right, I'll be back." You know, being a brash young man and not paying any attention to high command directives and so on and so forth, I landed back on board after dark, everything was all blacked out, radio silence, and reported to the captain -

Q: It must have been difficult, a deck landing at that point, wasn't it?

Adm. F.: Oh, they turn on the lights, the landing lights. I reported to Captain Duke Ramsey and told him what I'd promised, and he said, "Oh, my gosh, we've got orders to leave tomorrow." I said, "You can't leave, Captain, these guys still need air support. You just can't do it." Radio silence. He had his orders. He had to leave. He couldn't break the radio silence. He said, "All right, we'll launch tomorrow morning." I think he probably caught hell, but we stayed, and it was during this day that the Japanese started to attack.

The coast watchers were very good and we had intelligence. We knew that a whole swarm of Japanese were coming down to hit the transports that were offloading at Guadalcanal.

I came back and first I saw the Captain and he said, "Go up and talk to the Admiral." I went up and said, "Look, these guys are coming down and they're just going to literally clobber those transports."

"No, they won't attack the transports. They're going for us and get us." I said, "Look, between you and those Japanese, there's Guadalcanal in the first place and all these helpless targets down there. Let's get our fighters off and protect those fellows." Dave Richardson was in that fighter squadron.

Finally, he gave in and said all right, and our fighters arrived there just after the Japs had attacked, and the fighters did do a great job of shooting down airplanes.

Dave told me, incidentally, when I was talking to him yesterday, that he shot the first one down.

Well, we did pull out after that second attack. That was Guadalcanal.

Q: And was there any threat to the carrier during that time?

Adm. F.: No, the fighters never bothered after they saw all those juicy targets.

We pulled back and then started to operate some more. I'm leading up to the battle of August the - let's see, Guadalcanal was the first part of August - here we were steaming around, scouting, exercising, and we got word that a big Japanese group was coming down and I was launched with practically all of my air group to try and find these guys.

Q: Was this in what's called "the slot"?

Felt #2 - 109

Adm. F.: No. I ought to remember the name of this battle east of the Solomons. This was the lead-in to it. It was the Battle of the Eastern Solomons. We were launched to try to locate and attack this group and we ran into some just terrible pile of weather. Having confidence in my people, I put them out on what you might call a scouting line. In other words, a line abreast, by sections of airplanes, three in a section. We did have an automatic device in the airplane which would fly the airplane when you set it. We were going about 50 feet off the water, all spread out I don't know how many miles, this whole air group -

Q: How many were in the group?

Adm. F.: Oh, I had about three squadrons. Everybody on instruments. Wing men latched right on to the section leaders. We must have flown in this stuff for an hour, and all of a sudden broke through into an open area, and there was the whole damned group right there. Just magnificent discipline! And that's about where we expected to find these Japanese. They weren't there. We had a little consultation, and one fellow suggested that we look over in this direction, which we did, and didn't find them.

We'd launched pretty late in the afternoon and we had orders to land back in Guadalcanal and spend the night there.

Q: On the land?

Adm. F.: Yes. So we made our way back to Guadalcanal in all this bad weather, and the Marines were there, of course, and helped us get into the field. The Japanese on the perimeter of the field were shooting at us all the time. We got every one of them in there, this little old horrible field.

Q: This was Henderson Field?

Adm. F.: Henderson Field, parked the airplanes off to the side, and I went up and reported to the senior Marine, and it was agreed that we would stay in our airplanes that night and be ready for take-off in case the place was attacked. The only attack that occurred that night was a submarine bombardment. Meanwhile, it was raining hard and we managed to get a cup of coffee and eat what little bit of what was then emergency rations in the airplanes.

The next morning we sat through an alert and nothing developed. We dumped our bombs in the mud and gave them to the Marines and took off for the ship. We got back to the ship about eleven o'clock in the morning and they said, "Get ready to take off immediately. There's another outfit." Meanwhile, this first outfit we'd looked for, we found out later, had turned around and gone back north. I said, "How far away?" They told me and I said, "No, that's beyond our range. Let's just take it easy. This gang has flown all day yesterday, spent the night in their airplanes, flown back here to the ship. They need just a little bit of rest. You keep getting intelligence and when those things are within our range, we'll go," which we did about two thirty in the afternoon.

Q: What was considered your range?

Adm. F.: Oh, golly - meantime we had a different type airplane, an SBD - 200 miles maybe. Well, we found this outfit and I had a little trouble. My receiver indication thing went out. But we found and attacked this outfit. We weren't quite sure of the results, but it turned out later, yes, we did sink the Ryujo and were given credit for a cruiser and damaging some other ships.

The interesting part of this was that here was this carrier, big cruiser, and destroyers, and I elected to divide my forces. I put the majority of the force on the carrier and then told one division of my bombing squadron to take the cruiser, and, as the attack developed, I could see we were getting near misses but I couldn't see any hits on the carrier, so I rescinded the order and caught the division that had been told to attack the cruiser just as they were going into their dive, and they pulled out and came over and joined the attack on the carrier. With the result, as I say, of sinking it. Then I went off into the clouds and hung around a long while and finally made my way back to the ship.

Meanwhile, the Enterprise had been damaged, so the Saratoga had the job of taking aboard all the Saratoga planes and also a bunch of Enterprise planes. It was quite an operation that night, with planes put up on their noses to make more room.

Q: Stacked!

Adm. F.: They were stacked. But, getting back to this pro business, that attack was carried out just like a training exercise. By the way, it was dive bombers and torpedoes. Just like a training exercise! We didn't lose a plane or a pilot. Some of our people shot down some of theirs.

Let me jump ahead now. We've been mentioning Admiral Nimitz a lot. This jumps two months ahead. This was maybe shortly thereafter. I was called in to Admiral Nimitz' headquarters and ushered into his office, Admiral Nimitz and some of his senior officers, to orally report on this action. During the course of this I was criticized by at least one of Admiral Nimitz' officers for dividing my firepower. Admiral Nimitz asked me about it and I told him that I thought I had more than adequate force to take the carrier and I also wanted to hit that cruiser. But when I found out that it wasn't working like I had hoped, I countermanded the order and everything went on the carrier.

God bless him! He turned to that officer and said, "Gentlemen, Commander Felt was in command." That was the end of that.

Q: That was his philosophy.

Adm. F.: Well, now, to carry on.

Here was this battle - the Enterprise, the Saratoga. Then subsequently here we were operating around, crossing the same point time after time, and damned if we didn't get torpedoed again! Oh, boy they blew a big hole in us, and we went in to Tongatabu, where the repair people who did underwater stuff put on a big patch. And - an interesting sidelight - I believe this was the island that was commanded by a queen.

Q: Yes, the Tonga Island group.

Adm. F.: Right. She had gotten word that we were coming in. So, as we understood it, she sent all the girls to the mountains and released all the ponies! So when the men got ashore they had a heck of a good time riding the ponies!

Our people, of course, the Americans, no matter where they are, have to buy souvenirs, and riding back in a boat one day this fellow was sitting there fingering a meerschaum pipe - "Boy, just look at this bargain I got! Wow!" I said, "Let me see that." I turned it over and it was made in New Jersey! or made in USA!

Anyhow, we got out of there and this time the <u>Sara</u> was brought in to Pearl for repair, here to this Navy yard, and the decision was made that my air group, or at least most of it, would go ashore at Guadalcanal and help the Marines. I had my parachute bag all packed with my dirty khaki and was ready to go, and the skipper called me up and said, "Oh uh, you're not going. You're going back and organize a new air group." So I was stuck with that. I wasn't able to go with the boys to Guadalcanal.

Q: How did they do when they went?

Adm. F.: Fine, I believe Mangrum was the senior Marine aviator there.

Well, I got back and here I had the job of getting a new air group together. I brought back a handful of fighter pilots. These were the most wonderful enlisted APs, and that was all I had. I said, "Where am I going to get my squadrons?" And they said, "Well, there's one dive-bombing squadron ready." I said that's fine. There was a torpedo squadron with a new airplane that was going to be available. "Where do I get my fighters? Where do I get this other dive-bombing squadron?

"Well, we've got a lot of pilots around. You know they've thrown the airplanes off of the cruisers because in those battles down there, Savo Island - remember, fires because of aviation fuel, and so on and so forth." So they threw the airplanes off the cruisers and we got all these pilots.

The catch in this whole thing was that these pilots went to Pensacola pretty much on an expedited basis and had never flown a land plane, nothing but seaplanes. I said, "Well, I don't like it but I'll take a chance. We'll give it a try."

Q: Where were you doing this?

Adm. F.: Over at Kaneohe. There was only one runway and along the lefthand side of the runway were these big revetments. Our airplane was this airplane designation - I've forgotten - but I told you it was such a beast to handle on takeoff.

Q: Yes, it went in circles.

Adm. F.: We had a handful of those. So the procedure was something like this. The pilots, remember, were the kind hopefully being converted from a seaplane pilot to a fighter pilot. He'd be put into the cockpit and be given a dry run on the cockpit, with an AP leaning over his shoulder instructing him, and after feeling that the pilot had absorbed all the instruction, a pat on the back and saying, "OK, let's turn up and go." Well, the first two or three on their "go" went off in a round turn and crashed directly into one of these revetments. And that was the end of the experiment, as far as I was concerned.

Q: Maybe, this would be a good time to point out the major differences between a seaplane pilot and a carrier-based pilot?

Adm. F.: There are no particular measured differences. There's certainly a difference in technique in taking off a seaplane and taking off a land plane, but the problem was the idiosyncrasy of the airplane with the torque of the engine pulling it to the left and being able to control it with a full right rudder and full right tak, and if you lost control there you were. But that being the case, we dropped that experiment.

I found, however, there was a fighter squadron in this area. It was over on one of the other islands, completely organized and ready, and commanded by a fellow who later became an ace - David McCampbell, would that be the name?

Q: I don't know.

Adm. F.: Well, we finally got an air group together and when the ship's repair was finished, off we went again down to the South Pacific. This time with a new skipper, Gerry Bogan, having relieved Duke Ramsey.

Shortly thereafter I was relieved as the air group commander and took over as the air officer of Sara and spent a few months handling the flight deck and all that sort of thing. It was quite a job because, as you recall, the carriers in those days were straight-decked and after a couple of days of operations the deck would get pretty confused so you'd have to fall out and fall in again. The job of being the air officer was an all-day job and well into the night. You were lucky to report to the captain around eleven p.m. that the deck was ready for launching the next morning.

Then they had a system of requiring the more experienced officers to take a watch on the bridge as the supervisory watch to the officer of the deck, and I drew the watch of 4 to 8 in the morning every morning.

Q: After being up until midnight!

Adm. F.: So there wasn't much rest involved in this job.

Q: Why this supervisory watch? This was an auxiliary thing, was it?

Adm. F.: Looking back on it, darned if I know. I guess it was born of a feeling on the part of the skippers that the officers of the deck were pretty inexperienced and needed experienced supervision.

Q: Was this fleetwide?

Adm. F.: I think so. We didn't have any combat action during all this time. A lot of operational training. And it looked to me as if I should move on to something else, so I talked to the captain about it and he agreed, and I left the ship in the South Pacific with orders to go to Florida to report to Admiral A. B. Cook, who was in command of operational training. That command had a series of little airfields up and down Florida, where pilots were being trained in combat types.

When I reported in at Jacksonville I was told I could have command of the Naval Air Station at Daytona Beach, where we concentrated on training dive-bombing pilots. I did that for six months and then was transferred to Opa-Locka, outside of Miami.

Q: When you were training dive-bombers, how many passed through the course?

Adm. F.: Oh, gee, I don't know.

Q: What sort of an operation was it?

Adm. F.: These were pilots who were trained to fly an airplane and who could fly this particular type of airplane, but they'd never had any experience in combat tactics, and the object was to train them in gunnery, particularly in dive-bombing on land targets and floating targets, moving targets.

Q: What I was trying to get at was the flow of pilots going through a course like this. It had been increased greatly, I imagine?

Adm. F.: Oh, yes. You see, this command was set up after the war started to create a back-up for this real small group that was naval aviation at the beginning of the war. Of course, these were all Reserve officers.

Q: They were all U.S.? There were no British involved?

Adm. F.: Not at Daytona Beach. Our instructors were people who'd come out of combat, one with whom I'd served.

Then when I went to Opa-Locka it was a bigger operation. There was a bigger installation. When I arrived there was a conglomerate of airplanes which we straightened out, and we had fighter instruction, navigational instruction, dive-bombing instruction, and gunnery, and all that sort of thing.

This was where I made my first contact with WAVES. They had a headquarters barracks for WAVES which had been Al Capone's big gambling casino. We had a senior WAVE officer in charge of the WAVES, the object being that the WAVES could do anything a man could do and, sure enough, they could do a lot. They even worked on the line. Some of these airplanes were hand-cranked and they had a little difficulty with that. We had an overhaul shop there and they did work in it. It was a full-fledged air station.

Q: They did that kind of job?

Adm. F.: They worked in the overhaul shop and, of course, all the other kind of jobs - in the tower and all that sort of thing.

Q: I understand they did pretty well in the tower?

Adm. F.: Oh, great. The feminine voice in the tower came through just loud and clear, and they were cool. They were good.

My immediate problem with the WAVES was how to handle the disciplinary problem, getting back to mast. Here I didn't have the lovely experience that I had in VB-2 of having a blank mast book. I had to hold mast.

I consulted with the senior WAVE officer and we agreed that I should handle -

Q: Was she a commander?

Adm. F.: No, she was a lieutenant - that I should handle the WAVES in the same manner I handled the enlisted men - the male enlisted people. However, I decided I would hold separate masts. I wouldn't bring a WAVE up at the same mast I was having males, but if they were over leave the same thing was dealt out to them as was dealt out to a man. That seemed to be a correct decision to make.

We did have British under instruction there, and it was very interesting to see the competition. It was also interesting to see the way in which Americans could take it fed real fast, hard, fast tempo, whereas the British had to take it a bit slower. But in regard to the safety record, the British were better than our boys.

Q: Not quite as impulsive?

Adm. F.: Maybe. This was all supervised in the Washington area by a British officer, quite a character. He used to come down and see us every once in a while. Then what made the comparison too obvious was - and this was a strange thing. A system had developed in the basic training command to "plow under" is the word they used a fellow who had just completed his student training retain him, plow him under, and make him an instructor. By that time I guess the volume had increased to the point where there was more output than was required out in the fleet. So they converted a lot of these people who'd just gotten their wings to instructors. How they turned out as instructors I have no way of knowing and can't comment on.

But came a time while I was at Opa-Locka that they decided these fellows should now get ready to go out to combat and they came down to me. They were careless - this was the first time they'd flown a combat airplane, they'd just been flying trainer types. They knew it all. And they started cracking up all over the place, to the point where I had to personally get them together and read the riot act.

Q: Was it fear that induced this?

Adm. F.: No, it was overconfidence. I recall in the area of accidents - prone to hurt yourself - it goes in cycles, or it did in those days. Up to a certain number of flight hours, you were pretty safe, and then you thought "boy, I've got it now." Then, sure enough, something would happen. You'd pick it back up again and then you'd reach another one of these peaks where you relax a little bit and it happens to you again.

Felt #2 - 121

Q: And this pertains to the majority?

Adm. F.: I suspect this was the case. What the heck! They had been successful instructors in aviation. What can you tell me about flying an airplane?

Q: This raises a question about the age level.

Adm. F.: No, I don't think age had anything to do with it. These were youngsters. But it was interesting to see and it took a little time to straighten it out.

Q: Were you using new-type planes then?

Adm. F.: They were the current combat-type planes.

Q: And, again, were representatives of the manufacturers on hand?

Adm. F.: No, I don't think so down there. There might have been one in the overhaul.

Q: How closely was this operation viewed by BuAer? How close were they keeping to this training schedule?

Adm. F.: The whole thing in those days was under BuAer. As a matter of fact, Duke Ramsey after he left the Saratoga went to Washington and became a flag officer and he visited me in Miami. He was Chief of BuAer.

I don't think there was much outstanding in that experience. It was just regular routine training with all the problems that you have with training, unless I could comment on the Navy as it was developing in those days. Going back to Daytona Beach - I relieved a fellow who had been a squadron commander in my air group. The training officer was a regular and all the rest of them were Reserve officers - no, the instructors were regulars, I mean the station people were Reserve officers. When I went to Miami I found more of the same, but a little bit different.

At Daytona Beach I inherited a policy by which a man in disciplinary trouble would be told by the skipper at mast that he would be sent to combat - this was if a man got in trouble. I changed that and said the fellows who stay out of trouble go to combat, the fellows who are motivated to go to combat go to combat, and I think I created a spirit there among the men and these Reserve officers. They all wanted to get out into the fleet. That's why they came in in the first place.

Q: I would think the other policy would be a contrary -

Adm. F.: Oh, it was.

Q: A penalty to go to combat!

Adm. F.: Yes, like the bad boy who comes before a civilian judge and is told, well, I guess you'll have to go to the Army!

I want to go back a bit. There was a program that these Reserve officers came out of. I can't remember what it was called, but it was a program to get outstanding young men to come in and be a part of naval aviation.

Q: That was at Quonset.

Adm. F.: Yes, it was up at Quonset, but I've forgotten the name of that program.

Q: Gus Reade had something to do with that.

Adm. F.: And it was so successful that it apparently produced more officers than they had requirements for in the fleet.

Q: So they depopulated all the brokerage houses in New York!

Adm. F.: Yes - so they were shunted off to these various Air Stations, and I had some fine boys at Daytona.

Now, when I went to Miami I found the same situation but a little different. They were rich boys and they had no motivation to go to the fleet at all. They wanted to get back to Washington and get in the administrative business there and things like that, so I had a little difficulty.

Q: How did you instill in them a feeling of going to combat?

Adm. F.: I was not successful with some of these officers. As a matter of fact, I fired one because he laid it on the line quite clearly that he did not want to go into combat, he wouldn't go to combat, he had political pull, he was going back to Washington. I said, "All right, scram," and that's the way it was.

Q: What would happen to a lad like that?

Adm. F.: I think he made out all right, the war was over, and now the record shows that he served in the war.

I guess that about covers that experience. At what turned out to be the end of it, I got a telephone call one day from my good friend Duckworth on Admiral Cook's staff saying, "How would you like to go to Russia? No, don't answer that question. You are going to Russia." So that was the end of that.

Q: What was your reaction to that?

Adm. F.: I was going to Russia! So I started to try to prepare myself to go to Russia, meanwhile turning over the command to Slim Johnson. And Kathryn helped me a lot. We had no concept of what life would be like, but she went down to the dime store and bought me lots of lipsticks for all the girls that I would meet in Russia and things like that.

We got in the car and went up to Jacksonville and there I left Kathryn and Linn on their own, told them to head for the West Coast and make out the best they could. And I went to Washington. I was having the heck of a time finding out about Russia and what it was all about -

Q: They were pretty secretive about the assignment, weren't they?

Adm. F.: I don't know whether it was secrecy or just what it was, but one day I ran into Wu Duncan in the corridor and he asked me what I was doing. I told him and he said, "Come over with me and I'll help you." And he dug out files and reports which gave me some idea of what to expect.

I could expect no laundry, so I loaded with soap. I loaded with a whole raft of paper collars - in those days we were still wearing the shirt with the collar button and a stiff collar. The stiff collar couldn't get starched, so I got a lot of awful things. I got some heavy clothes, of course, and did the best I could to learn a little bit about Russia. And one day, of a Sunday morning, I was going in to old Main Navy - that's where everybody was in those days - and out in front of the building was Admiral McCain, the father of Jack, Jr., here. He was fumbling around in his pockets and it was quite clear he wanted to buy a Sunday newspaper. I said, "What's the matter, Admiral?" and I bought him a paper. He looked at me and said, "Oh, yes." Admiral McCain was Chief of BuAer then. Remember I said, Ramsey was chief? Maybe he was assistant chief. Anyhow he was the head man. He looked at me and he said, "Oh, yes. You're that fellow who's going to Russia." And I said, "Yes, that's right, Admiral."

Now, it was Admiral McCain who made the decision to send a naval aviator to Russia, the idea being that there was no naval aviator over there and they thought it would be a good idea to have a naval aviator on the Military Mission in Moscow.

He looked at me and he said, "Well, I don't think you're going to accomplish anything." That was my send-off!

Q: Was there any attempt at indoctrination, I mean other than the kind of clothes you would take and so forth? Was there any attempt at telling you what they thought you might achieve?

Adm. F.: No. Nobody had any idea of what I might achieve.

Q: And what about the language barrier?

Adm. F.: Well, I could do nothing about the language. I was only in Washington a few days. Of course, I realized that it was going to be a heck of a barrier, but the only thing that I got help on was what I might expect in a living way, an existence way.

Finally, somehow or other, I joined up with another fellow who was also being ordered to the Mission.

Q: Olsen was already there, was he?

Adm. F.: Yes. This was Zonderak, and Zondarak was one of a small group of youngsters who, years before that, had been over in China and been given a Russian course. Kemp Tolley was one of them. So he could speak Russian and I thought this was great.

So we loaded up and I had a great big wooden box which they allowed me to take plus my hand baggage, and the last thing that happened before departure was a call from either the medical center at Bethesda or the hospital at Bethesda, or something, saying we've got a crate of white rats we want taken to Moscow. They're all inoculated with all the horrible diseases, each one inoculated with a different disease. All you have to do is deliver them.

Q: And feed them on the way?

Adm. F.: No. I said, now what about it? "Oh, no, you don't have to feed them. Maybe put a little water in once in a while."

Well, we took off, and I've forgotten our mode of travel, across Africa -

Q: By way of Teheran?

Adm. F.: By way of, first Cairo. By this time that crate was commencing to smell pretty high and the crew would put it way back in the tail of the airplane. We got to Cairo and there I had a problem. Something had to be done about those rats. Nobody would touch them. Incidentally, I was a captain and in those days when we checked through an Army Air Corps place I was the rank of Captain, Army Air Corps, you see, and it was difficult to establish that I was a colonel, but after having established that I was a colonel, they showed me a place up on the second deck of one of the buildings which was loaded with unclaimed baggage, and said, "You can put your rats up there, if you stay with them!" So I deposited the rats up there and the next day, we took off for Teheran. There I found a Navy medical unit and they took these rats off my hands and cleaned the thing out. I believe I had half of them still surviving and they gave them back to me. I managed to deliver about half of them in Moscow!

But, in Teheran - of course, this was my first experience in that part of the world - it was quite interesting to see how the Russians were behaving, completely disciplined, segregated unto themselves, and it was interesting to see how the community water system worked, particularly the system of flooding these deep gutters from the mountain streams, one by one, and learning that these people believed that water having flowed over three stones was pure and watching how they used the water. That was all quite interesting.

Well, we finally arranged for Zondo and me to go up to Moscow in a Russian airplane.

Q: That was another experience!

Adm. F.: And we got up there early, out to the airfield early. Nobody around and there was the airplane sitting there. Finally the pilot showed up and he went around kicking various things to check the airplane out, and Zondo pointed at one of the wheel's flat tire. The Russian shook his head and cursed a bit, and went in and got a bottle and pumped the tire up. They had no spare tires - just pumped it up, kicked it again, and said something. I asked Zondo what he said and he said the Russian said, "Oh, that goddamned American rubber."

Then we watched them load. They loaded the plane full of people, one of the persons being a woman who had been the interpreter at the Teheran Conference, who could speak some English. It was just flabbergasting to see the way they loaded that airplane. It was bucket seats, and everybody had big cartons of everything under the sun and a heck of a lot of vodka that they were taking from Persia up to Russia. Nothing tied down - nothing.

Q: No seat belts?

Adm. F.: No. And all this heavy stuff that they put in - nothing tied down. And we knew doggone well when that airplane landed that tire was going to go flat again. Well, it happened. The tire went flat, but fortunately the pilot controlled the airplane and none of this stuff started to rattle around inside. But there we were. We were at Baku. Again no spare wheel, so we were stranded.

We went into the operations building and got the usual cup of tea - glass of tea - and while there, a Russian general showed up in his airplane. He was going to Moscow, having been on duty some place in North Africa, and was senior enough - I guess he was a lieutenant general - to have been provided an airplane. He said, all right, I'll take you. So we climbed aboard and here again, as in the early days of my flying cross country, in Russia - this was in 1944 - there were no aids to navigation, all VFR and all daytime flying, and our first stop was Stalingrad. This was shortly after the Russians had successfully defended Stalingrad.

Q: Pretty much of a mess, wasn't it?

Adm. F.: Yes, it sure was. The general took us on a tour right away and we saw what had happened to Stalingrad. Again, being a typical American, I wandered off the beaten path and went out into the field and everybody was screaming at me "watch out for the mines." However, I picked up a key about six inches long, all rusted and burned, and I called it my key to Stalingrad! I have it with my medals.

That night I was introduced to the standard way of holding a Russian meeting. A chair like this I'm sitting in, a long table with a red cover on it, and chairs along each side, the head man sitting in this chair, and here comes the vodka treatment, which I'd never experienced. The idea, which I'm convinced of and learned later, when vodka is available to a Russian there's only one objective, and that's get drunk, and if there's an American around, get him as drunk as you are! And I was exposed to this "dodna" (bottoms up). Well, that went on - I think we had something to eat, but it was a pretty gay party. Nobody was feeling any pain. It was time to go to bed, and we went into a great big, open room just with Army cots, wooden canvas type. Then this general and I got into an argument. He gave this woman the cot next to him. So I said, "No, Sir, General, I don't trust you. She's not going to sleep in that cot." Apparently, after arguing a bit, I went sound asleep!

The next day we went up to Moscow. It was early May or April. When is that day the Russians - ?

Q: May Day.

Adm. F.: May Day! I think it was a Sunday and, again, thank goodness, I had Zondarak along, because there we were. Nobody meeting us, just lost. Of course, we had our papers and the Russians weren't bothering us any, but they weren't helping us any either!

Zondarak knew enough to get on the telephone, and finally somebody came out and picked us up.

Q: From the embassy, from the Mission?

Adm. F.: Yes. We were put into a hotel, and first of all the bedding and beds were something I'd never seen before. It took a little time to figure out how to handle all those big pillows and the way they made a bed up. Secondly, hospitality was offered immediately of the kind that we didn't dare accept and there were knocks on the door. Thirdly, the eating problem was difficult. The meals you got in the hotel were very meager and right soon it was agreed, Kemp Tolley and Vlada agreed that they would take us in for breakfast.

Q: They were married by that time?

Adm. F.: Yes. They'd take us in for breakfast in their apartment in the embassy. That tided us over.

It wasn't too long after that that Tolley was ordered out. I've never known exactly why, but I think it was because he'd married a Russian girl. You probably know more about this than I. He was ordered out and Vlada had to stay behind. As you know, she got out later.

Zondy and I and another fellow who'd shown up - Denny Knoll, an aerologist - took over Tolley's apartment, and there we had a cook and a maid. Then I found out that living wasn't as rugged as I'd been taught at the Navy Department, as I was trying to

Felt #2 - 132

prepare myself for this. The cook washed all the clothes in the bath tub every day, and the maid cleaned up. We had the privilege of buying at the Russian store. Well, we had one egg every morning for breakfast, which was quite a privilege. The cook and the maid couldn't understand why we preferred Russian black bread to the white bread, which was kind of gray bread, which we could have bought. We were allowed to buy vodka and things like that.

The cook was a German refugee. I'm not clear on the whole story, but there were a bunch of Germans down in the Ukraine some place who had been displaced and had lived there for years. I guess the Germans did pretty badly by them. Some of them escaped this, and this woman - Kemp had employed her, we inherited her - had to report to the NKVD every week.

Q: About your activities?

Adm. F.: About our activities. She had a little cubby hole off the kitchen where she slept, and the only time she dared go out was when she'd meet some friend on the street. That was the only place where Russians could talk openly, where they wouldn't be overheard and reported on. Our phone was bugged. We knew that - not bugged, but tapped. Every time we'd pick it up we'd hear all the connections being made by the fellow who lived in the hotel next door.

The apartment might have been bugged. We didn't know and we didn't much care, because we had a little game going on of having conversations saying what we thought about certain things, hoping that it would be taped.

Felt #2 - 133

Q: You mean about conditions and that sort of thing?

Adm. F.: Yes, and about certain people!

Q: You were daring them to lay hands on you!

Adm. F.: You brought up the question as to what I was supposed to do there. Of course, I wanted an interview with a Russian authority - naval authority - as soon as I could get one. This was put into the paper mill.

Meanwhile, shortly after I got there, Admiral Olsen, who was the attache - naval attache - had been invited to go up and visit the Russian fleet at Leningrad and he asked me to come along. That was a trip in one of these international coach jobs, with private rooms and bunks, you know, and a wash room. The only thing provided was a samovar of tea that the train people provided. We had to take our own food, the first time I'd done this on one of these little burners, you know, that sort of thing, crawling along about the pace of a fast jog on the railroad which had been put back together after the Germans had practically destroyed it. Quite a long trip getting in to Leningrad, going to a hotel, and then meeting a wonderful guy, a commodore, a Russian naval officer, our host, who took us the next day out to visit the fleet all along the Neva River.

We visited a submarine, all red-carpeted, no torpedoes on board, shined up to beat the band, a destroyer, watched them go through a gun drill, a gun battery ashore firing into Finland, and lunch on the old battleship that was established there with the admiral in command. I asked the commodore if I had his permission to take pictures. I'd never known anything about photography but before I left Moscow the boys provided me with a camera and gave me instructions as to how to load it, which button to push. The commodore said, sure, anything you want. So I had a ball. I pushed that button and I changed the film, took two rolls of film, of all the ships being built in the ways along the Neva River, the beginning of their modern navy.

The next day we kind of went sightseeing and I took pictures again. I think the outstanding feature of the sightseeing trip was two things - seeing the museum they've set up depicting the attack on Leningrad and going to some palace outside of Leningrad.

Q: The Hermitage!

Adm. F.: Yes - completely destroyed and now restored in all of its glory, I understand.

Oh, yes, and we visited an aviation unit. Somebody discouraged me from trying to fly one of their airplanes and I never was sure whether they meant it when they said I could!

When we came back, all of the pictures I took on sightseeing day came out nicely developed, but none of the pictures I took on the previous day came out. What I had done, like a stupid neophyte, was I had left the film in the hotel room.

Q: That was a catastrophe, that was the intelligence-gathering that didn't work!

Adm. F.: Everybody knew about the thing, I suppose, but there were pictures of the ships themselves, some of them almost completed.

The other thing that I was introduced to for the first time was the manner of gorging their guests through that Intourist agency. Four meals a day was minimum and each meal was the same, a big spread of all that kind of Russian food, including vodka all the time.

Q: For breakfast, too?

Adm. F.: Oh, sure. We finally made a plea to knock off some of this. We'd have breakfast, we'd have lunch, we'd have a meal at I guess British teatime or thereabouts, and then after going to the ballet or something at night, another meal about 11:00 p.m. All the same, this great spread.

Q: Was it a smorgasbord?

Adm. F.: All kinds of fish, caviar, of course, chicken, cucumbers. I can't remember the names, but about a dozen items on the menu and many courses - overpowering.

I guess the principal reaction I got from that visit, not then knowing much about the history of the Russian Navy during World War II, was, first, the successful defense of Leningrad and while defending it still producing - the factories though badly damaged were still producing. That lesson, and the other the complete ineffectiveness of the Russian Navy, having been bottled in, having tried to break the barrier, you know, that mine barrier.

Q: Yes.

Adm. F.: Well, that was that. Shall we go on with Russia a little bit? All these things seem to be coming back to me.

I mentioned that I wanted an interview and it came about finally. It took thirty days before I was granted a meeting, and I met with a senior naval officer. Meanwhile I'd been turning over in my mind what am I going to say to these fellows, how can I make an approach that might attract them. I finally hit on this: to tell them that I had been impressed with the way they used their aviation in support of troops and to tell them, if they didn't know it, that this was exactly our U.S. naval aviation concept, amphibious attack, the support of troops, and, by golly, that caught. Not too long after that they offered me a trip and provided, I learned later, the only transport aircraft the Russian Navy owned - an R-4D, I think it was, with a Hero of the Soviet Union to go along as escort and a Russian crew for the airplane.

We went down to the Crimea. The Russians had just been cleared out of the Crimea. We went to an air base called Taganrog, right in the center of the Crimean Peninsula, where I was welcomed with the news that they had a hot bath ready for me. We were taken into a barracks building, a long narrow building, and the front door was in the end of this oblong, on the right, as you entered, was the kitchen, on the left was a head - and if you haven't seen Russian heads you haven't seen anything, then into the living spaces, a dining room and individual rooms. We were put up in there and immediately taken over to a bath house. The attendants were there, the towels were there, the hot water was on, and I had a quick shower and everybody was amazed, disappointed, because they thought Americans bathed at least an hour long and wanted the water just steaming hot. So you see they didn't know much more about Americans than we knew about them.

Q: They thought you were going to take a Turkish-type bath!

Adm. F.: Yes. By the way, I had another officer along with me, a U.S. naval officer Reserve, born of Russian parents, and very good with the Russian language. While we were down in the Crimea they couldn't believe that he was American, they thought he was Russian. He was great.

Q: What was his name?

Adm. F.: I can't remember it. I'll try to look it up.

After the bath, I guess the next thing to do was to have a meal, and it was the same kind of Intourist-provided meal. In other words, the commanding officer had been provided funds and Intourist had provided the supplies to put on this kind of a spread. We sat down at this table with his officers and my group, all men. Meanwhile, I knew he had a wife there and I said, "Where is your wife?" He said, "Oh, she's back in the room.

Would you like for her to come and be with us?" I said, "Of course," so she came, and that livened up the thing from then on.

I flew with him in a Stormavik, which we'd heard so much about. I went out in a transport type, having examined their torpedoes and having been given a ground demonstration of how they put the torpedoes on and what not, and watched them drop these torpedoes. With this tactic they had just panicked the Germans. This torpedo went floating down under the canopy of a parachute, hit the water, took off in decreasing diameter circles. Apparently they had these German ships just running crazy with this torpedo running crazy around them.

Q: Then it finally zeroed in?

Adm. F.: Yes. Well, something ran into something eventually, they hoped! I got a swastika off one of the shot-down airplanes which I kept for a long time, but it's disappeared some place.

Then a trip was set up to go down to Sevastopol and Yalta. This was before the Yalta Conference, just after the Germans had been cleared out. We got into Sevastopol and saw what had happened there, cruised all around, the harbor completely deserted.

Q: It was still mined, wasn't it?

Adm. F.: I don't know. Got an explanation of Russian defense, which I learned more about later - which was throw the troops in and take the casualties, mass 'em and throw 'em. Listened to the air boys brag about the job they'd done on a catch-as-catch-can basis. This was a caravan of a couple of trucks and a couple of cars, I guess, all kinds of spares, tires, fuel drums, food, kitchenware, dinnerware, a couple of maids, and what not. All the time we were taking pictures with this man's wife centered in the picutres because she was a kind of pretty girl.

Q: She was the legitimate wife, was she?

Adm. F.: Yes. We got to Yalta. It's a lovely place really, all white buildings, villa-type things. Unannounced, the Hero of the Soviet Union did two things immediately. He picked out the one he would like us to use and went in and commandeered it, just moved whoever was in it out. So we moved in, got ourselves established somewhat, and decided we'd like to go swimming. Meanwhile, he'd been to the beach, this Hero had, and had observed that the Russians were down there bathing in the nude, and he cleared them all off the beach because he knew the Americans wouldn't like that. We got to the beach. I suppose you've seen these kind of beaches, nothing but smooth rocks, with a problem. Here we are in normal clothes, how to get shifted into a pair of trunks. This young man I was telling you about, the fellow who spoke such fluent Russian, and I resolved it by just sitting down and changing - that was all. The maid took off all of her clothes except her under shorts, and her undershorts were typical Russian red! And we enjoyed the water.

Meanwhile, sunburn started to take its effect on some of these white-skinned Russians who hadn't exposed their skin, and the commanding officer of the air station acquired a horrible sunburn. They got rummaging around and found some wine which the Germans hadn't discovered, and brought it to the beach and we started to drink. Again, in typical Russian fashion - water glasses full of wine, lock arms, put it down.

Q: No moderation there!

Adm. F.: No moderation or pleasure out of it. I finally demurred and asked if they'd ever taken the time to taste that wine. It was beautiful wine. They said no, and were puzzled why I would ask such a question. I said, "Well, let's try it, just sip." They thought, gee, that's pretty good, never thought about tasting it before!

Well, that wound up successfully. We had a pretty nice time, made friends, went to a dinner party one night - this was after the Yalta thing, I believe - oh, no, this was at the Stormovik school area, men and women, toasts, of course, as happens at all these parties. A Russian commissar present, of course, making a typical commissar-type speech and Felt maliciously making a different kind of speech. Presents for the hostess, chocolate candy and things like that. It was very successful, very friendly. Questions asked, well, gee, can we visit you? Why, sure, we'd be delighted if you ever get to Moscow. Where do you live? In the embassy. Oh. That was the end of that.

Q: Off bounds!

Adm. F.: They wouldn't dare try.

That was one visit, and now I think I've practically told my story of Russia, other than enjoying the ballet - we had privileges for getting good tickets to things like that.

This was a trip down to the area where our prisoners of war were encamped, way down in the southwest corner, an area of vegetation and groves and what not. The name of this town doesn't come immediately to mind, but it will before I've finished, I hope.

The idea was for an Army doctor and I, again with a Hero of the Soviet Union to escort, to fly down to take medicines and playing cards and paperbacks and anything we could think of -

Q: Was this Kharkov?

Adm. F.: No.

Q: Kiev?

Adm. F.: No, the southeast corner - to our prisoners of war. Now these prisoners of war were people who had been flying TVs out of Alaska to the Kamchatka Peninsula area, and if they got any kind of a combat thing at all they would run out of gas. They were really extended on those operations and had to force land in Kamchatka. The Russians would pick them up there and send them down to this place, far removed from any Japanese eyes, because, remember, Russia and Japan were not at war at this time. Those were the Navy pilots and personnel. The Air Force personnel were the ones who had gone down in the Maritime Province area around Vladivostok and so forth. There was quite a group of them down there.

Tashkent!

We went out to the camp, after checking into a hotel, and just barged in and you've never seen expressions like that on these fellows' faces. I wore my naval aviation green uniform with my wings on it, and of course the doctor had his Army uniform on. They just couldn't believe - this was an apparition. Well, the doctor inoculated everybody. There was a Russian woman doctor in attendance there but she had very little to work with. He gave them all shots, we distributed supplies, ate with them, talked with them, watched their recreational activities. They organized softball by taking - I don't know - an old soccer ball and making a soft ball out of it, and cutting a limb off of a tree to make a bat, things like that. They taught the Russians how to play softball, while at the same time being beaten badly at volleyball by the Russians, who are expert at that. We left with an understanding that an arrangement would be made for these people to escape. This was something that Stalin agreed to. Only one man in the whole group was to know about this, but the word would be put out suddenly one day that we're going to shift you fellows from this camp to another camp. All right, get your belongings, climb in those trucks, and the route taken by the trucks was right along the northern border of Persia, and suddenly there'd be a little breakdown and the convoy would come to a halt, and the one man in the know would say, "Hey, that's Persia. Let's go." And off they were, you see. This was all agreed to. They'd been there over six months already.

You know what happened?

Drew Pearson learned of this and he published it in the paper, about this plan. It showed up in - well, I won't say which Washington paper - the day these guys were on the road. Stalin got it, he countermanded the order, the convoy turned around, and those guys had another six months back in the camp.

Felt #3 - 144

Interview No. 3 with Admiral Harry D. Felt, U.S. Navy (Retired)

Place: BOQ, Makalapa, Pearl Harbor, Hawaii

Date: Monday morning, 6 March 1972

Subject: Biography

By: John T. Mason, Jr.

Q: Well, it's good to see you again this morning, Admiral, and I'm looking forward to a day of real accomplishment here.

Last time, when you broke off, you were in Tashkent with the American prisoners, and I think you have a great deal more to say about your tour of duty in Moscow.

Adm. F.: It's nice to be with you again, Dr. Mason. I hope you had a nice weekend and did some sightseeing in Honolulu.

I went through the old worn-out archives at home yesterday -

Q: Good, good!

Adm. F.: - and found that I'd gotten things a little mixed up, that is chronologically, in respect to my Russian tour. I have in hand here some excerpts of letters I wrote to Kathryn, my wife, during the early part of the tour there.

Q: Splendid. Are you going to read them into the record?

Adm. F.: I might read a little bit. I'm reminded first of all that apparently it was my first trip out of Moscow - it's not clear whether it was the first, but anyhow it was going down to Poltava to be present when the first American bombers landed in

Russia. This arrangement had been made whereby the American bombers taking off from Italy and bombing the oilfields in Ploesti and thereabouts would continue on, instead of turning back, and land in Poltava.

Q: That was an ideal arrangement actually.

Adm. F.: Yes, it shortened the range and what not.

Q: It enabled them to really flatten those installations.

Adm. F.: Well, it was a good idea. I remember the takeoof from the airport in Moscow very vividly. I heard a lot about Russian pilots' contempt for ordinary safety precautions that we took. For instance, I'd heard they never warmed up their engines before giving them the gun in below-freezing temperatures. I didn't realize they took off down wind, however.

I was put up in the bow, in the gunner's bubble, of a B-17, standing in there. They turned the engines up, gave it the gun, and took off down wind, and all I could see coming at me was the forest. We fortunately pulled up just clear.

Q: They had a different concept of life, didn't they?

Adm. F.: They certainly did! Well, I watched the bombers land at Poltava, met some of the people, stayed there that night, watched them disperse the bombers and service them. I believe it was one of the Andersons - I've forgotten which Anderson - Major General Anderson who led the flight. I was particularly interested in how the Russians would protect these planes while they were on the ground. Asking questions, I was told that, oh, the Russian fighters would take care of that. "That's interesting. I'd like to see some of that," and about that time two of the fighters landed with women pilots. That was the fighter defense of Poltava, I was told.

I went back to Moscow the next day and shortly thereafter the planes at Poltava were destroyed by Germans who came in, having, of course, spotted the whole operation and apparently knowing full well the defense would be inadequate. They really raised havoc - and that was the last of that operation. It was not repeated again.

It was interesting to learn how the Russians cleared the field of the mines. The Germans had dropped little mines all over the field. They did it with human beings. They just formed a scrimmage line - you might describe it as such - with a lot of people and just swept across the field, blowing up the mines.

There was one other interesting little incident subsequent to this. Of course, the airplanes having been pretty well beat up, there were a lot of people sort of stranded at Poltava and they allowed some of them to come up to Moscow on, as we call it nowadays, R and R. In those days everybody wore their side arms. The Russians always wore those, so they permitted our American airmen to wear their side arms as they came up to Moscow.

It so happened that my roommate, Zonderack, went to the one and only night club and found there these airmen from Poltava, American airmen. And at another table were some Japanese.

Remember, the other day I mentioned that, of course, Russia wasn't at war with Japan. Well, one of these airmen apparently got a little high and he pulled out his .45, I guess it was, pulled the clip out, counted the bullets, and then with a finger, looking over at the Japanese table, counted, one, two, three, four, five, six - then looked at his clip. It was quite obvious what the man had in mind. Zonderack went over and put a stop to that, but I've often wondered what might have happened if this really had come about.

Q: Yes, an international incident.

Adm. F.: Yes. Well, that's the Poltava story.

Remember, we were talking about the trip to Leningrad the other day?

Q: Yes.

Adm. F.: And I couldn't accurately identify the palace we visited that had been destroyed by the Germans. Well, I found some pictures of that visit. The second roll. Remember I told you I flunked at being an agent when the first roll didn't come out? Here are some pictures of that visit. I believe you said that you'd seen some of these?

Q: Yes, from Mrs. Olsen.

Adm. F.: Yes, well, a picture of Olie and our Russian host. Here it is, "Admiral Olsen and Commodore Alexandrov." Is that the same one you've seen?

Felt #3 - 148

Q: Yes.

Adm. F.: Now, on the palace, there are several pictures here of it. It's the palace of Catherine II at Pushkin. Pushkin's the name of the town. Here's the great big ballroom with the floor all torn up, all the tapestries torn. Here's a picture of the cathedral in Leningrad. You see, no damage done. Here's another picture of that ballroom. Here's a picture of the marble staircase, all torn up, with a pretty Russian girl who was showing us around.

Well, that's kind of filling in where my memory was vague last time we met. You asked me, I believe, about the meals we had. One of these letters has a description of the meals, all the same four times a day. The toasts, all that sort of thing. I remember I disturbed them quite a bit because the toasts were all to Roosevelt, Stalin, to the Navy, to the Army, to the armed forces, and all that. I finally got a little tired of this and offered a toast to the ladies! That stunned the Russians. They'd never heard of such a thing.

I think we needn't say anything more about that, except I note here in these excerpts that I wrote Kathryn upon returning to Moscow after a six-day trip I had a bath. I do recall now that in the hotel there was a bath tub but no water. It called for a celebration.

Q: Are there any paragraphs in there that are worthy of preserving in this record?

Adm. F.: Well, let's see. There's a lot about the Leningrad trip, a lot about the rail travel, an interesting description of Leningrad itself, how devastated it was but the people were still working. Some place in here there are some statistics on people.

I might read this into it. This has to do with Leningrad: We saw the works from automobile, boat, by walking and by visiting ships, airfield, the naval base at Kronstad, and palaces of the Czars and Queens. I was permitted to take pictures at some places and will send some of those that turned out well. The city and its defenses had withstood a 900-day siege, during which it was both shelled and bombed. Some of it was horribly shattered and, of course, all of it run down. About half of its prewar populace was evacuated and of that population about a million and a half were killed or died from starvation or disease during the siege. About 250,000 had returned to the city, but this is being controlled in ratio to the city's capacity to provide housing and food. Everybody remaining was employed in building defenses, converting industry to war production, or fighting. Each, whether soldier, worker, man or woman, who fought the Battle of Leningrad wears a military medal award. The streets are strangely free of people when one compares with Moscow, but they are chesty and proud. Incidentally, the theater kept showing and factories kept producing, although being tumbled down by gunfire.

Felt #3 - 150

Peterhof and Pushkin were the two palaces I mentioned. I mentioned going to a museum the other day?

Q: Yes.

Adm. F.: This was the first of this sort of thing I'd ever seen. I'd seen a similar thing in Australia, but this was the first of this. Now, this was shortly after Leningrad had been relieved - not too long after - and this is a description of the museum:

> Depicting the siege and defense of Leningrad, huge paintings, maps, pictures, scale panoramic arrangements and equipment spread throughout many rooms. It was the most graphic thing I've ever seen.

Well, that's, I guess, plenty on Leningrad. Now, let's see, what have we covered? We've covered Poltava, we've covered the trip down to Tashkent, Yalta.

Yes, Yalta. I found some pictures of the Yalta visit. I'll just show them quickly to you. Here are the Russian aviators. Here's the skipper greeting me. I went along the line and spoke to each one of the aviators, then they took a group picture.

Q: Would you say a little about the attitude of the Russian military toward you? They seem to have been friendly and receptive.

Adm. F.: Oh, very, very friendly. By the way, the young man interpreter, Joe Chase was his name. Remember, the young man I said they thought couldn't possibly be American?

Q: Yes.

Adm. F.: Oh, yes, we became just good friends. Here are some pictures of Sevastopol, the harbor and looking at some of the monuments. Group pictures of the party. Here we are at the dinner table after we'd arrived at Yalta. That's after the convoy had been unloaded. There's the wife of the commanding officer.

Just a few comments about some of these pictures. Here's one just before or just after I'd flown in a Stormovik. My visit to the Stormovik school. I mentioned this the other day but I really didn't have my thoughts well organized.

Q: No, you didn't, you just mentioned it actually.

Adm. F.: This was at a different place than the air base in Yalta, still in the Crimean area, however. I remember a few minutes after arrival I excused myself and when I came back my companion interpreter, Joe Chase, was kind of flapping, and I said, "What's up?"

He said, "These Russians are very puzzled."

"What about?"

You asked me a moment ago how they were, you know, how they accepted us.

"Well," he said, "as you were out of the room, they were talking about you and they said, 'We expected him to be like a Britisher, austere and hard to talk to. Instead, they say, you're just like a Russian.'"

There is that aspect of the Russian people. They're basically friendly and outgoing, similar to the way Americans are.

Q: May I ask - you spoke about Poltava and the clearing of the mines and how they simply had the local peasantry walk out and -

Adm. F.: Oh, these were soldiers.

Q: Oh. Well, now, do they do this willingly?

Adm. F.: I don't think there's any choice. That's part of the dictatorial, authoritarian way of life there. Of course, it was war, too.

Now, let's see.

Q: You were going to tell me about Archangel.

Adm. F.: Before I get to that. We've talked about some trips I made. Came the time when Admiral Olsen realized that this wasn't a fifty-fifty shake between the Americans and the Russians on this matter of seeing and visiting places. Here, in America, the Russians would come over with authority to go into all of our factories, carrying their notebooks, making sketches - there were practically no restrictions, whereas in Russia, other than these couple of things I've mentioned like down to the Crimea, it was the arranged red-carpet treatment. Everything staged. Then Olsen decided that he'd better go back and talk to Admiral King and recommend that we not ask for any more trips. This was done, and then we had the problem of what are we going to do with ourselves. We can't just have parties and go to the ballet and all that sort of thing. We've got to be active some way or other.

So we decided to start to plan, to plan on the problem of whether the Russians could whip the Japanese out in Manchuria and the Maritime Province area. The thought being that the Japanese would make their last defense on the mainland. Now, this was a mistake. There was one officer there in the Military Mission who had a reputation, at least, of knowing the Japanese mind. It's always dangerous if you rely on one man who says, I know. Anyhow, he said that the Japanese would make their last stand on the mainland and not in the home islands.

On this basis was generated the thought that we'd better get Russia into the war. So we started to plan to see how it might come out.

Q: This was prior to the Yalta Conference?

Adm. F.: Oh, yes, several months prior to the Yalta Conference. We thought we had little or no intelligence, but as it developed it came out that the Russians would have no problem really.

Now, to make that story a bit shorter, came the Yalta Conference, at which Stalin was enticed to come into the war -

Q: For a price!

Adm. F.: Right. He made a promise that I believe it was thirty days after VE Day-or thirty days after some date, I've forgotten which - he would attack the Japanese. The thirty days was necessary for him to group and get across on the Transsiberian and so on and so forth.

Finally, I got a set of orders to take command of a small carrier in the Pacific. I had a little trouble convincing my people in Moscow that I should be sprung, but they agreed that if I had a chance to take command of a carrier, I ought to be dismissed. I left Moscow in Secretary of State Stettinius' airplane with the Secretary of State after the Yalta Conference, this time without any white rats! Down through Teheran, Cairo, across North Africa is the usual route, where I was dumped off but given a priority. As I remember it, Stettinius and his crowd went to Mexico City and then to San Francisco for the first conference on - what did they call it, it was the beginning of the United Nations. And, with a priority, I got a ride to Washington, sitting alongside of a courier who had just come from the Red Sea and had witnessed the meeting between President Roosevelt and the King of Saudi Arabia.

Q: Ibn Saud?

Adm. F.: Yes. I checked in in Washington and found that, yes, I had my carrier orders intact. Went across country and had I don't know how long with the family, probably a couple of days. Incidentally, going across country by air transport in those days was going in a cargo plane and sleeping on top of a bunch of crates. Then across here to Honolulu in a Mars. Do you remember the big seaplanes?

Q: Yes.

Adm. F.: Checked in here, tried to find out where my ship was, and onward to Guam and so on and so forth. I finally caught up with the ship just after the Okinawa campaign started. You remember that was an 80-some days' campaign?

This carrier of mine was one of the converted tankers, the Chenango. There were four of these, and we operated as a four-ship unit during that Okinawa operation, fortunately undamaged.

Q: I thought this was a projection forward, because you were making a point. But you haven't told me about your visit to Archangel yet, while you were still on duty in Moscow?

Adm. F.: Oh, I forgot. I'd been in Russia so long, that is on this tape, that I thought it best to leave!

We had two officers up north. One in Murmansk and one in Archangel, to deal with the Russians there and particularly, at least in Archangel, to deal with the shipping that was coming in to supply Russia.

Q: The lease-lend material?

Adm. F.: The lease-lend shipping. Our man in Archangel fell ill and was brought down to Moscow to have some sort of surgery, as I recall it, and, lo and behold, I was detailed to take his place. I've forgotten how long I stayed there, but it was a routine of checking the waterfront, going aboard ships, meeting with and talking with the ships' skippers, and, while I was there, they were all - at least most of them - were British.

They would come in in a convoy, of course, then there would be a party for them that night hosted by the Russians. I only attended one of these while I was there. I guess only one convoy came in while I was there. It was very strange to witness the attitudes. The British skippers would be off to one side and the Russians off to this side. Remember, now, the Russians are hosting this party. With no communication whatsoever between them. It was clear to me right off the bat that the merchant ship skippers, in the eyes of the Russians, were inferior to the Russian naval officers.

Well, I bridged this gap and apparently didn't suffer any damage from it. But I just couldn't stand there and do nothing, seeing all of this.

Q: Basically, the Russians didn't like the British, either, did they?

Adm. F.: Well, I didn't get that impression. I didn't get that impression in Moscow, for example. But the impression I got here was a sort of a class distinction.

Q: Ironical, in that the Russian merchant marine is now actually a part of the Russian Navy, isn't it?

Adm. F.: Right. Of course, when you go to Russian parties like that, there's always competition in respect to entertainment. The Russians dance, most of them can play some sort of instrument, and it's a lot of fun. The sad part of it is that we Americans weren't talented.

Q: And couldn't communicate very well either!

Adm. F.: The communications with Moscow had to be through the Russian wire system, so we had a code thing that was a laborious thing to work out every night. I remember I'd be up every night till midnight working out this simple but time-consuming code.

Q: Did you supervise the unloading of the cargoes at Archangel?

Adm. F.: No.

Q: To make some accurate check of what came in actually?

Adm. F.: No, I don't recall that we did. We had just a very small staff.

A little impression of people and Archangel itself. It reminded me somewhat of good-looking Kansas in my very early days, wooden sidewalks, dirt roads, down-to-earth, simple people, friendly.

Q: Did you have any contact with the over-all Russian naval commander who was a hero of the Russian state?

Adm. F.: As I recall, yes. There was a Russian naval officer who had established a reputation and, after the war, became quite famous, I believe, in arctic operations. I can't remember just where I met this fellow, because I did go over to Murmansk and visit there. Of course, Murmansk was a much larger operation. There was a great deal of military activity going on there. I can't remember this man's name. You said it might be Popoff?

Felt #3 - 158

Q: Something of that sort.

Adm. F.: Could be. But that was just an interesting interlude. Cold weather, of course.

Q: Was Archangel under air attack from the Germans?

Adm. F.: No, not when I was there.

Q: Had it been?

Adm. F.: I don't recall that Archangel was targeted. Murmansk, of course, was. They were under fire almost constantly and, of course, were dug in real good.

Q: You said you had to travel there by train?

Adm. F.: Yes, I went up by train.

Q: Which was a pretty arduous journey, wasn't it?

Adm. F.: It's pretty long but, as I recall it, it was much better than the trip to Leningrad because the rail line, I guess, hadn't been destroyed.

Q: Did you have anything to do with the preparations for the Yalta Conference?

Adm. F.: No, nor was I present at the Yalta Conference. Admiral Olsen went down, Joe Chase, this young fellow I mentioned, and I stayed in Moscow, having been instructed by Admiral Olsen to keep the lines of communication open with the Yalta people and also with Washington.

Q: Did you have any personal contact with Harriman?

Adm. F.: Oh, yes, he was the ambassador, of course, the whole time I was there. I saw him frequently.

Q: How did he function as an ambassador?

Adm. F.: A little bit differently than I had imagined an ambassador to function. He worked out of the embassy residence, in his upstairs sittingroom, instead of out of the embassy offices. When we started this planning procedure he was present quite often, as we'd brief and critique some of these things.

Q: Were you, as a group of planners, to involve the Russians in the Far Eastern conflict, were you all in agreement that this was a good step?

Adm. F.: No, that wasn't the object of the drill, to make up our minds whether or not Russia should be brought into the war. The problem was, should Russia be brought into the war, would they be able to handle or defeat the Japanese. At first, it looked to us that they'd have a very tough time of it, but as we studied the problem more and more it became clear that the Russians could do it hands down, so to speak, and that's, as a matter of fact, the way it turned out.

Q: Admiral Olsen made a point and I wonder if you saw evidence of what he said, and that was that the Russians, as a whole, thinking in terms of lease-lend, were always anxious to get everything they could, regardless of whether they could use it at the moment or not. Their thoughts were on the postwar period and building up a granary, so to speak, of supplies.

Adm. F.: Well, let me talk to that just a little bit. He had a better view of this than I, of course, but generally speaking I would agree completely with that. Just what the object of acquiring all this stuff was was not quite clear in my mind, because things would come in in bulk and sit on the side and just deteriorate, never be used, never be assembled. Of course, there was a lot of dishonesty in this thing, too. I say "dishonesty." I'll try to tell you what I mean by this.

Red Cross supplies would come in and they'd be confiscated immediately or be turned over to them, and it would never be shown to the people in Russia that they were American Red Cross supplies. They showed up in the stores that were available only to the members of the Communist Party and to senior officers. Locomotives would come in with the markings on them, "made in USA by so and so," all of those would be eliminated and Russian things would be marked on them.

One of the things that I recall so vividly was that we provided them with I believe they were P-38 airplanes - that's a twin-boom fighter, I believe. As I recall it, they were assembled and test-flown in Teheran and then turned over to the Russians, and the Russians just couldn't handle them. They started killing themselves in that airplane, to the point where they had to come to the Military Mission - we had an Air Force colonel on this Mission - and request assistance and we had to send some pilots over there to teach them how to fly them. That was pretty amazing.

To get back to the thought that Admiral Olsen had. When I came back from Russia and before I came back out here to the Pacific, many people, knowing that I'd had this experience, would come to me and say, what about Russia? And then, without waiting for an answer, they would tell me what they thought, which is human nature. Finally, I'd say, "Do you read the newspapers?"

"Yes, but we don't believe a damned word in the newspapers."

Well, it turns out then that the commentators, the columnists, knew what they were talking about and were trying to tell America about Communism and about the long-range objectives of the USSR. Our people wouldn't believe it, of course.

When I did get a chance to talk to people or when they'd listen, I would tell them that the Russians had just gone out 100 percent for technical education. I don't know just how this is going to come out, but every kid, every boy, every girl, wants a technical education, and if their families can qualify under the Communist system they're getting it. The schools are just full of boys and girls studying to be engineers. Now, when I left there they couldn't put a piece of machinery together and I predicted that it would be <u>years</u> before they'd make any technological advance. But I qualified it by saying, here are the kids being educated. And look what happened! It didn't take them very long, did it?

Felt #3 - 162

I was amazed at the speed with which they started to catch up.

Q: But their great advancement, was it not predicated on the fact that they borrowed from what the Germans knew, they borrowed from what we knew, and presumably from what the British knew? So they filled in the gaps.

Adm. F.: That's true, but on the other hand Russia - well, traditionally great scientists have been Russians. Of course, the purges stopped a lot of that, but as you say remember the United States and Russia were after the German scientists.

Q: The Penndemunde people.

Adm. F.: Yes, the rocket scientists - copying. What was the most modern bomber that Hap Arnold had in the war, the B what? B-36?

Q: B-36, wasn't it?

Adm. F.: I don't remember but it was the most modern thing that the Air Force had. One of them went down out in the Maritime Provinces and, at a party one night, I was talking to the head of the Russian Air Force and he said, "I've flown that airplane." And I said:

"Now, wait a minute, General, don't try to kid me like that."

He said, "Yes, I have."

I found out that what he said was true. He'd gone all the way out there. The plane wasn't badly damaged apparently, and he'd flown it. I said, "Where is it now?"

He said, "It's coming here to our research and development center."

"What are you going to do with it?"

"We're going to tear it apart, piece by piece, and examine it, and then we're going to build one of our own." And that's what they did.

I said, "Why do you do that? Why don't you say to the United States, look, we've got one of your airplanes, how about giving us some more? We're giving you everything you ask for!"

"No," he said, "I've got longer-range plans."

Q: You said that you flew back, part way, to the States in Stettinius' plane, and he was just coming from the Yalta Conference. Was there any brush-off from him as to what transpired at Yalta? What was his attitude?

Adm. F.: Oh, the Americans were elated, just absolutely elated. They thought - well, they did, they accomplished everything they wanted to accomplish, which was to get the Russians to come into the war.

After we took off from Moscow he asked me to come and sit with him and talk with him. He talked about the Conference and how successful it was, and then he broke out an article in _Readers Digest_ about the Secretary of State, how he had just

Felt #3 - 164

taken over, and how he was organizing. He was quite proud of himself!

Q: Did he say anything about the President, and the President's state of health at that point? Was there any concern?

Adm. F.: No, I don't remember any discussion at all on the President's state of health. I've forgotten what I read subsequently. I'd left Moscow the day after the group came back from Yalta to Moscow, and I don't recall any discussion at all about the President's health.

Q: Shall we proceed with the Chenango?

Adm. F.: I won't try to go into those many, many days of the Okinawan campaign, except to say that I had a crew practically all Reserves. As exec I had a graduate of the Naval Academy. All the remainder of the officers, including the heads of departments, were either Reserves or ex chief petty officers.

Q: What sort of a complement did she have?

Adm. F.: Oh, gosh! I don't know.

Q: Well, how many planes?

Adm. F.: We had a fighter squadron and a torpedo squadron.

Getting back to the composition of my crew, it was just absolutely marvelous. The officers of the deck, I've never seen a more proficient group of officers of the deck. Remember now, at nighttime we were all blacked out, operating in formation using radar, of course. Our method of replenishment in those days - we didn't have to replenish oil because we were a tanker converted to a carrier, and the tanker bottoms were all full of oil so we replenished from ourselves.

Q: That, in one sense, added to the danger, I would think?

Adm. F.: Yes. But for ammunition we had to go into a place called Kerama Retto, a little island harbor, and the routine was to break off from the formation at night and arrive at Kerama Retto at sunup, usually searching for the entrance in a fog and I was fortunately successful each time I went in there, then opening the ship wide and taking on all this ammunition. Invariably there'd be attacks during these periods. We were never hit, but the Sangamon was hit very, very badly and beat up terribly.

I mentioned the officers of the deck. I never will forget the first night after VJ Day, I guess it was, when we turned on the lights and my beautiful officers of the deck were so confused! They had never stood the deck with the lights on at night! All these lights all over the place!

I have some pictures of the Chenango. There's a picture of the American flag and the V - the VJ Day victory - flown from the mast.

Q: That was the heyday of the kamikaze, was it not?

Adm. F.: Oh, yes. They flew over us at night every once in a while with their bombers but they never were able to locate us apparently or spot us, because we were being very quiet and as invisible as we could make ourselves. The kamikazes hit the destroyers very badly, of course, which were up on picket duty, and, of course, hit some of the carriers which were operating to the north of us.

Q: What was your particular assignment in the battle?

Adm. F.: We were to keep an island and its air installations out of business, a little bit south of Okinawa. We worked on that all the time. As I recall it, we would leave station every once in a while and the British would take over but from a different position. They'd take over from a position between the mainland and Okinawa, and the Japanese would always clobber them on the way through their fleet. We took a position north, and never suffered any casualties at night.

An interesting thing was the number of mines we would pick up in the daytime. Every day we'd pick up mines and destroy them with rifle fire, but at nighttime somehow or other we never saw a mine, and never got hit with one.

Q: What kind of mines were they?

Adm. F.: Just these floating big round things.

Q: How did the British perform as part of the - ?

Felt #3 - 167

Adm. F.: We never actually saw them. As I say, the thing that impressed us was that they took a position where they were a target all the time.

Okinawa was over now, and there are two things I want to talk about as briefly as I can.

One was evacuating Okinawa Harbor because of a typhoon coming in. I had put my little air group ashore. There was a little field there they could operate from. I attended a conference and the admiral issued orders that we would all evacuate as a group. I told him that I had to get out right now and recover my airplanes, and he said: "All right. You're on your own."

Q: Who was this?

Adm. F.: I can't remember now. He was a cruiser division admiral.

Shortly after I left the harbor I picked up a friend of mine who was just arriving in a 105 class, which is a copy of the old tankers. He was to report in and I said:

"No use going in there. Everybody's evacuating." and he said:

"All right, I'll join you."

Before it was over I picked up a couple more and we lit off south to get across the front of this typhoon, and just barely made it, but by the time we made it there was some terribly rough weather. We were all the way down off the Philippines, but we got across the front.

Felt #3 - 168

The other thing that I want to talk about is that finally came the time for the invasion of Japan, the big, big operation. This was to be the climax of the war.

Q: Olympia, was it?

Adm. F.: I think that was the code name for it. We were on our way to Japan to participate and suddenly came the word "The Japanese have surrendered. We want you to go up to Nagasaki and pick up our prisoners of war."

So I turned around and flew off the air group and collected as many cots and blankets as I could and went in to Nagasaki. Is this right now? Is that where the second bomb was dropped?

Q: Hiroshima, the next?

Adm. F.: Right. We were the first to go in after this bomb and were the first to walk around and witness the damage that had been done by an atomic bomb. I have many pictures of it.

We had a hospital ship tied up at the dock. We were at a buoy out in the stream. Sure enough, down came the POWs and they were processed ashore, given a bath and supplies, and brought out to my ship. It turned out that most of them were British. However, I did have the survivors of the Houston, and you remember I'd served in the Houston at one time.

Q: They'd been there the whole period of the war?

Adm. F.: These were people who had come to the Houston after

I'd left, but were the people who'd been captured in the Battle of the Makassar Straits. I have some pictures of all of this, getting these people on board and -

Q: Were they in camps near Nagasaki?

Adm. F.: They apparently were in camps on the west side of Japan. Here they all are - clean clothes. Here they are having taken a bath with clean underwear.

Q: What sort of condition were they in?

Adm. F.: Well, here's a picture of three British characters, stark naked with their sea bags in front of them. You can see they look like they're in pretty good shape, don't they?

Q: Yes.

Adm. F.: A bit on the skinny side, but they certainly don't look like they've been starving, do they?

Q: No.

Adm. F.: Well, we brought all of these people back.

Q: How were you received by people at Nagasaki?

Adm. F.: Oh, Japanese bowing, no show of resentment. They'd accepted what had happened. No problems whatsoever, except our surprise. We'd expected to see hatred in people's eyes and that sort of thing, but we couldn't detect it. It was there probably, but we couldn't detect it.

I've forgotten where we disembarked that group but anyhow we went around and picked up subsequently a bunch of our own POWs and came back to the United States, disembarked them at San Diego and then went up to Long Beach Navy Yard, as I recall it, and got ourselves fitted to do this job correctly. Put temporary showers and heads in the hangar and cleared out the hangar completely and put bunks and whatnot in it, and off we went on another what they called Magic Carpet trip.

This time we had Christmas at sea on the way back to Japan and the ship's company had a Christmas party in the hangar. No, I take that back. After we had picked up the POWs, all U.S. Army, we had Christmas at sea and the ship's company put on a party. It so happened that there was a man in the Army group who was a professional entertainer and he said:

"Now, we are going to put on the New Year's party," which they did and it was a lot of fun. A little difficult in some respects because aboard ship in the Navy gambling was not permitted. Of course, there was gambling, everybody knew that, but it wasn't open. However, down in the hangar, where I think we had 1,000 of these people, my exec told me there was quite a bit of gambling going on and I said:

"Well, that's all right as long as it's restricted to the hangar."

But, lo and behold, one day a group came up on the flight deck with their dice and started throwing dice up on the flight deck right under my nose, so we stopped gambling.

It was an experience that was, I won't say enjoyable, but interesting -

Q: Maybe "rewarding" would be the word?

Adm. F.: Yes. And when we got back I saw an officer on the dock and he had in his hand a set of orders to relieve me. I had yet gotten no orders. The ship, incidentally, was scheduled for decommissioning.

So he relieved me and I went back to Washington - I went to Washington.

Q: Were you glad of that opportunity, or did you want to do some more ferrying of POWs?

Adm. F.: Well, the ship was due to go round to the East Coast and be mothballed in Boston Navy Yard and that was fine with me.

Incidentally, the time we were in Long Beach getting ready for the second Magic Carpet trip my mother and father and my sister and nephew came up to the ship. My mother had a little difficulty getting around so the men made a sedan chair for her, just an ordinary chair with some rods to carry her up the gangway. My little nephew just fell in love with that ship. Subsequently, after she was mothballed in Boston Navy Yard and he was then living in Milton, Mass., he'd go over to the Boston Navy Yard every once in a while just to take a look. One day he played hooky and went over and asked if he could go aboard. They said, sure. So he went aboard, rummaged around in the dark down there, and in the ready room he found photographs of all the officers and what not, and he stripped them off the board. He sent them to me and I have my picture which was taken off the board, a picture of the exec, and so forth. And he said it looked just the same.

Q: In mothballs?

Adm. F.: In mothballs, it looked just the same. The furniture and everything was just left there.

Q: Maybe this would be a good point to ask you if you want to comment on the seemingly inevitable policy of rapid demobilization after a war and the consequences, since you were later involved in political things as well as military.

Adm. F.: Yes. I think that's a very good point and if I may take a moment here, again going back to letters from Moscow.

"It is hard to predict the future and evaluate my usefulness here. There is a suspicion that I could be doing a hell of a lot more towards winning this war in another theatre and liking it more. When someone pumps a silly lot of bunk at me about the importance of these contacts I've been making to the final settlement of all our troubles I try to believe it, but I'm not completely sold. I'd rather help kill Japs."

Well, let's get into the Chenango again.

Q: All right.

Adm. F.: The war is over. Remember now, the crew is Reserve. They've built up points for demobilization. Around my sea cabin was a walk way, one level above the bridge, and the flight deck crews would come up to that walk way to smoke. They couldn't smoke on the flight deck but they'd come up to that walk way to smoke. And I could overhear their conversations, and I heard this:

"Damn it, I've got points, I've had enough of this."

"Well, you know, the captain has told us that we must stay here. We've been ordered to stay here, we still have a job to do, and if he says we've got a job to do, let's do it."

That was the attitude of the enlisted men.

On the other hand, I found that some of the officers, particularly those who really didn't like the military at all, the free-lance writers and that type, they wanted out right now and they got out just as fast as they could, regardless of the fact that I'd said we'd got to stick together and do this. This was this evacuation job I was talking about.

Well, as to the problem of demobilization. I was ordered to Washington, for the first time ever, duty in Washington, to Aviation Personnel. In those days naval aviation officer detailing was under the Deputy Chief of Naval Operations for Air, Op-05, and, of course, in that position I was sitting in the observation tower, so to speak, as to what was happening to the Navy. Quick demobilization. The war is over. There'll be no more wars. And the Navy just slid down the drafts.

Q: A state of euphoria!

Adm. F.: It was pretty bad. Ships tied up, not in mothballs but with just a skeleton crew on board. I'll get to that a little bit later, but let me continue with this personnel business.

There are two things that stand out in my mind. One is that during this two-year tour was the beginning of the program to consolidate all personnel detailing into the Bureau of Personnel. Of course, we argued and argued and argued to have safety clauses in all of this.

The other thing that stands out is I believe it was my second year in this personnel business, the National War College was being established and there was a problem in selecting people to attend the first class of the National War College. The Army and the Air Force had adopted a policy that every officer ordered to the first class would be preselected for general rank, flag rank, and we in the Navy said no, we can't do this because we have a selection system which we think is far superior to anything you fellows have, and we can't preselect.

So we had a heck of a time trying to determine what Navy personnel would be ordered to this first class. I asked if I could take it over, and I said, "I think I can solve this problem for you. I can find people well qualified to matriculate, whose normal tours of duty are coming to an end about time to enter the National War College."

They said all right, and I made out a list.

Q: Were you talking in terms of 25 men or what?

Adm. F.: Talking in terms of maybe 15. I'm very vague on that number. Anyhow that's the way it was done, and it turned out that I would say at least half, maybe a majority, of those captains sent to that first class eventually made flag rank. Some did not. Maybe the percentage was higher than that, but it was good. You probably know a lot of them. Savvy Sides. Oh, no, beg your pardon, he was in my class. I went to the second class, after two years of that I was ordered to the National War College.

I don't know whether it's on this tape or not, perhaps not, just in our off-to-the-side conversation way back when we were talking about public speaking I mentioned that so many of our naval officers were, I won't say frightened, but -

Q: Deterred from asking questions?

Adm. F.: Deterred from getting up on their feet and talking, but we had a fine group in my class.

Q: Could I ask you to lap back just a second and perhaps give me your opinion of the policy which we always enforce, that is, rapid demobilization, and what could be done to do it in a saner fashion?

Adm. F.: In a what kind of fashion?

Q: In a less emotional fashion?

Adm. F.: Are you talking about demobilization?

Q: Yes, demobilization. Going back to my original question.

Adm. F.: I don't know. Public opinion, of course, is, I believe, controlling. Look at what's happening today. Public opinion then was "bring the boys home no matter what. The war is over." I'll never understand public opinion that apparently comes to the conclusion that you can deal from weakness, and people didn't understand what Communism meant. After all, during the war we were buddy-buddy. We'd given everything the Russians wanted. Some people tried to alert the American public of the long-range objectives of Stalin and Communism, but it didn't take.

Q: It's a very short-range point of view that we accept as our policy.

Adm. F.: That's right. Remember that the Navy at the beginning of World War II - I'm just going to talk about the Navy now - was very small and grew to be a tremendous organization, all filled in with Reserves, and these Reserves had done their duty and they wanted out, everybody else wanted them out. So therefore, the ships, the squadrons, couldn't be manned.

Your question is how do you solve that problem -

Q: How do you slow things down in the face of the international picture?

Felt #3 - 177

Adm. F.: Well, there wasn't any international crisis in the American mind. The crisis was over. Not all of our wars but at least in my lifetime - the first one in my lifetime was World War I. That won the war for peace, didn't it? Wilson was going to have his - what was it? President Wilson. Not the United Nations.

Q: The League of Nations.

Adm. F.: The League of Nations.

Q: Well, would you tell me a little more about your duties in Op-54 because they have bearing on this whole subject, too? And some of the headaches which were yours.

Adm. F.: The headaches, I suppose, were trying to do justice to the individual. Everybody aspired to bigger and better jobs and it was a question of filling the slots with the most proficient people. I think that the one thing, if there was one thing, I did to help the situation was to establish personal contact with everybody. In other words, I encouraged people to come and see me or write and tell me what they thought.

Q: People who were being re-assigned?

Adm. F.: Yes. I encouraged people to come into the office and look at it from my point of view. In other words, this fellow was being re-assigned, perhaps he wanted something as Number One priority. I'd sit him down and show him the situation and usually that satisfied, at least it helped to satisfy, the people if I could show them that it just wouldn't work out that way. In other words, the personnel business, I thought, was a person-to-person business, and that's why we wanted to preserve Op-54 under Op-05.

Q: To continue that policy?

Adm. F.: For naval aviation's policies because we did have this two-way communication and we didn't believe that the big mill over in BuPers had it as well as we had. Arrangement was finally made that Op-54 would sort of go intact and the consideration for aviation personnel would be continued. I didn't stay to actually see it work.

Later on, when I get up to the point where I'm back in the Pentagon in a much more senior position, I'll say a little bit about one of my good friends in BuPers.

Q: Who was head of Op-05 at that point?

Adm. F.: John Cassidy, I believe it was.

Q: Did you have any contact at all with Admiral Nimitz who was then CNO, was he not?

Adm. F.: Not then. No, he wasn't CNO then, was he?

Q: He succeeded King.

Adm. F.: Well, I had I guess you could call it a contact, but it was later. Remind me to mention this. This was later. He was CNO at the time I'm talking about.

Q: He was CNO from 1945 to 1947.

Adm. F.: Are you sure of those dates? Wasn't he CNO a little longer than that?

Q: Two years.

Adm. F.: Two years?

Well, I'll tell you what happened. The timing is a little off, I believe, but anyhow I went to a meeting in the Navy Department at which staff members from the Naval War College presented the solution to a problem. Admiral Nimitz was sitting in the back of the room. This was a presentation to him and staff people, and it was done pretty poorly. The War College hadn't learned yet how to use graphics or really how to present, and the solution wasn't very good either.

At the end of this meeting, after the War College people had made their presentation, Admiral Nimitz walked down front and he said:

"Gentlemen, I'd just like to comment that what you've just heard is one solution to a problem, not necessarily the best solution."

Then he went back to his office. What I'm going to say now is second-hand but I think absolutely true. He immediately called for someone and said to him:

"Who is that aviator you've been talking about?"

"Oh, Cat Brown."

"Get him going. Get him up to the War College as fast as you can."

So Cat Brown went up to the War College to be the chief of staff.

Q: Under Admiral Harry Hill?

Adm. F.: No, this was the Naval War College.

Q: Oh, I see.

Adm. F.: Under Admiral Spruance, with a chief of staff - I may be wrong in this name - W. W. Smith. Would that be right?

Q: Could be.

Adm. F.: And Cat was subjected to a very sophisticated several months of hazing, but he eventually took over and changed the War College.

Q: Does this imply that they knew he was Nimitz' man?

Adm. F.: I don't know, but the War College was still a surface Navy war college, a Battle of Jutland war college.

Q: I suppose that follows!

Adm. F.: Where they worked out tactical problems all the time on that game floor up there, and when aviation was introduced into a problem it was always decided by the umpires that it was zero-zero weather and the aviation was grounded. Well, the one big thing that Cat did, as soon as he survived all this hazing and took over as chief of staff, was to change the curriculum completely to strategic problems, instead of tactical problems on the game board. He kept in one tactical problem on the game board and changed it to broad-picture strategic.

Now, that's getting way ahead of my story, but it is an interesting development insofar as the War College is concerned, and I'm glad to tell it because I went up and relieved Cat subsequently at the Naval War College.

One more thing that struck me. Here we are demobilized, ships tied up with skeleton crews, all of the big ships practically, and a friend of mine, classmate of mine, on duty in BuPers was to go to sea and apparently had a choice whether to be skipper, captain, of a cruiser tied up immobile or a destroyer squadron commander operative. Now here comes the big-ship complex into the picture.

Q: Yes.

Adm. F.: He chose the cruiser! Now he was the head detail officer over in BuPers and I guess he knew what he was doing because he made rear admiral subsequently and, incidentally, worked for me subsequently as a vice admiral. But I was amazed. If it had been me, I would have chosen the active operating job, the destroyer squadron job.

Q: But under the system then obtaining, your chance of flag rank would have been lessened?

Adm. F.: That's the way it worked, I guess. Yes. In other words, he wanted command of a big ship, and he got it operating eventually.

Q: The story you tell about Admiral Nimitz and the Naval War College is kind of a watershed thing, isn't it? I mean his sending Cat Brown up there to inaugurate a new approach to things, is indicative of the new thinking that was taking place within the Navy.

Adm. F.: I think so.

I'm sorry to have mentioned that it was Admiral Spruance who was President of the Naval War College at that time. I have no way of knowing, because Admiral Spruance was gone by the time I got there, but my strong impression is that it was not Admiral Spruance who was dictating the policy there and sticking to this tactical surface concept with aviation grounded. It was the chief of staff.

I'm just reminded of something that goes way back, back a couple of days ago so far as this little game we're playing here is concerned. But talking about the Naval War College brings this to mind.

At one time - I guess I was a lieutenant by this time - I applied for what was then called the junior course at the Naval War College. I didn't make it. They chopped it off up ahead of me, but I enrolled in the correspondence course and did the first assignment, dragged my feet on the second assignment, the third assignment I ignored and received several letters asking why. I finally wrote back and said, "If you people up there at the Naval War College will stop fighting the Battle of Jutland and construct your correspondence course around the future, I'll re-enroll. You know as well as I know that the next war is with Japan."

Now, that's when I was a lieutenant and, looking back, I think I knew ever since graduation from the Naval Academy that some day we were going to have to face Japan.

I want to go back and insert something with regard to the time I was in Russia.

I found yesterday among my odds and ends of papers an invitation and a program to a concert in Moscow of American and Soviet music sponsored by the USSR Society for Cultural Relations with Foreign Countries and by the Moscow State Philharmonic. Here's the program. They played the national anthem of the USSR and the national anthem of the USA. Part One is all American - Roy Harris, Fifth Symphony dedicated to the peoples of the Soviet Union, the first performance in the USSR. Wallingford Riegger, Canon and Fugue for strings, first performance in the USSR. Samuel Barber, Overture to the School for Scandal, and here we go - American songs. I can recall the Russians coming out on the stage and singing these songs - Stephen Foster, Swanee River; Jerome Kern, Smoke Gets in Your Eyes; and George Gershwin,

Love Came In - and it names the person who sang all these songs.

Part Two was all Russian music. But I thought that was quite interesting. It shows how close the relations were, really.

By the way, these relations became this way only after Stalin was convinced that we were going to fight on a second front, invade Europe. When I arrived there, the atmosphere was pretty chilly and a lot of propaganda and complaint as to why we didn't open the second front.

Q: Am I not right in saying that it came to an abrupt halt immediately after the armistice?

Adm. F.: I'm afraid so. Of course, I wasn't there, but I do recall - and now here I'm back in Op-54 - this fellow being ordered to Russia, to Moscow, and he had pretty fancy ideas of what it would be like. For instance, he thought he'd be able to fly either his own airplane or be allowed to get out of the country to fly, neither of which was possible. He apparently thought that the social life would be on the Czarist level, because he bought himself civilian tails and all kinds of fancy clothes. It turned out that he could not get tickets to the Bolshoi. It turned out that he had nothing to do. Life was just as dull as could be.

Does that answer your question?

Q: Now, we're going to the National War College, and I wish you would tell me in some detail about the set-up as you found it.

It was under Admiral Harry Hill at that point, was it not?

Adm. F.: That's correct, and he had relieved -

Q: He'd set it up.

Adm. F.: Maybe his Number Two was General Al Gruenther. It was set up well, I thought. I think the reason Harry Hill was there was because during the latter part of the war he had organized - I've forgotten the name of it, but some sort of educational thing for military people, maybe just naval officers. I don't remember. Anyhow, Harry Hill was there and was fine. Lemnitzer was the deputy at that time - maybe not all that time but at least most of that time.

The system was we divided up into committees, all services in each committee, and were given problems to solve, try to solve, at the end of which we critiqued them. I found at the very beginning that the Army - and well, of course, the Air Force, an offshoot of the Army - were much more proficient at doing this kind of staff work that was necessary.

Q: Why?

Adm. F.: Because they were - well, as I've always said, the U. S. Army was the best educated army in the world, back to the days when it was a very small professional army with no troops to speak of, and they all went to schools. They knew how to go about these things very readily.

On the other hand, when it came to judgment I felt that the naval officers were at least their equals, if not a little bit better. But as far as the techniques of solving a problem were concerned, the Army was already educated in this field.

We had to write a thesis. I've forgotten where it was at the end of the whole year or at the end of the first semester, you might call it.

The first semester was devoted to political-military affairs. We had professors on sabbatical leave from various universities.

Q: And they were A No. 1, weren't they?

Adm. F.: They were, they were tops.

The second semester, and the civilian professors then were not present, was devoted primarily to military affairs. A lecture perhaps every day and an excellent choice of lecturers.

Q: You had the choice from the whole government set-up!

Adm. F.: That's right. Lectures on various places in the world, lectures on techniques of planning, how it was done in the Department of Defense. I remember one by George Kennan, where he got up with an old envelope in his hand with a few notes on it, and spoke extemporaneously. In those days, that was quite an innovation.

By the way, George Kennan was Number Two in the embassy in Moscow during Yalta.

I don't know how to sum this up. At the beginning of the year, Admiral Hill would say to us:

"Now, this is a period provided you, a one-year sabbatical from your military, to think."

My complaint was they didn't give us much time to think. They piled it on pretty heavy! Perhaps not as hard as a Harvard business administration course.

This may not be the correct place to record this story, but I'll do it anyhow.

One of my good friends in the Air Force, a brigadier general, was at a dinner party at the old Wardman Park and present was Jacqueline Cochran - is that correct?

Q: Mrs. Odlum, yes.

Adm. F.: That's right. During the course of the dinner she kept asking my friend, "What do you do at the National War College?"

He said, "Oh, we're given problems, and we solve the problems."

She said, "Give me an example."

So this is the example he gave: What do you do about the Jewish situation? Everybody picked up their ears and said, "Oh, that's excellent, that's very timely." Well, what do you do about it?

Well, our solution was that when they cut that little piece off, they should throw the other part away!

She just roared, and she rushed to the telephone and called her husband up out in California to repeat the story!

He had a way about him, that fellow.

Q: There were State Department people there, too?

Adm. F.: Oh, yes.

Q: And these contacts were useful to you, weren't they?

Adm. F.: Very, and one of the best things I got out of it was the contacts with other services and with State. Nowadays they come from other government departments, but in my day, other than the military, there was just State. Oh, and by the way, we had representatives from Britain and Canada, military people.

We organized driving squads and I thought I was quite fortunate in mine. There was a Marine, an Army officer, a State Department officer, and myself.

Q: A daily car pool!

Adm. F.: That's right, and driving back and forth, of course, there was a great deal of discussion. I recall one of them particularly having to do with intelligence. There was great concern in those days, as there always is, about how to handle intelligence, and a lot of people feeling that the subject was compartmented too much. Each separate service, including State, had its own intelligence organization, and I started to argue that it should all be put under one roof, be brought together. And the statement that was made to me by my State Department carmate was:

"Absolutely, no. Do you think the State Department would ever share its intelligence with the military?"

Just think how far we've come!

Q: And speaking of intelligence and having foreign officers present, how was this handled when you talked about military matters?

Adm. F.: Well, later they had to stop that, and, as I recall it, we had to stop it at the Naval War College, too. This didn't happen until the atomic weapon and strategic considerations of nuclear war came into it. But in those days they were cleared and there were no restrictions. I think the nuclear weapons finally brought it about.

Q: The Atomic Energy Act, which bars the divulging of information.

Adm. F.: Yes. Of course, nobody in a school like that had access to numbers but they did have access to developing techniques and thoughts about realization.

Q: Was the Industrial War College in being then?

Adm. F.: Yes.

Q: What was your relationship there?

Adm. F.: They were in the same area. The National War College, of course, took over the buildings and the library of the old Army War College. The Army, I think, made a mistake during the war. They closed down completely, and when the thought was born of establishing a National War College, there the Army War College installation was available and moved right in.

I don't know when the Industrial College was started. I never thought to look into that, but they were right next door in temporary buildings. They attended our lectures. On the athletic field there was competition between the National College and the Industrial College.

Q: Did you get on the athletic field?

Adm. F.: Oh, one of the first things that Harry Hill did - you know how he is - was to circulate and find out who was interested and if you weren't interested, why not. We organized a softball league right away. Let me see, there was the Army, the Air Force, the State Department, and the Navy. On the Navy team Savvy Sides was the pitcher and I was the catcher or sometimes second baseman. Lemnitzer played first base on the State-staff team. He was good. Harry Hill played left field, remarkable, too. Then, as I recall it, the winner of that league played the Industrial College.

Let's see if there's anything else in my mind that stands out particularly about the National War College.

Q: There were social events attached to life at the National War College, were there not?

Adm. F.: Yes, but not overdone. There'd be a party every once in a while. That's where I became acquainted with General Barnes, and I'll get to General Barnes later on. He was a classmate of mine there, a colonel.

In the Navy group we were all captains. In the Army and Air Force some were brigadiers. I remember one lieutenant colonel in the Army group who was talking a lot about China. Was this subsequent to the Marshall attempt to solve the China problem? This was 1948.

Well, this fellow had an idea which he expounded. It made a lot of sense to me. The charge was made that the graft in Chiang's outfit was what destroyed the whole United States effort, that whatever we put in immediately went into the pockets of senior people. And he said that if we had established a Military Assistance Group, like were established later on in my time, where we would have been able to control supplies which we put in, it could have turned out quite differently. Now, that's conjecture, but the idea of a Military Assistance Group had not yet been born apparently.

Q: When did MAAG come into being?

Adm. F.: I don't know. I inherited it when I became CinCPac. I don't know when they started it. I guess it was after Dulles and Company negotiated and made all these security treaties, after SEATO was established and things like that.

I started to talk about the composition of the groups. It's been very interesting to see how members of that class made out later, particularly the State Department people. Many of them became ambassadors. As a matter of fact, the United States Ambassador to the Republic of China, Walter McConnaghy, was a classmate.

Q: Which probably facilitated your dealings?

Adm. F.: Oh yes. The State Department was very enthusiastic about this National War College concept. The National War College became rated as the Number One choice for officers of all services who wanted to go to a war college. That was changed somewhat later, at least modified somewhat later.

Q: I suppose it had direct bearing on the fact that so much effort was made to get top-flight people as instructors?

Adm. F.: That's right, and, I suppose, kicked off by the policy adopted by the Army and the Air Force at the beginning, that students would be preselected for flag rank.

The other thing that sticks in my mind, and again we come to Harry Hill. He was a strong advocate of carrier aviation and, on the other hand, this was in the days of interservice controversy particularly on that subject. But Harry Hill tried to use me and another classmate of mine in the class to support everything that he had to say about it, but we got to a point where we couldn't quite do it because I remember his turning to Paddy Kane, this other classmate of mine, and saying:

"Paddy, wouldn't you take your carriers into the Black Sea and up the river?"

We allowed as, no, that wasn't quite the way to do it!

Q: Well, Hill became sold on carriers because of his amphibious operations, I suppose.

Adm. F.: That's it, but we had to kind of tamp him down a little bit as to the practicality of some of the things.

There was a great - not a great, I'm overstating that, but there was an effort to enlist me and convert me into an Air Force officer. This was done by two or three of the Air Force students in the class.

Q: In midstream? I mean change?

Adm. F.: Yes, the argument being that here I was a captain at a certain age and if I was in the Air Force, gee, I could be a brigadier general at least, and if I'd just turn in my blue suit and take on their suit I'd be promoted immediately. But I managed to sort of destroy that idea!

Q: Was there any of that going on, actually? Shifting services?

Adm. F.: No, but I believe there was something in the wind that it could be done. I don't recall any of this accurately, but there was a thought going around that people could shift from one service to another.

Q: Had you any contact with Admiral Hill when he was in charge of the operation at Okinawa?

Adm. F.: No. No, you see, we didn't support directly - I'm saying that badly. We didn't support the amphibious operations on Okinawa itself. Our job with our four little carriers was to keep this other place out of business so it couldn't disturb the operations there.

Felt #3 - 194

No, I didn't know Harry Hill until I went to the National War College.

Q: Well, that year there turned out to be a very profitable one for you, not only in having you think a great deal but also in the contacts you made?

Adm. F.: Yes. I don't know what the result of the thinking process was! But the contacts were good and invaluable. And I think it did something towards creating a unified feeling. It didn't solve it, but it was a good beginning, you might say, for people to understand the other fellow's problems.

Did you read the article about Bataan in the last Shipmate?

Q: No.

Adm. F.: Oh, it's a beautiful article written by a Captain, USNR, named Chaplain, I believe, but it comes out loud and clear in this article, talking about Wainwright and others. Communication between the Army and the Navy was nil to start with but finally worked out.

At the end of the one year at the National War College, of course the graduates were supposed to be well versed in planning and many of them went to their service headquarters as planners or some similar function. I went to sea, to take command of the FDR - the Roosevelt.

Q: This was a plum, wasn't it?

Adm. F.: Sure was, one of the three largest carriers in the Navy at that time, the Coral Sea, Midway, and FDR.

Remember we were talking some time ago about demobilization and the condition of the Navy during this period?

I took command of the FDR after she had survived this bad period, halfway in its training period at Guantanamo, and I want to walk back a little bit and recite what happened to the FDR.

First of all, there she was alongside of a pier, denuded of men, just a skeleton crew on board, the ship apparently filthy because they just couldn't handle the housekeeping, and it was decided okay, now the situation has changed, we're going to be back in business. And, as I got the story, they filled out the complement of the crew with a large group of enlisted men whose IQs were not high enough to warrant sending them to school.

Q: They were bodies!

Adm. F.: They were bodies, and they got the ship out from the Navy Yard at Norfolk and anchored in Hampton Roads. The skipper, Binny Williamson, heaved a great sigh of relief. That was accomplishment Number One. Then they finally picked up and went out to sea, and this is the story that Binny tells:

He was out on the open part of the bridge, the closed part being where the wheel is, the helmsman, and the ship started to wander around. He said, "Mind your helm." The ship still wandered. "Mind your helm." No change. Finally, he looked around and behind the wheel was a great big black boy with his

Felt #3 - 196

arms behind his back, and the wheel was kind of going around, back and forth.

"Mind your helm. Put your hands on that helm. Come back on course."

"No, Sir, Boss, no, Sir, Boss, I ain't never seen one of these things. I ain't going to touch it."

So that was the way they started.

Well, I found them in Guantanamo Bay. Binny said, "Everything's going pretty well. The air group is just great, the flight deck is great, the engineers are doing fine, everything's fine except the gunnery department and, if you will fire the gunnery officer, I'll take him back with me when I go back north."

He did that and then the gunnery department started to improve. What he said about the rest of the ship was true. They'd done very well. This was the Training Group, Guantanamo. Preceding us into this training cycle was the Coral Sea, which had been built subsequent to the FDR and, as was the case - I guess it still is, a new ship gets manned with capable people. And they'd gone through the training there with just flying colors. Well, when we'd finished they said that we were equally as good as the Coral Sea, which was really something and what a tribute to Binny Williamson's leadership, bringing that ship out from the condition he found it in to turn it over to me under way.

While we were there, just before we finished our training, our division flag officer came down to visit, and he was aghast at the appearance of the FDR - rusty, it looked awful, but we could operate. He raised hell with us about our appearance.

We got back to Norfolk after an interesting experience. There was a hurricane up ahead of us and the young officers in the ship had never experienced any kind of rough weather at sea, and they thought this ship was so doggone big that nothing could disturb it.

"Well," I said, "all right. Lash everything down and up." I wasn't content until it was lashed up as well as down, so there wouldn't be any bouncing. I said:

"We're going to do a full-power run," which we did and, at the end of the full-power run, I arranged it so that we'd run into this hurricane to give them a taste of it. That made sailors out of these young officers! After a horrible night of getting around the back end of the hurricane on the Carolina coast, thousands of ships and everything, we got into Norfolk.

Then we learned that we were going to go to the Sixth Fleet, to the Mediterranean, and only had a handful of days to get ready, which meant that we had to offload all the training ammunition and onload the service ammunition.

Q: This was for a three-month tour?

Adm. F.: Yes. And because the admiral had raised so much hell with our appearance, we painted the ship from top to bottom and tried to indoctrinate our people that, in addition to being operational, we had to be spit and polish and know something about protocol. My exec resented this terribly, but I said: "Chuck, we've just got to do it."

Q: Why did he resent this?

Adm. F.: Because, "Damn it, we're operational and to hell with this spit and polish business" and so on and so forth.

Q: It's a kind of a diplomatic assignment?

Adm. F.: That's right.

Well, we got over that hump, operated well, looked good, and Forrest Sherman was Commander, Sixth Fleet, in those days. I remember the first meeting aboard his flagship, where all of us captains arrived in our gigs, went to the meeting, and he showed us off and observed the boats. I told my people that I wanted my gig and my boat's crew to be every bit as sharp as the Italian boats' crews were. And Forrest Sherman complimented me. We wound up with a very nice message from him when we finished our tour.

A few words on the tour. We had many, many visitors, groups of people who came aboard, civilians. One group was headed up by the then Secretary of the Army - Mr. Royal?

Q: Yes, Kenneth Royal.

Adm. F.: Yes, and instead of bringing just staff members he brought a bunch of fellows from the civilian world with him. Quite a large group. I didn't have an admiral on board so there was my cabin and the admiral's cabin available for these people. Of course, I couldn't keep track of them all, but one day we were sitting around having a discussion and one of these fellows showed up a little late and I asked him where he'd been. He said:

"Oh, I've been looking around."

"What did you do? What did you see?"

He said: "I went all over and I asked a lot of questions."

I said: "What did you ask?"

"Well, I asked these men all around the ship, what's your job, they told me, and you know every one of those men told me 'I've got an important job,' and they were dedicated to that job."

That was really something. I was, of course, delighted to hear this.

The cruising routine went something like this. We visited North African ports first, all along the North African coast, and then finally Greece and Naples and so on and so forth, the Riviera. There weren't any emergencies or any crises during that period. We had a wonderful air group and a wonderful ship. Everything was fine. The flag officer who sort of insisted I go out on the town with him a lot and couldn't understand why I'd excuse myself and go back to the ship relatively early. He used to kind of pull my leg about it, but I think eventually realized that my responsibility was to the ship and not to the social thing on the beach.

Q: Who was in command of the Sixth Fleet?

Adm. F.: Sherman.

Q: That's right, Sherman. During the whole period?

Adm. F.: Yes.

Q: Now that was the day of the economy drive, too, was it not?

Adm. F.: Well, no, things were picking up. The tempo of operations wasn't as high as we would have liked it to be. There was a little bit too much time in port relative to time at sea, and this always concerns a skipper of a carrier because he gets concerned about his pilots. If they lay off too long, you're asking for trouble. We didn't have any significant aircraft casualties, except one. One of our pilots had a fighter whose wings came off. This was in Aegean waters, as I recall it, and they had a very fine ceremony aboard ship.

Q: Did you use any foreign port facilities? Did you use any fields like Wheelus in your operations?

Adm. F.: We were restricted very much, and when I learn what they've got now "restricted" is not adequate to describe it.

We had one SNJ and we took the wings off of it and parked it in a motor launch when we were at sea. Then when we came into port we'd pull it out and put it up on the flight deck and put it together. Occasionally we'd have permission to fly it ashore, and occasionally we'd have permission to put, maybe, some of the scouting dive-bomber types ashore, but very rarely.

An incident that I remember so vividly was when we were in Sfax, North Africa replenishing - and in those days it was an at-anchor replenishment with supplies coming aboard by barge - and we had some planes ashore. I went ashore to fly, as did some other people. I believe there was an account of a crash recently over in that area. But I got through the mountains and landed at, would it be Tunis?

Q: Could be.

Adm. F.: Where there were two fields, a naval field and an Air Force field adjoining, turned around and got back through. I found out that my other people were scattered all over. They hadn't been able to get through, or something. Anyhow, they were out of fuel and didn't have enough fuel to get back and land aboard ship. Somebody from the ship had come over and told me about all this and I said:

"All right. Get some fuel some place or other in drums. I'm going back to the ship."

Here the fleet was still at anchor. I saw the admiral and said, "I want to get under way right away." Meanwhile they had found some fuel and gased these planes up. So we took off down this way, Sfax, 90° to the wind. The wind was blowing across the short dimension of this sort of bay and we were churning up the mud astern, and my navigator was saying, "We've got two feet under the keel," and the admiral was chewing his hair, "What in the hell are you doing?"

I said, "I'm trying to get sea room to turn into the wind and recover all these planes."

We did. We turned back to join the fleet. They were under way by this time, we made a round turn and joined the formation, and out we went. Perfect timing. I guess I've been close to going aground may times, but I don't think I've ever been closer than that.

Q: Two feet!

Adm. F.: Yes!

Q: You say you were very limited in terms of what you could do in foreign ports. Did you look in at Malta or anything of that sort?

Adm. F.: When I had the FDR, yes. Yes, we looked in at Malta. I get confused between this tour and when I was Sixth Fleet commander.

Yes, and I recall the approach to Malta. We had one heck of a time distinguishing anything to get cross bearings on and visibility wasn't very good. Of course, Malta's just all brown, you know, and there hadn't been any rain there in months. We went ashore and went around sightseeing a little bit and found that water restrictions - I believe all the faucets in the people's houses were locked, except one in the kitchen - and, by gosh, that day it rained. There was nothing outstanding from a diplomatic point of view. It was just a normal visit.

Q: Actually, it was perhaps the first thoroughgoing experience of that sort that you had, wasn't it?

Adm. F.: Yes. Well, it was my first experience in the Atlantic Ocean, and my first in the Mediterranean, of course. I never had served in the Atlantic area, except when I went to the Houston and made that one fishing trip with President Roosevelt.

Q: Yes.

Adm. F.: Well, let's see.

Q: You might talk a little about the FDR as a carrier, her virtues and, in the light of future developments, her defects?

Adm. F.: You probably know that the FDR, Midway, and Coral Sea were laid down to be invulnerable ships in the war with the Japanese. The concept was to defeat the kamikaze, so we had an armored flight deck and below chopped up into many, many small compartments. For example, the officers' wardroom was way aft and the officers lived spread around forward. I remember my exec telling me that he was having the heck of a time with these junior people who were division officers.

Let me go back to my story about the Mississippi when I told you I came aboard as a junior division officer. In this ship there was one officer per gun division, first, second, third, and so forth, Reserve officers, probably ensigns, maybe

JGs, who had very little opportunity to get all of his people together in one group because of the way the ship was split up and because he couldn't get them up on the flight deck because we were flying. They were pretty frustrated and the way the exec solved this was - well, they all wanted to get the heck off of this - he said:

"Look, you've had the greatest experience any young officer could possibly have. You've experienced all of the bad things, all of the difficult things, and you have overcome these. From now on it's just going to be downhill for you."

These are the people who kept the morale of the ship together.

Q: It was done this way because the damage control was the thought?

Adm. F.: Yes, the damage control was the controlling thought. Operationally and from the point of view of the flight deck it was fine.

Q: The armor plate didn't make any difference?

Adm. F.: No, except there was a question of covering on deck. They experimented with several coverings. Remember we were all prop airplanes, so there'd be an awful lot of oil on the decks, and slippery, and of course, this was still in the days when you parked your airplanes just inches apart, pre take-off. They weren't catapulted. So a slippery deck would let the chocks slip every once in a while and chew up somebody's tail. There was that problem.

Q: Was the armor sufficient? Would it have been sufficient to stop the kamikaze?

Adm. F.: Well, it was never tested. As I recall it, the hangar deck was also armored.

Q: What about the sides of the ship? This was also a favorite place for a kamikaze attack, was it not?

Adm. F.: No, it wasn't armored. We had a vast array of anti-aircraft guns.

There was just one carrier attached to the Sixth Fleet. No, wait a minute, let me back up on that. I think only one. However, it was the concept of World War II, operating in a circular screen.

I'm trying not to get confused with my Sixth Fleet experience.

Q: Yes, Keep that as a separate entity. Were these carriers reconstructed later?

Adm. F.: Twice, I think.

Q: Did they eliminate all this warren - ?

Adm. F.: Well, no, they're still armored deck. I think they solved that part satisfactorily, and of course they now have the angled deck. They're not as good as the Forrestal and that class of carrier, but they're quite adequate. I don't know what they call these modernization programs, but I think perhaps only two of the three have had refits.

Q: Wasn't that a part of what they called FRAM?

Adm. F.: FRAM was for destroyers.

Q: Oh, only for destroyers?

Adm. F.: Yes.

Well, we came out of the Mediterranean after what was then a normal tour, three or four months, I guess, and back to the coast, back to Norfolk. There it was an entirely different routine. The first thing that happened was that we got the first jet-engine squadron. The very first one carrier-based. And there was a great deal of concern on the part of everybody as to whether or not our flight-deck crew could accommodate themselves to keeping out from under whirling propellers, as they were trained to do, and at the same time keep from getting sucked into the tail of a jet. But we didn't have any particular problem there.

Then they broke up my wonderful air group, and a new system came into being. Up until this time, this was from my beginnings in naval aviation, a carrier air group was assigned to the carrier. Of course, there were marriage problems because the carrier air group was ashore a lot of the time. They were supposed to belong to each other. Somehow or other, the decision was made not to carry on this policy, but a carrier would just pick up whatever was available. So I picked up what was available and lost my wonderful air group. One of the pick-ups was this jet squadron, and I suppose for a period of five weeks - that's approximate - I received a group of Secretary of the Navy guests every weekend to go to sea and demonstrate.

Q: With the jets?

Adm. F.: No, with the whole works.

Q: Oh, I see.

Adm. F.: I learned a lot about shiphandling during this business because always at anchor in Hampton Roads and usually pointed the wrong way, the immediate problem to get the ship turned around 180° and get out into the operating area as quickly as possible. One particular morning, I remember. We got out into the operating area and were doing all right. We had a good wind, weren't bothered with fog. And the chief engineer came up to the bridge with two buckets full of oysters and clam shells and what not. I said, "What the heck have you got there, Chief?"

He said, "Well, half of your power plant's been out of operation ever since you turned the ship around."

And what I did was I used too darn much power and the main injection was right in the bottom of the ship and all I did was suck all this stuff up into the evaporators. Fortunately we had wind and nobody knew about it, except the Chief and me!

Q: Had you prior knowledge of jets? I mean intimate knowledge? Had you flown jets?

Adm. F.: No.

Q: How did you prepare yourself for - ?

Adm. F.: We just had to learn by doing. Of course, the squadron was proficient, but operating from a carrier was something we had to develop.

Oh, speaking of development, one of the things that seemed spectacular at the time - I have a picture of it, and what the object was I can't for the life of me reconstruct - but we landed a blimp on board and took it off from the flight deck.

Q: A Navy blimp?

Adm. F.: Yes. You know Chick Hayward, don't you?

Q: Yes.

Adm. F.: Well, Chick was flying a multi-engine airplane. Maybe it was a PV. He'd come out and make passes, carrier-landing passes.

Q: Wasn't that the squadron he'd taken from Sandia to the coast?

Adm. F.: I think he was operating out of Patuxent. Everything looked good and he kept bugging me and asking me could he land, and I said no. I never landed him. We hoisted him aboard several times and took him off with jayto assistance. Chick has never forgiven me for not letting him try to land on board. If I'd had an angled deck, I think I would have, but I wasn't sure of the arresting gear, whether the arresting gear could take it, and I didn't want him marching up into the barrier.

Q: The angled deck hadn't been conceived, had it?

Adm. F.: No, it hadn't.

Q: Did you have any set procedure for dealing with the VIPs?

Adm. F.: Yes, there was. It was amusing a little bit. CinCLant Fleet would be the host and somehow or other ComAirLant was charged with the operation, and that was Felix Stump, and he in turn gave the job of organizing the thing and propagandizing the thing to Jimmie Flatley. Jimmie would come aboard and set up his then-crude public announcing system. These people would come on board early in the morning. One time they came on board the night before and spent the night, but it was usually early in the morning, assemble in the wardroom, and the script went something like this.

I would be in the wardroom and welcome them aboard and then excuse myself and go to the bridge and get the ship under way. Then Jimmie and Admiral Stump would brief them. I think I'd have my people brief them on safety precautions. Then they'd come up topside and observe operations.

I got a little tangled with my dear friend Felix Stump one time because I went a little beyond just saying "hello, good morning, gentlemen, excuse me I must go and get the ship under way." Being the captain, I thought, by God, I ought to have something to say, and he'd reserved all that for himself and Jimmie Flatley!

They spent the whole day, the night, and then I would make my way back into harbor in the early morning hours. Some of those experiences were a little rugged because of fog and sometimes the only way you could find the channel would be by CIC and radar. Sometimes buoys would be missing. We'd disembark them the next morning.

Q: What was their purpose largely in visiting? Were these members of Congress?

Adm. F.: Sometimes, but mostly prominent people in the business world.

Q: Why were they - ?

Adm. F.: Just to acquaint them with naval aviation, carrier aviation.

Q: An educational process and they were taxpayers.

Adm. F.: They're still doing it. Groups arrive out here in Honolulu, Secretary of the Navy guests, who make a trip from the West Coast out here in a carrier. And then there was a thing called the Department of Defense something or other and there are graduates of this. A group of people get together every year. I've forgotten the terminology of this, but anyhow when it started they'd go down to Eglin and see the Air Force demonstration, go down to Fort Bragg and see the Army demonstration, and then come to Norfolk and see the Navy demonstration. That would be part of it.

I remember one time, we were in the Caribbean and I guess there'd been some big amphibious operation down there. I left from our formation at sea and went into some island, into the Harbor - can't remember the name of the island - and picked up a whole group of congressional people. One of them was Mendel Rivers, and I picked up a British admiral who knew something about carrier aviation, and then we headed out for the fleet with full power on, knowing approximately where they were, finally picking them up on radar, hoisting a signal from the yardarm saying, "I'm preparing to fly. Air planes all turning up."

Wu Duncan, commander of the Second Fleet out there, and I was anticipating and hoping and apparatly he was anticipating and hoping. He had everything all set for an operation. I came boiling in at 32 knots, settled right in the middle of the formation, and boom, off went the airplanes. Wu and I were tickled to death. We'd been reading each other's minds.

Q: Were these people overwhelmed by the tremendous striking power of the carrier?

Adm. F.: I don't know what the civilian reaction was. Remember

I said I didn't keep a diary? I find I do have a photographic diary, starting with the FDR, and in that - I looked at it yesterday - are letters from many, many of these people expressing gratitude and you get the idea they were impressed. But to answer your question more directly, we'd have Air Force guys come aboard every once in a while, and I remember one colonel saying, "It's just impossible! It can't happen! I don't believe it!" A carrier-deck operation is really fantastic.

Oh, racism! I remember people looking down on our flight deck and seeing white and black boys running back and forth doing their jobs on the flight deck, shaking their heads and saying, "How do you do it?"

"I don't know. We just do it, that's all."

Q: What about the press? They came on, too, didn't they?

Adm. F.: Yes. I stumbled onto a photograph in that album yesterday of a woman press person, the first woman to come aboard while at sea.

Q: This was verboten, was it not?

Adm. F.: Oh, sure. We had a little problem, so we put her up in my sea cabin. No, in the chief of staff's sea cabin, I guess, and put a Marine guard on her!

Q: Now, this is another type of question. As skipper of a tremendous unit of the fleet, how did you react to the tremendous power which you had under your command?

Adm. F.: Oh, gee, I guess you can take your responsibilities too heavily or too lightly. I never let it bear me down.

Q: Or change your point of view on life?

Adm. F.: No, that's part of command. Either you accept it or you don't.

Q: I asked that of a young fellow in our office a year or so ago who was on a visit to a carrier and he came back just overwhelmed by the whole thing. He thought that this must do something psychologically to the men who were involved in the operation of the carrier. It must make them think that they're invincible. This was his reaction.

Adm. F.: No, no, I don't think there's any of that sort of feeling. I know there was a great pride of accomplishment, particularly to old fellows like me who weren't early birds but started out in the game relatively early, watching this thing develop, overcoming the many handicaps, including lack of understanding on the part of our fellow officers. I think the Air Corps never understood why we didn't split off from the Navy like they did from the Army. Thank goodness we didn't.

Q: Growing up with it that way and seeing all the defects and seeing them develop, this sort of helped to keep an even keel, didn't it?

Adm. F.: Sure, that's right.

To try to kind of wind up this Roosevelt tour. It came at the time I was about to be relieved. The decision on what they called the Meatball, meaning Number One, we won it. Starting, as I've described, from Binny Williamson's taking the ship out with a black boy who said, "No, Sir, Boss, I ain't goin' a touch that thing."

That just about covers the FDR, I believe. Oh, no, there's one other little story I want to tell.

I don't suppose very many stories are told about Forrest Sherman which are not completely complimentary. We were the FDR. President Roosevelt and Mrs. Roosevelt loved the FDR, and on a hangar door expanse, a big wide expanse, was that famous cartoon of FDR with his cigarette in a long holder sticking up at an angle of about 60°.

Q: And the jaw jutting out under it!

Adm. F.: Yes, right. We had a vehicle ashore, a pick-up truck with a canopy over it and that cartoon plastered on the side. I guess this was probably in Naples. Admiral Sherman saw it and he called for me and he just read me up and down. He said that was disgraceful, derogatory to the President of the United States. I finally managed to get in a word and told him that the President had authorized this cartoon to be put on the hangar door where thousands of visitors had seen it, and I didn't see anything wrong with putting it on the vehicle. So, he sort of cooled off and that was the end of that, but I think I took it off that vehicle! I'm sure I did.

Q: There's a story you want to tell me about the men from the FDR as tourists in Paris.

Adm. F.: It isn't just the FDR. I want to talk about white hats. I recall hearing stories told by tourists and particularly by Mrs. Roosevelt who, while in Paris, spotted sailors on the street. The stories were always, "Gee, look at those beautiful Americans." A white hat meant American to our American tourists over there. This brings to mind also the conduct of our men ashore. We installed the so-called "buddy system," and the conduct ashore was just fantastic. The lack of disciplinary reports was just something to be very proud of, and I categorized our enlisted people as "the white-hat American ambassadors."

Q: Well, did you have any sort of program on board the carrier before coming to a new port? Were the men lectured as to proper behavior and local customs and that sort of thing?

Adm. F.: Yes, and it was something that I suppose the Chaplain was in charge of. Each time when we'd move on to another port there were brochures put out and talks made after the movies about the customs and traditions of the next place we might go to. Remember I told you that at the beginning of that cruise we visited North African ports?

Q: Yes.

Adm. F.: That was the first introduction for all of us, I guess, to the Arab world, and of course we had to understand

Felt #3 - 216

something about their customs and traditions. Otherwise, we were in the soup. This was an active program and quite successful.

Q: That leads me to another question. What kind of an educational program did you have on board such a great ship as the FDR?

Adm. F.: I can't recall whether the program of getting high-school diplomas by correspondence had been started. I don't think it had. There was a library. We had two chaplains, one Catholic and one Protestant, and the Catholic chaplain was very active with the men. He was all around the ship, very active in athletic programs. I don't remember that there was any formal program to help people enlarge on their grade-school education. There probably was, but I don't believe it was anything of any great emphasis in those days. Lots of emphasis on venereal and all that sort of thing, conduct, behavior.

Q: Well, indeed they are ambassadors in their own way.

Adm. F.: That's right, they certainly are.

I might jump ahead because I get confused all the time between my tour over there as skipper of the FDR and as Commander, Sixth Fleet. I was talking about white hats. I'm sure I've got this tagged correctly now. It was while I was Commander, Sixth Fleet, that the suggestion became alive and was debated quite heatedly about changing the sailors' uniform, doing away with the white hat. As you know, the uniform has been changed dramatically recently.

Well, I listened to the sailors discuss all of this and got into the discussions with them, remembering the white hat ashore and the fine impression he made ashore, and finally put it up to a vote of a group of enlisted men, and they all elected to retain the white hats, which delighted me. They felt a little bit underdressed, of course, when they went ashore compared to the other sailors of the European countries because they had fancier hats, and fancier uniforms, and such, but it was distinctive as American.

Q: I take it you spent a good deal of time associating with your men?

Adm. F.: Yes, I guess that's true. After all, when you start out as a junior division officer and spend all your life practically with the men, it's only the natural thing to do -

Q: It pays dividends, too, doesn't it?

Adm. F.: Well, it brings a lot of satisfaction to an old man now retired several years after 45 years of active service to get letters from these people every once in a while.

Q: Now, when you got a new assignment it was to go to the Naval War College.

Adm. F.: Yes, that's correct. I was under the impression I

was going up there as the chief of staff to relieve Cat Brown. I don't know what happened, but there was a delay in that and Cat stayed on for a few months after I got there.

Q: You went in July of 1949, I think, did you not?

Adm. F.: 1949, that's correct, and I was assigned as the head of the Intelligence Department. You've been telling me about your background in intelligence and I'd had none, except when I flunked the course in Moscow trying to be an agent on the Neva River. And I was the butt of a lot of joking because of this.

I suppose the big part of the job was taking charge of the lecture program, and, at the Naval War College, I think we had as good a mix of lectures as they had at the National War College. It was a bit more difficult to get lecturers there because Newport is isolated somewhat. It's not as convenient for the Washington people, but they'd come up by train to Providence and be driven to Newport for a morning lecture.

There were some outstanding men on that lecture platform. One of them was the President of Brown University, and he had established himself as an expert on strategy.

Q: A curious thing, isn't it?

Adm. F.: Yes. I remember the first time Rickover came up. It was quite a performance. It wasn't a very good performance from our point of view. You know Rickover's quite a character. But he walked to the front of the stage and announced to the group that he was going to talk about nuclear energy and that nobody in the audience understood anything about it. He was the only man who understood anything about it. Nevertheless, he was going to talk on the subject! He established a very fine rapport with his audience immediately!

Q: That saves me a question!

Adm. F.: I remember another one when we invited Curt Lemay up. There'd been a great discussion as to whether we would invite him. We made the decision we would and that we'd behave like gentlemen. But he announced his view that the Navy should have zero carriers, none whatsoever. So there was that argument wide open.

But, all in all, it was a fine lecture program. As I said earlier, Cat Brown had changed the whole course around so that the students were in the strategic field primarily, rather than in the tactical field. But there was another very important point that impressed me.

The charge has been made time after time after time in our history that each service had no understanding of how the other service thought, and at the beginning of the academic year, a program was set up to try to introduce each service to the other services, not only by lectures, some of them given by students themselves, some by staff members, but by visits to installations in that Newport area. And then an introduction to what you might call the tactical instructions of each service. And out of this came a very interesting observation. The Navy tactical instructions were guidance but not doctrine, not the Bible. The best guidance that could be given in a certain set of circumstances that you didn't necessarily have to follow. Whereas the other services' books on doctrine were laying the law down. The other services had a little difficulty accepting this, that is that this was the Navy program.

Q: Greater flexibility?

Adm. F.: Yes.

Well, I found when I arrived that I was accepted but with suspicion.

Q: Why?

Adm. F.: I wasn't a graduate of the Naval War College. I was a graduate of the National War College.

Q: The arch rival?

Adm. F.: Yes, and it took some time to lay that one to bed. An experience of the Naval War College in one field was this. That as the selection process ground itself, very few graduates of the Naval War College in those days made flag rank, and this was because of the method of detailing officers. The ones that were the best prospects for flag rank went to the National War College or the Industrial College. After I relieved Cat and became chief of staff I made several trips down to Washington to try to get this changed and managed to get an agreement that the detailing of officers would no longer be made according to that pattern. Let's say naval officers were sent to the National, Industrial, Naval, the Army War College and the Air War College, and I got them to agree, insofar as detailing was concerned, they'd all be on the same level, with the result that after another year or so the record for selection of Naval War College students was as good as the National War College.

Q: That sounds like a fair and equitable way of doing it.

Adm. F.: I thought so. And the course at the Naval War College was different than at the National, yes, concentrating more on planning techniques, the science of planning. On the other hand, the lecture program was every bit as broadening as the one at the National War College, and working solutions to strategic problems was very valuable to these people.

The President of the Naval War College was Donald Beary.

Q: Spruance was there when you first went there, was he?

Adm. F.: No. Don Beary had taken over. I had bumped into him, not personally but by an exchange of messages, during the war. I guess in one of those interludes out there. You remember the occasion when Halsey's group got clobbered very badly with a hurricane?

Q: Yes.

Adm. F.: Ships were damaged, some ships were sunk, capsized. With Chenango I was ordered to join Beary's logistics force after this hurricane because the big carrier which had given them support had its flight deck all rolled up. Shortly after I got there a message came over, "How do you ride best in a hurricane? Into the wind, or the wind on your bow, or with your stern to the wind?"

I couldn't believe being asked such a question, but I sent back, "I don't know. I've always been able to avoid going into a hurricane." And the response was, "Say again."! I think it was Beary's chief of staff on the other end. Then they said, "I wish you'd go find the hospital ship." It had gotten dispersed during all this bad weather and, you know, the hospital ship was not supposed to be part of a combat group but was always somewhere around.

Well, we found it and came back and reported we'd found it and where they were, and said that we'd been invited aboard but weren't able quite to make it. You know, having a little fun and I understand Zumwalt is reviving fun now. But I found no sense of humor over on that staff, so I wondered about Admiral Beary but he turned out to be great, just great, and they all apparently forgot that I was not quite legal, not having graduated from the Naval War College. Then after becoming chief of staff, the big job was revising the curriculum, a lot of work spent on that.

Q: How did you go about doing it?

Adm. F.: I had what you might call a task group that met all the time.

Q: Were any of the civilian instructors included in this?

Adm. F.: I can't recall that we had any civilian instructors. There were a lot of civilians around in various administrative positions, but our instructors were all in uniform. One of them, incidentally, a Coast Guard officer, who was very brilliant, very good.

That was the main job. While there, the Army was reestablishing its Army War College, and they made two or three visits to us to find out how we were doing and get some ideas on getting their Army War College going again.

Q: Where was this? Carlisle?

Adm. F.: It was at Carlisle, that's where they set it up.

I suggested that they set it up at whatever that fort is across the harbor from the Naval War College and Naval Station. Anyhow, the Naval War College after I left took over all the quarters on that point. I suggested that they set it up over at that fort and then we could share our lecturers, and they said, gee, that's a good idea, but it was too late. They'd already got themselves settled on going to Carlisle. Subsequently, I went to Carlisle a couple of times when I was CinCPac to make a talk there and I understand how difficult it is to get in and out of Carlisle in the wintertime.

But, getting back to the Naval War College, that's about it. Admiral Beary while I was there had a heart attack. We saved him because his aide came running down the corridor hollering for me and I hollered for a doctor who was in class, and he fortunately had the kind of thing that you puncture a guy with and sent him to the hospital under a tent. But he had to retire as a result of this, and then there was a big fuss as to who would be temporary president of the Naval War College. They assigned, first, the base commander, Admiral Cooley, and then, for a very short time, a fellow who was there, retired but on active duty writing history - you probably know him, Bates?

Q: No, I don't know him.

Adm. F.: Commodore Bates.

Q: I know about him, but I don't know him.

Adm. F.: And then they finally assigned me as the Acting President of the War College. I held that for I don't know how long. Not very long, till Admiral Connolly came in from CinCNelm to do that.

Q: What changes did you actually effect in the curriculum?

Adm. F.: I wouldn't claim to have effected any significant change. What I did was carry on the line that Cat Brown had already established and sort of refine it. If there was anything a little bit extracurricular we put in, we encouraged people to take speech classes and rapid reading.

Q: You actually had instructors in those areas?

Adm. F.: Yes. Oh, and we set the groundwork for computerizing a problem. The ground hadn't been broken when I left. The idea was a computerized arrangement. We never got all the money we needed for it, where you could crank into this thing speeds from 2 knots to 1,000. So you could get information on any kind of a problem. Now we were getting back into the tactical field, you see, working back from this ground tactical, floor tactical, with the air grounded, to all strategic, back to a better mix where we could not only put the current air into the air but also anticipating missiles, with missile speeds and what not.

Q: Has this been developed?

Adm. F.: It's been done and developed. The idea was that not only would it be used by the Naval War College but also by the fleet, by Lant Fleet, and this has come about. It's probably a lot more sophisticated than we visualized then. We thought we were pretty sophisticated then.

One other feature of the War College when I was there. There was a senior course, a logistics course, and this was the cause of much unhappiness at the beginning of each academic year on the part of officers, particularly aviators, assigned to the logistics course. Logistics, in those days, was categorized as just nuts and bolts. The idea, of course, was to benefit from the lessons gained in World War II and make people realize that logistics is the heart of any military effort.

Q: I should think the example of ComServPac was so flagrant that they would have learned already?

Adm. F.: No, it was difficult for particularly the aviators to take because, you know, it wasn't operational. After a short while all of this discontent faded out because then they started realizing that they had a course every bit as good as the senior course, and the lectures were shared by both. The man in charge of the logistics course was Henry Eccles, who has written voluminously on the subject of logistics, lectured there, and after retirement went on a contract with George Washington University, your alma mater, and is still an authority on the subject.

While I was there we started up a new course, different, a new course - what did we call it, junior, I guess, junior something or other - for younger officers.

Q: This was inaugurated at that time?

Adm. F.: Yes, that's right - lieutenant commanders. That thing was in existence one of my two years there. We started it. I selected the personnel to head it up. Here again, they had their own lectures. This was down on a lower level of military learning, but they came to the senior-course lectures also, and one of the features we put into this was learning how to run a committee. Naval officers had had little, if any, education in

Felt #3, 227

carrying or participating in committee work -

Q: The elementary rules and things like that?

Adm. F.: Right. We put that in and that caught on very well. Cat Brown had started the - now, what was the name of this, it was a thing that was done in June at the end of an academic year where a bunch of Reserve officers were called in to active duty for a couple of weeks and civilians from all over the United States were invited to the global strategy meetings. I carried that on and it's still being carried on. The Naval War College was the first to do anything like this. This was very good and particularly that second year because our students had learned how to run a meeting, and we put all these youngsters in as chairmen of these committees.

Q: In the realm of curriculum, did you make any attempt to assess the impact of the Naval War College course on men who then went out and achieved things in their naval careers? Did you make any attempt to check on this and learn from it?

Adm. F.: I don't believe I can answer that question. I can go back and say that the quality of officers assigned to the War College was improved. In other words, the prospects of future success were increased just by the fact that they were higher-quality men. The broadening of their knowledge as to how the other services worked, as to what the situation all around the world was, of course, helped them and, no matter where they went from the Naval War College, they had a knowledge - at least some knowledge - of what made other people tick.

Q: I was thinking of it from the other side of the coin. From the men who went out and were confronted with certain problems and what-have-you, were you able to learn things that would help you to adjust the curriculum?

Adm. F.: You're talking about feedback?

Q: Yes.

Adm. F.: No, I can't remember any significant feedback. You mean somebody goes out and he has an experience and his student days at the Naval War College helped him solve something. I can't remember that kind of feedback.

We've just been talking off the record here about what Admiral Nimitz said about the value of his student days at the Naval War College, which reminds me of something I've heard and I'm sure it's true - that the war in the Pacific, that is the business of wrapping up the islands and so forth, was planned at the Naval War College many, many years before World War II.

Q: And the tie-in with this story about Nimitz.

Adm. F.: Yes. Whether or not that study at the Naval War College visualized the use of carrier air and amphibious operations I would sort of doubt -

Q: But the basic concept was.

Adm. F.: To get back to that question of feedback - we've been talking about it off the record and you tell me now that a thing has been set up at the Naval War College to put in oral history - I think that I was a little unfair in saying that I wasn't conscious of any feedback, because I was thinking in terms of an officer saying - who was out in the field, at sea, writing back and saying, "Look, this is what helped me," but as I think about it more, our instructors were graduates of the Naval War College and experienced with the fleet. And, as we worked up these programs, their experience and judgment were woven into these programs. So, in that way, there was feedback.

Q: Yes. It wasn't a self-conscious thing, but it was there.

Adm. F.: Right.

One other thing about the War College. While I was there we had foreign officers. We had British, Canadian. I think that was all, and there was one Canadian officer who was really a sparky guy. He was really British, with a hyphenated name, but was in the Canadian Navy and an aviator. After every lecture, he'd always be on his feet asking questions and making comments. He was pretty sharp, but one line he followed all the time was that naval aviation had no business crossing the shoreline. Naval aviation's business was at sea and it should stay at sea. I had quite a time with him on that one.

Q: Well, this was born of the Fleet Air Arm, I suppose?

Adm. F.: This was born of the British so-called naval aviation, where, of course, they operated just at sea and didn't have the capability of doing anything else.

Another thing I remember. Cat Brown had instigated this, and that was what we called the "murder board" to help people in the preparation of staff presentations.

Q: Is this where this term originated?

Adm. F.: I think it originated there. I hadn't heard of it before that, anyhow. But apparently the staff presentations had been pretty awful - you know, reading a dull paper - and he insisted that people train themselves to get up and make a speech. So we had these murder boards, and I never will forget how I sweated through the preparation of my first one, which was on carrier aviation. At my first murder board, I gave my presentation and an officer got up on his feet and said, "Captain, I don't think you should give that speech."

And I said, "Why?"

He said, "Because it's controversial."

Well, I hit the ceiling a couple of times but then gathered myself together and said:

"What's the purpose of this War College? Are we to throw out everything controversial? I thought the purpose of this War College was to look at all the problems."

I was very amazed.

Q: Did he make flag rank?

Adm. F.: Yes!

Now, let's see.

Q: The other services were represented in the student body?

Adm. F.: Oh, yes.

Q: What percentage? Preponderantly Navy, weren't they?

Adm. F.: I wouldn't say preponderantly. There was a good percentage of Air Force, Army, and of course, there were Navy and Marine, a couple of Coast Guard students. As I say, some foreign officers, and that again was stopped, as it had been at the National War College later on.

On the staff were officers of the Army and Air Force, as well as Navy-Marines. I've never been a student at the Army War College or the Air War College, but I visited both making talks there later on and found the same thing there - a mixture of all services.

Q: At this stage, how did you handle sensitive material with British and Canadian officers being present?

Adm. F.: There may have been some wraps on it, but at this stage, as I recall it, the lecture was announced as being confidential or secret and there were no restrictions as far as the student body was concerned. The only restriction was that we used to invite retired people to come to the lectures, but if there was the classification of secret they wouldn't be invited.

But I don't recall any restrictions insofar as the foreign officers were concerned.

Q: Did you ever, in the course of your career, visit with the Imperial War College?

Adm. F.: No. I had an experience with a portion of the student body in my next tour of duty, out in the Persian Gulf, but I've never been there.

Q: Were there very many American officers who did get to the Imperial War College?

Adm. F.: A few. I don't know how many each year. In this group that came to the Persian Gulf, there was I think only one naval officer. There may have been more. That was just one group of them.

During my time at the Naval War College there was never any trip, indoctrinational trip, to various service installations except in the immediate area, during that early part of the first term.

Q: Was this a matter of expense?

Adm. F.: I guess so. I asked for it, but I was never successful in getting it. The National War College, when I was there, started the business of trips and now it's very extensive. It goes all over the world. But in my day we went to Fort Knox, weren't allowed to get into the vaults! I saw a program the

Army was conducting then - I've forgotten what the heck they called it, but it was a bunch of recruits and they separated the blacks from the whites. Fort Knox was an armored business, I believe. We saw an Army day-and-night exercise there, but that was about it. I never got a trip for our people at the Naval War College.

Q: Well, we're still at the Naval War College.

Adm. F.: I guess that's about it on the Naval War College. In the early spring or late summer of 1951, the selection list came out and I found my name on it, having been selected to flag rank. So I got in an airplane one day and flew down to Washington to find out what would be next. Forrest Sherman was CNO then. He learned I was in town and called me in and said:

"I want you to get going right away to the Middle East to take over the Middle East force. I want you to get there by a certain date." So off I went.

Q: Why the urgency of it?

Adm. F.: I've never been quite sure.

Q: Was there any crisis brewing at that point?

Adm. F.: Yes. The Abadan thing was hot, and our commander of the Middle East force in the Persian Gulf was Judge Eller, and I relieved Judge.

Q: How large a force was it?

Adm. F.: A little flagship, a little aircraft tender painted white and air-conditioned, and that was it.

Q: Was it a symbolic sort of force?

Adm. F.: Yes, showing the flag. I relieved Judge up in the northern end of the Persian Gulf and stayed there for quite a while. We were not permitted to go up the river or go into Persia. We just stayed there showing the flag and watched the British come in with a lot of their amphibious-type operations.

Q: They were there in force, were they?

Adm. F.: Somewhat in force. In miserable shape because of the heat. This was one of the very worst summers that had been experienced there in the Persian Gulf.

Q: How high does the temperature get?

Adm. F.: Oh, gee, 112° or something like that.

Q: And humidity?

Adm. F.: Yes, very high humidity, and the British being very proud of the fact that they'd set up a salt-water shower on the fantail. People walking around in a daze, their equipment going to pot because of the humidity. But on the way in - I flew in commercial and stopped at - oh, that town right across the river from Persia.

Q: Baghdad? Did you go through Baghdad?

Adm. F.: No, this was down on the river, down south. I bumped into a lot of the refugees, the American refugees, that had come across from Persia, having been told to get out right now and being permitted to take one suitcase with them. It was pretty bad.

Well, this went on for a time and eventually I was invited to come up to Teheran. Our ambassador there was giving a garden party for some charity and I met - I don't think I met the Shah, but I met both of his sisters and some of the other relatives and the foreign minister. We had a naval attaché up there, a young fellow, a lieutenant commander, who had taken the language course at Anacostia and had married a girl in North Africa, the daughter of a French general, so he and his wife both handled the language well. And in the course of that visit, on the Sunday we were invited out to their Persian residence, out in the foothills, where gathered were a bunch of Persian businessmen and what not. This young man was doing a magnificent job. He was traveling around, getting information that none of the people in the embassy could get. Just magnificent.

The rest of the time I cruised around the Gulf. I had to try to figure out what I could do to keep myself occupied, and it was divided between three things. One was to try to provide some kind of recreation for the crew: they couldn't go ashore except in a conducted party, which the chaplain would arrange, and that's pretty dull.

Q: Did they feel inclined for exercise in such terrific heat?

Adm. F.: Oh, yes. American boys - well, interpret that word "exercise" in all of its connotations!

Q: Yes, I see! Pretty dangerous in an Arab country!

Adm. F.: That's right, and their efforts were not very successful. They were allowed to go ashore at Bahrein, where the British had a little base and we had a unit ashore to help with the oil business. That came under me.

But what I did was provide fishing, and we'd go out to some of these unoccupied, unpopulated, islands and let them go ashore with their beer and have a beer bust - islands populated with turtles and birds, and that was all. That was one thing.

The other thing was calling on the sheiks.

Q: In the various sheikdoms?

Adm. F.: Yes, and I had enough sense before going over there to collect as much as I could get my hands on telling about the customs and traditions. This really paid off because I found that it was very necessary to know some of these customs when you were received by a sheik - very formal and all that sort of thing. Not only did I make calls on them, but attended dinners that they gave, eating in Arab fashion.

Q: That must have been a chore!

Adm. F.: Well, yes and no. It just depended on how well informed you were and how well you conducted yourself. I forced every officer in the flagship to go with me, and that was difficult. They didn't want to do this. But when I told them that all you have to do is be careful not to drink any water and be careful what you eat and eat with the correct hand, they were all right.

This was rewarding. I made some good friends with these sheiks and I learned to respect them. I suppose the most interesting was a trip that I made up to the governor of a province at an oasis in the middle of the Saudi Arabian Desert. The Consul General went with me. My party was small and at the various occasions I always took the enlisted crew of the airplane who'd gotten their uniforms all clean and pressed. It was the usual kind of reception. The sheik greeting us, the Consul General's interpreter sitting on the floor in front of the sheik, and the sheik's entourage banked along the walls of this big court room, you might say. The Consul General had taken a whole bag full of money, because he knew the customs on tipping - all coins, incidentally, no paper. Then a fellow took charge of us, who was, oh, I suppose you might call him a foreign minister. He spoke very fine English but he'd never been out of the country, and he took us on a tour around the oasis. One of the things that impressed me immediately was watching bathing in the pools at this oasis. Pretty large pools, the water coming in from a well at one end, and at that big pool men and their donkeys were bathing. The donkeys, of course, reacting as many people do when they put their feet in the water. They reacted accordingly -

Q: Purified the water!

Adm. F.: Yes, purified the water. I finally asked where do the women bathe. I hadn't seen any women and I knew there had to be some around. Well, they were on the other side of a wall, where the water from Number One Pool flowed into their pool!

Then, that evening, after a big Arab dinner - a word about that dinner. Here again, orange crates with a sheet on them and all these little dishes of all sorts of things around here, mostly American canned goods, and sitting on the deck with your feet all curled up under you, getting cramped. Behind me was oh, a brigand, a sort of dangerous-looking man, with swords and guns, and the sheep was a little bit far out for me to reach it with my right hand unless I got up, and I was having trouble unwinding myself. With that, this pirate back of me walks out into the middle of the table with big, black, dirty feet, and took his great big knife and went whack, whack, whack, whack, and plopped onto my plate. I got the very best bit of that sheep, however, I found out later, that's the piece right around the backbone.

Not once in all my experiences at sharing a meal with the Arabs was I ever given the pope's nose or an eye. You know the stories told about how they treat Americans?

Q: Yes.

Adm. F.: I don't know why, but they never did it to me.

Anyhow, we stayed there approximately three days, as I remember - not quite, because any visit is supposed to be at least three days and I think I pleaded with the sheik and he said all right, cut it a little short. Well, on the last morning we'd been asked if we wouldn't like to go out and see his horses, which we did. One of them was a beauty. And at the farewell audience, he asked me what we'd been doing. I told him we'd been out to see his horses and he said:

"Well, did you see anything you liked?"

I opened my mouth to say yes, and the Consul General gave me a very hard kick in the shins, which closed my mouth, because I was about to say yes, which would have meant I would have had the horse!

So that was that visit. Oh, by the way, one evening, I guess the first evening, remember I said this man who spoke good English took us around sightseeing? That evening we gathered on the roof. It was fairly cool in that oasis, up on the roof at night. Here was an Arab, never having been out of his country, who broke out cigars and whiskey, which he helped us to consume. Then finally we got to a point where we were taking pictures with our cameras, and we got this pirate to join us in having his picture taken with us. He was a dangerous-looking fellow, but I found he was just like a lot of other people - he liked to be mugged, having his picture taken.

Q: That's a violation of their rules, too, isn't it?

Adm. F.: That was, yes. The oil people had quite a problem with that.

Oh, by the way, while I'm on the enlisted crew subject, going back to it. I had a discussion with the captain as to what working hours should be observed. We were observing a working routine where they got up early in the morning and went to work up topside, scraping the stack in these high temperatures and so forth, then taking a blow every once in a while down in their quarters which were air-conditioned, and then knocking off at one o'clock. And I thought, gee, maybe that's too much spare time on their hands. We decided, however, to retain the whatever it was, six to one o'clock routine, and not work them topside during the real hot part of the day - go fishing or something like that if we were at sea. Incidentally, the temperature of the water at sea was about - I think the intake main injection temperature was something like 104°. So swimming was like swimming in a hot bath.

Q: Not invigorating at all!

Adm. F.: The first thing was working with the Americans over there on their evacuation plans, and this was a real live subject. That's why I went up to Teheran, to work with those people on their evacuation plans. I said I went up there to attend this garden party, but thinking back, that was the main reason for going up there.

I found the oil people very superior types of people.

Q: These were the Aramco people?

Adm. F.: Yes. Particularly the Aramco people. They ran a school in New Jersey for their enlistees, and the attrition was pretty high in that school, getting them prepared to deal with the situation there. There were problems, of course. One was the picture-taking problem, which had been solved by the time I got there. The other was liquor. They did have liquor privileges —

Q: Within their compound?

Adm. F.: Within their compound, and about the time I was leaving that was withdrawn, and that was a real hardship on those rough, tough guys who worked out in the fields.

Q: Why was it withdrawn?

Adm. F.: Just because of the Arab custom. I suppose some of this liquor was percolating out into the community, too. I don't know. Another feature was the air base at Dhahran. We were in charge. An American Air Force officer who, incidentally, was a classmate of mine at the National War College, was in command, in charge of the whole operation, while at the same time training the Saudi Arabians. The Saudi Arabians finally took it over completely. However, we still had landing privileges there. All of that's changed and I don't know exactly what it's like there now. I doubt if there are any Americans there.

I visited all the oil people up and down the coast at various places. One of the men I remember meeting was up north and he was drilling offshore. He hadn't found oil yet when I left. Subsequently they have found oil there. They had gotten an old Navy LST and converted it into a hotel barracks ship, air-conditioned it, and I had lunch with him one day. Fortunately my supplies had come in. So-called fresh, maybe frozen, I don't remember, came by commercial ship out of New Jersey, after stopping God knows how many times on the way to the Persian Gulf, so when our stuff arrived it wasn't very fresh. But every once in a while we'd get celery, and I took to this luncheon all the celery I'd gotten, put it in the middle of the table, and you've never seen men go so hog wild about anything in your life! They just went after that celery. They hadn't seen it for months and months and months, I guess.

Q: I understand that was true in the Far East, too, wasn't it?

Adm. F.: I don't think I've ever seen celery in the Far East, come to think of it.

I mentioned the evacuation plans. We worked these out together. There was a problem of how much they could do, how much the Navy could do, and how much the oil shipping could do. All that sort of thing. Trying to put the whole thing together.

Q: Did you have any other naval ships on call to augment your - ?

Adm. F.: While I was there the policy was established for having a couple of destroyers come in every once in a while, which happened.

Q: From the Mediterranean?

Adm. F.: Yes, and incidentally, before I got there, Wu Duncan had taken a carrier task group into the Persian Gulf, and he wrote up a very fine report which apparently didn't accomplish anything. He told about the difficulty of operating in those high temperatures and the necessity to put air-conditioning in our ships. It took a long, long time for that ever to come about.

I entertained aboard ship. I had a little cabin. I could seat about eight people. The sheiks would return my calls. They'd come aboard with all their pirates and I'd send them back on the fantail and the crew would give them ice cream, while the sheik and his son, or somebody, would come in.

Q: Did you feed them lamb?

Adm. F.: Probably beef.

After I relieved Judge, that was up north, we came down to Ras Tanura, an oil town just north of Bahrein, and that was my entrance into Saudi Arabia. The Consul General was there, and I fired a 21-gun salute to the Saudi Arabian nation. The Consul General said:

"Ooh, they can't return this salute. They can't possibly return this salute, so you shouldn't have done that, maybe."

I said: "All right. Never mind. It's done, and we're just going to wait and see."

They returned the salute. I think it took them six hours to get off twenty-one guns! But they returned it.

Q: I imagine they can do better now?

Adm. F.: Oh, yes.

Then I went to Bahrein, and here I had an experience. I went ashore to call on a British gentleman who became a good friend of mine after a while. And I arranged to call on the sheiks at Bahrein and he went with me, and he said:

"Now, the return calls will be made at my office."

I said, "Uh-huh. If there is to be a return call it will be made under the American flag in my flagship."

Well, we communicated back and forth by means of flag lieutenants and what not for a couple of days. I stuck to my guns and word came back:

"Well, the sheik gets seasick." This was in Bahrein Harbor where the water's as smooth as this carpet. So that didn't mean anything. But they finally compromised and sent the sheik's brother out, which was all right. The call was returned officially! But I found that this had been accepted by my predecessors, to have their calls returned under the British flag.

Later, on calling on the sheik in Kuwait - that's where I relieved Judge - a delightful fellow.

Q: He was Oxford-educated, wasn't he?

Adm. F.: He might have been. It was on a Sunday morning - it wasn't Sunday for them, of course - and it was during Ramadan. Usually during Ramadan I had to wait until after sunset for my calls, but they made an exception. The only thing was they wouldn't serve any tea or anything like that.

Q: Fasting!

Adm. F.: Yes. We conversed, and there was a British Foreign Service gentleman there, and again I found that everything was to be done under the British flag.

I said to the sheik: "Gee, I would hope that you could return my call." He looked at this British fellow, then he looked at me, his eyes just sparkling, and said:

"I'd like to do that."

I said, "That's fine. When?"

"Right now!" I said: "All right. Give me a chance to get back to the ship. Now, this is our Sabbath. There's church going on. Let me go back to the ship and finish church, and then I'll be ready to receive you."

Sure enough, he came out. He was just like a naughty small boy!

Q: Pulling something!

Adm. F.: Yes.

Q: I take it that was British policy, rather than - ?

Adm. F.: Right.

During the time I was in the Gulf I went down to Oman, would that be it?

Q: Yes. The Sultan of Oman.

Adm. F.: Yes, and made a call on him.

Q: That's part of what they call the Trucial States.

Adm. F.: Yes, the Trucial States. Somebody had alerted me that baseball had been introduced. So I loaded up with some softball baseball gear and took it down.

I was rowed ashore in his gig. I have a picture of it. A canopy, oarsmen, and I have the tiller, going in to the castle. I've forgotten exactly the sequence of events, but I think somebody called on me first and it wasn't the sheik. Again, it was a relative, and I have a picture of him and the startled expression as he came on board because he didn't know what to expect, apparently. And again, the British were calling the signals down there and apparently weren't calling them in our favor. But that worked out all right.

Q: Admiral, with such close control as the British apparently maintained over these little sheikdoms, the wrench must be the greater now that the British have pulled out.

Adm. F.: Yes.

Q: Quite bereft, they must be.

Adm. F.: They sure must. Like pulling out of Bahrein. I never thought the British would do this.

The other place that comes to mind and at least was interesting to me was visiting Qatar and, while there, I went into a shop where they were overhauling engines, in-line, reciprocating engines. The foreman was British and the workmen were all Arabs. I asked if any of these workmen could qualify themselves to take their jobs, said I to the foreman and British officials standing around. The answer was a sharp, No, of course not. They couldn't possibly qualify to take over my job.

This was in such sharp contrast with the policy of Aramco, who had a policy that the sky's the limit as far as you are concerned. If you can learn, we'll advance you, and they did that. That was the American policy, in contrast to the British policy.

I guess the end of my story comes when finally I got permission to leave the Gulf. My area included all of the Saudi Arabian Peninsula and, incidentally, I went over to the Red Sea and called on our ambassador over there.

Q: Stationed at Jidda?

Adm. F.: Yes. What's that big gulf south of the Saudi Arabian Peninsula, west of India, that big body of water? That was in my area, and Pakistan and India were in my area, but despite my numerous requests to leave the Persian Gulf I was denied because of all this oil fuss up at Abadan and so forth. They wanted me to stick around.

Finally I got permission to leave, provided I would restrict the trip to one port in Pakistan and one port in India. I went to Pakistan first, went through the various formalities, protocol, meeting various people, talking with various people, among whom were the chief of the Army - oh, and I had my airplane down there, so I flew around in it quite a bit. The chief of staff of the Army wanted me to come up to the front, where they were confronting the Indians. The Kashmir thing was still very hot. I refused to do it. Our ambassador wanted me to, but I said no. I didn't want to be part of any controversy or have my actions be interpreted as being a part of any controversy between India and Pakistan.

I found out later that I was correct because when I went to Bombay and exchanged visits with officials there, the first question asked me was "where did you come from?" Answer, Karachi.

"Oh! How long did you stay in Pakistan?"

"Five days."

"How long are you going to be here?"

"Five days."

In other words, I balanced it off. It was all right.

Communications were very difficult in these days. We had a communications station in Ethiopia, a naval communications station.

Q: At Addis?

Adm. F.: Yes. But there were gaps in this, and communications were quite difficult.

Q: Did you have any units of your fleet in Indian waters?

Adm. F.: No. Just as I say, there was one flagship and occasionally a couple of destroyers would come in.

We had visits from the people in London. Mick Carney was in Naples. They were just setting up in Naples. They'd always come down in the wintertime when it was cooler. That summer was a terrific summer. In the oil business there were many, many casualties in the civilian tankers just from heat prostration.

By the way, our little outfit ashore had to do with inspecting oil. You see, the Navy acquired a great percentage of the oil out of there, and this was to satisfy Navy specifications.

It was a six months' tour.

Q: And actually you were under the London command, were you?

Adm. F.: Yes, under CinCNelm.

A six months' tour without dependents. My successor brought his wife over and that broke that.

Q: Agnes, you mean, Judge's wife?

Adm. F.: No. Not my predecessor, my successor, who was Massie

Hughes. No, he's one removed, I guess. He talked to me in Washington before he went out there. Anyhow, they finally set it up and got a house and made it a -

Q: Where would it be?

Adm. F.: In Bahrein - and made it a one-year tour.

Q: Did you touch down at any of the islands in the Indian Ocean where the British had installations?

Adm. F.: No. As I say, the only time I got out was the short visit to those two places.

Q: Well, that certainly was an educational tour, wasn't it?

Adm. F.: Very much so.

Q: And later on, when you became CinCPac, was this area not under your jurisdiction?

Adm. F.: No.

Q: Not India?

Adm. F.: No. My line - and it still was so until just recently when Admiral McCain's line was extended to take in most of the Indian Ocean, as you know he's over in Ceylon right now.

Q: This reflects changing policies.

Adm. F.: Yes. It was discussed during my time but never acted on.

Q: Well, the British fleet was still in evidence, wasn't it, in that area?

Adm. F.: Yes, the British had a unit in the Persian Gulf, which was a permanent thing.

Q: They always maintained a cruiser there, I think, didn't they?

Adm. F.: No. They'd bring in a cruiser every once in a while, but the flagship was what they called a frigate.

I had one very amusing little incident. This was up in Kuwait again, alongside the oil pier. They had two frigates alongside, tied up, one outboard the other, and they gave a reception and invited me. I walked down the pier and went aboard and was met by an aide and escorted aboard. Drinks were being passed around, a punch-type thing, and the aide asked me if I'd like a drink and I said that I'd appreciate that very much. He handed me a menu, and every kind of drink that anybody ever thought of. Amongst them was rum, and I hadn't had a drink of rum for an awful long while and I knew that British rum was awfully good. So I ordered rum and water. He turned to somebody and gave the order and time went on and time went on and I looked at the aide. He was just staring straight ahead. Nothing happened for, oh, I don't know how long. Finally, I grinned and said, "What's the problem?"

He said: "Well, Admiral, I'm very embarrassed but you know in the British Navy officers don't drink rum, and we had to send down to the enlisted quarters to get your rum!" And I laughed because the only thing he knew about the British Navy was that British Navy over there that drank Scotch all the time, but I was well aware that the British Navy in the Caribbean drank rum all the time!

Well, so much for the Persian Gulf. As you say, it was an education and subsequently that part of the world became very important in our strategic thinking, and there were not too many people who knew much about it. That, and the fact that I learned to appreciate these Arabs and their way of life. I didn't appreciate their way of life, but I appreciated their integrity, and it was another lesson in my course of learning. The first being visiting Arab ports as a captain when I had the FDR and we weren't very well informed, and then really learning something about the Arabs. We were thinking in terms of what the Soviets might do. I found many places that were ideal fjord-type places where a submarine tender could tend submarines unobserved for months on end.

Q: Was there any interference or attempt at interference by the Russians at that time?

Adm. F.: No. We never saw anything of the Russians. One other thing I can think of, and this is a black mark on the United

States. The U.S. government was going to supply the Saudi Arabians with military equipment and it decided to send a team over to work out the terms and agreement. One member of the team was a Jewish man, an Army officer. The Arabs discovered this immediately and that stopped negotiations right now. How short-sighted it was for the American government to put this man there.

Q: I suppose it was understandable in one sense, in that normally we don't think of such things.

Adm. F.: Yes, but we did understand it. I had visas to all the countries I went to on the way, in anticipation on the way back I was instructed not to go into Israel unless I just had to, and my passport clearly indicated that I'd not been to Israel and wasn't going there. I did have a separate letter that covered me if I had to go. But we knew the situation. It was just an administrative error.

Q: Admiral, in the light of the fact that you were there in the Persian Gulf, even though the British were still very much in evidence, in the light of the fact that you were there and had that experience, what would you say about the advisability of our being there now and doing something in terms of fleet and so forth?

Adm. F.: Here you run into what I think is the paramount question. What are our national interests and where? It's clear in my mind today that the President of the United States has declared that it is in our national interest to support Europe. The Nixon Doctrine is fuzzy on that point, insofar as I'm concerned, in respect to the Pacific and Asian free countries. In regard to the Persian Gulf I haven't seen any statement that it is in our national interest to retain our interest and show the flag, but I assume a decision has been made because something is being done there. The Americans are staying there. This much we know. Just what the arrangement is is unclear to me. I haven't been informed. I believe that we're going to stay with some people ashore in Bahrein and I understand that we're going to continue to maintain a token naval force in the Persian Gulf. How dependent the United States is on that oil, I'm not really qualified to say. We've become less dependent on it than we were in these days in 1951 that I was talking about. However, I think that we still are dependent to a great extent on the oil that comes out of there. I know Europe is, although there's been some relief from the oil findings in North Africa. But that again is –

Q: Pretty precarious, isn't it?

Adm. F.: Yes, because of politics. The thing that immediately comes to mind, and stands out in my mind, however, is the dependence of Japan on that oil. It's my understanding that the industrial complex of Japan is almost completely dependent on the oil from the Persian Gulf and its transport through the

Makassar Straits and on up.

That's the strategic situation, briefly, as I see it.

Q: Well, it's an interesting observation.

Adm. F.: Therefore, getting back to our national interest, it's involved. It's involved not only with our requirements, but the requirements of Europe, the requirements of our friends the Japanese. Over-all I'd say very definitely - I'm talking from the left-field bleachers now - that it's in our national interest to try to see that the Soviets don't take over.

You asked a question about the Soviets. When I was there, we didn't see them, but there was great concern on the part of the oil people about possible capture of the area by the Soviets, and plans were made to deny their oil to the Soviets, as they evacuated. That was the threat always hanging over the whole picture there.

I recall working on strategic problems - I can't remember whether this was at the War College or later in the Navy Department - as to how to defend that area in case the Russians attacked. It was quite a controversial subject as to how to do this.

Q: Especially lacking substantial force in the area to begin with!

Adm. F.: Yes. I met a gentleman while I was there and went over to his island. The king, I guess, had granted him an island all unto himself.

Q: The King of Saudi Arabia?

Adm. F.: Yes. I spent a Sunday with him. I wish I could remember the name of this gentleman. He worked for the Shah at one time. He was an oil expert, worked in our State Department, and went to Persia to draw up a seven-year plan, which the Shah never adopted. But I understand now they have a seven-year plan. Finally, I don't know just why, he had to leave Persia. He was granted this island. But he had foresight about the development of Persia.

At the time I was there the Shah was just starting on some land reform.

Q: Against great handicaps!

Adm. F.: Yes. There was one very delightful sister and one witch of a sister, and the airplane going back home, landing in Paris, I found that a co-passenger was this witch of a sister. I didn't know she was aboard until we disembarked.

Well, so much for the Persian Gulf, unless you have a question or more.

Q: I can't think of anything.

Adm. F.: OK. I went back to Newport and picked up my family. They'd stayed there while I was in the Persian Gulf. And we went back to Washington, where I was brought in as Number Two in the Navy Strategic Plans Section. Shortly thereafter, Arleigh Burke came in and took over as Number One. That was the beginning - I think I can say this without any question - of Burke and Felt working together as a team.

Q: A tandem.

Adm. F.: Yes.

Q: Had you known him before that time?

Adm. F.: Oh, yes. We're classmates. We'd known each other at the Naval Academy, bumped into each other from time to time in our separate careers, and I did my best to keep up with that fast-moving Burke. Of course, that was an introduction into the interservice problems. Representing Burke down in what they called the tank at the Joint Chiefs' meetings - no, no. I'm getting ahead of myself again. No, we were the planners, yes. We would go up and brief the CNO before he'd go to these meetings on the various papers that came before the Chiefs.

Q: What sort of thing were you planning in 1951 and 1953?

Adm. F.: Force levels, all sorts of strategic plans. I suspect that nuclear weapons plans started to be developed in those days. The whole gamut of strategic thinking. And here is where my experience in the Persian Gulf paid off, because that was still a very hot spot.

I spent two years there.

Q: How closely did you work with R & D in your planning?

Adm. F.: There wasn't any real close association. The plans people, if they're going to do their job properly, have to be cognizant of what's going on in the technical field, of course. When budget discussions came up, we always supported strongly the continuation of budget money for all aspects of Research and Development.

In the personnel business I found that there was more than a tendency to keep rotating people in and out of this business. A person might come once, go away, and come back. You know, sort of continuation of the same cycle of people, and we weren't injecting any young brains into this thing. I reminded Arleigh of this thing we'd set up at the Naval War College, this junior course?

Q: Yes.

Adm. F.: And the high caliber of people who'd graduated from this. So we started to bring in some of these people, inject them into the system, and this was a very fine thing to do. Most of these kids were flag officers now. And that's about it on that. Hard work, long hours.

Q: Anything with Admiral Burke is long hours apparently!

Adm. F.: Yes. Arleigh and I had different concepts, however, as to how to do this kind of work. Arleigh's the type of guy - he's a bulldog, you know. He's tireless and as long as there's a problem to chew on, he'll stay right there and chew on it well into the night, which means a lot of other people have to stick around while he's chewing.

On the other hand, I felt that there comes a point of no return in a man's capability to concentrate, and I would knock off, oh, at six or something in the evening and go home, have a bite to eat, and then go to my briefcase afterwards. This was true all the way through our association. He would stick to it right at the office, and I'd carry it away.

Q: Didn't he need any kind of break or relaxation?

Adm. F.: He didn't seem to. Maybe it broke up his continuity of thought.

Q: Did he have any hobbies?

Adm. F.: Yes. He bought a farm, a piece of land out in the country, and with his own hands built a house on it, and spent a little time in it afterwards. The sad thing about it was that he put all of his tropies, World War II trophies, out in that house and somebody broke into it and stole them all. But that's the only hobby I knew of.

Q: Did this job put you in touch with the congressional people?

Adm. F.: Not in that planning job, no. I didn't go up on the Hill. That was a job for somebody up the line.

Q: How large a staff did this section have? What was it Op- ?

Adm. F.: Op-30 in those days. It's now Op-60. Gee, I don't know how many people were in it. There were various different sections, broken up into areas.

Q: In your planning, how closely did you work with Intelligence and how much of a feed-in from them did you have?

Adm. F.: We had to have very close relationship there. Any strategic thinking has to be based on an appreciation. Of course, I'd learned my lesson long ago to try to get that appreciation from as many sources as you can get it.

Q: Exactly. I was about to ask you about that. I mean, did you rely only on the naval intelligence or did you go out on a little broader scale?

Adm. F.: Remember what I told you about how my fellow State Department student while I was a student at the National War College reacted. Some of that still existed, although I believe the move was on to try to break the barriers down between the intelligence agencies. You were there what year now? In ONI?

Q: I was there during the war period and left in 1946.

Adm. F.: Did you see all these barriers?

Off the record Dr. Mason was telling me some of his experiences during the war in the intelligence business. I think I tipped it off by asking about barriers. All it does is bring to mind the, I think, fundamental thought that no service can be

Felt #3 - 261

independent of another service. It took a long time for this thought to really develop into any kind of unified thinking.

You asked what we did in strategic planning and I mentioned force levels. Well, that was a very unproductive, long-drawn-out, hard argument, which produced nothing of value to the Secretary of Defense because it was the Navy's appreciation of what they needed, the Army's appreciation of what they needed - the Marines were with the Navy, and the Air Force's appreciation of what they needed, and nobody willing to make any kind of a compromise and try to bring this down to a level that could reasonably be supported by a budget.

Q: A coordinated thing?

Adm. F.: Yes. Just a useless thing. And, of course, not only did we have current plans but we had long-range plans and papers that led up to long-range plans. When you got into the long-range thing, it was frustrating. Nobody would give an inch, and everybody overpadded everything, too, I suspect.

Q: Where was it ultimately boiled down into a unified thing then?

Adm. F.: Well, it was just a question of time. Time and gradually the birth or the growth of a concept. I suppose the beginning was - what did they call it? The National Security Act of 1947? And then a succession of Secretaries of Defense who handled it in their different manners.

Q: At the point that you served there with Admiral Burke, was he still suffering from the impact on him personally of the National Defense Act? I mean, the unification struggle.

Adm. F.: I don't quite understand your question.

Q: Well, he more or less got a kind of a black eye for his role in that, did he not?

Adm. F.: Oh, you mean the Op-23 operation?

Q: Yes. Was he still suffering from that?

Adm. F.: I don't think so. No, that had been, so far as I could tell, buried. Probably he benefited from it really. It helped his image, at least in the Navy hierarchy, in that he was recognized as having a big head full of big brains.

Q: Somebody told me once about in this very period an order coming in from Admiral Burke to the planning force to develop a plan for the Navy during the Eisenhower administration. I mean a long-range concept for them. Is this an illustration of the sort of thing you did in terms of long-range planning?

Adm. F.: I never heard it spoken of in those kind of terms. It was always spoken of in terms of a three- or a five-year projection.

Well, let's move on. Let's take a few more minutes and move on to another area. Is that all right?

Q: Surely.

Adm. F.: I received orders after two years of working with Burke and Company, having been relieved, incidentally, by George Anderson, and was given a carrier command. This was in the hunter/killer business. In those days the flagship was World War type jeep carrier, and this was back to the Pacific.

Q: Under the Seventh Fleet?

Adm. F.: Yes. Mel Pride had the Seventh Fleet. The Navy hadn't been in this kind of business very long. The Atlantic and the Pacific had different concepts and, as I understood it, the Atlantic organized permanent task groups, sort of thing, to work out the tactics for this finding and killing submarines. In the Pacific we had a different concept, which was to train as many people as possible in the fundamentals of it.

Now, we went out to the western Pacific and I operated from between Japan and Okinawa. The carrier and the flying people in the carrier were permanent. It was a combination of a type of airplane with equipment in it that could do something towards locating and destroying submarines and helicopters. It was the beginning of the helicopter engagement in this kind of work, the very beginning of it.

We'd get together in Japan with a bunch of destroyers and their skippers and we'd have a little preliminary instruction, indoctrination, for the destroyer people in how to handle the helicopters. We were very cautious about handling helicopters in those days.

Felt #3 - 264

Q: Had you flown one yourself?

Adm. F.: No. The helicopter hadn't really proven itself yet and they were having technical troubles, the engine overheating, and hovering, and things like that. So we had to be very careful in handling them. For instance, never allowing them out of sight of someone in control. So the destroyer people had to learn the rudiments of this.

And then the tactics of a bent-line screen - I don't quite know how to describe it - were quite different than the tactics of a circular screen, and they had to be introduced to these basic tactics. It was not only a daytime operation but it was a nighttime operation was all blacked out.

These destroyer people would come to me and say:

"Admiral, we just can't do it." And I'd say, Yes, you can. You're going to do it. Now let's go."

This was after this little preliminary. Not only indoctrination in conferences, but a little experience in actually handling helicopters around the waters of Japan. Off we'd go to sea and cruise down to Okinawa, most of the time operating just with ourselves and a submarine and the patrol planes coordinating into this. Sometimes working with other units of the fleet, trying to get through their protection or protecting units of the fleet from submarine attack.

Arriving in Okinawa, we'd have a critique of the operation, and then, as I remember, we'd pick up another group of destroyers and repeat the process going back to Japan, with the result that we at least inoculated, if this is the way to say it, a great many destroyer people and worked out tactics for our own air people in coordinating the carrier air with the patrol air, which I thought was right useful. For me personally, it got me acquainted with a great many destroyer people who, incidentally, did cut the butter. Some of those associations were continued on afterwards.

It was a hard working job for me because sometimes I was up twenty-four hours a day -

Q: A continuous strain, I would think.

Adm. F.: Yes, because it was day and night until I got my chief of staff well enough indoctrinated so he could take over and I could grab a little sleep. And it was a dangerous thing because the night maneuvers, unless they were done precisely, could involve collisions, where you'd have the ship just screen back and forth.

Q: How many helicopters were you working with?

Adm. F.: Oh, I don't remember. I suppose we must have had not more than half a dozen.

Q: And what make were they?

Adm. F.: Sikorsky, I guess. These were the ones that had the trailing sonar that they put in the water and hovered, then picked up and recovered the sonar in the water.

This thing went on for about four months and then, one night at the officers' club at Yokosuka, my chief of staff came boiling in and said:

"You'd better get back to the ship. There's a message there for you."

I did, and I found a message telling me that I should get going immediately, which I did that morning - next morning - down to the Philippines and relieve as Carrier Division Three. Now I was in the attack carriers, from the hunter/killer ones. And I found there Sol Phillips, Vice Admiral Sol Phillips, Commander, First Fleet, and two or three carriers.

Q: Commanded the First Fleet? Based on San Diego?

Adm. F.: Yes, but he was out there. I took over, immediately had a conference ashore of all the skippers of all the ships and told them how I expected to operate. Felix Stump was there, CinCPacFlt. He happened to be in town and attended this talk, having talked to them before I took over.

Q: May I ask, how could you achieve this? I mean, being so precipitously put into that job without any forewarning. How would you be able then to immediately take it up and say, this is the way I want it done?

Adm. F.: Well, remember now, I'd been skipper of a carrier, I'd been CarDiv of this smaller, somewhat different type thing, I'd been skipper of a smaller carrier in the war. I knew my carrier aviation, and all I did at this conference was tell people some of the simple things about tactical operations. For instance, you know how hot it is down in that part of the world and you know that in certain seasons of the year there is all sorts of rain all over the place and the winds are light and variable. We had some airplanes that couldn't be catapulted unless there was a good bit of wind. There'd been a turret accident in the Randolph, I believe, up in the Newport area - not a turret accident, a catapult accident - with the result there were restrictions on our catapult.

Well, the gist of my talk was something like this:

We'll go to sea and be as comfortable as we can possibly make it for you. I will not start flying at five or six o'clock in the morning. I won't start flying until eight o'clock or a little later perhaps, so that the crew can enjoy the only comfortable sleeping hours of the twenty-four, those late hours of the morning when it cools off a little bit.

We will steam darkened ship at night but I want you to take off all those damned things that close up all the air - those curtains, take them off and let some air into your ships, and at night, while we're cruising, I'll set the course so that we're cruising in the wind to get some ventilation into your ships. I want you destroyer people to understand that you need not follow that carrier around at 25 or 30 knots, hanging on to that carrier's tail, just because you might pick up an aviator. You will cut corners and use only half boiler power instead of full boiler power.

And, you know, made life a little simpler for them.

Q: This was the voice of experience!

Adm. F.: So off we went. Sol, a nonaviator in one carrier, I was in the other, and, according to Sol, having written to Felix Stump saying, "I thought I knew something about operating a carrier task group, but I found out I didn't know a damned thing."

No, it was just simple common sense, that's all.

Well, shortly thereafter we got an "open when ready" set of orders to go to the South China Sea and operated up into the Gulf of Tonkin.

Q: There were two carriers involved in this?

Adm. F.: Right. This was just standard operating in a different area, that was all.

Then an incident happened. The Red Chinese shot down a civilian transport plane en route Hong Kong to Saigon, no survivors, and we instigated a search. Couldn't find anything, went at it again, with instructions to stay at least twelve miles off the coast. We violated that somewhat every once in a while. Then I set up a trap. I sent the usual SBDs out at low altitude searching for survivors and, stacked above them, were two levels of fighters and other SBDs, and, sure enough, the cheese smelled pretty good and a couple of Chinese fighters came out, turned towards these two sitting ducks down there, and were shot down before they knew what it was all about. That was publicized. It wasn't kept secret, but not one word came out of Communist China.

Q: What sort of a communication did you get from your - ?

Adm. F.: Well, we were in communication with CinCPacFlt and he, in turn, with the CNO, oh, hourly, I suppose, while we were searching. After one or two days of it, we withdrew and we were directed to go back and do it again.

Q: Who was CNO? Carney?

Adm. F.: Carney. But we weren't given any orders like were given in the Cuban crisis of telling us how to fly our airplanes or what kind of tactics to use. We were just told - to Sol and him to me to go there and told us what they expected of us.

That just about sums up that experience.

Q: Maybe this is an appropriate time to ask you a question like this, if not, tell me so. You were able to use your own good judgment in this case and you weren't told from Washington in detail what you should do. What about the virtues of that vis-a-vis the Cuban operation?

Adm. F.: I was not in the Cuban operation, but I do know that orders came out of Washington to individual pilots of airplanes, and let's project this into the Vietnam situation. Signals were called from the quarterback in Washington all the time.

Q: The commander of the fleet, who was in charge of the quarantine operation, told me that he thought this was right because it was not basically a military operation. It was a political one.

Adm. F.: Well, aren't all military operations the result of a political decision, either the inability to effect a political arrangement or a decision - well, not "either." A military operation is never commenced - that is, I'm talking about a combat military operation - until there's a failure on the diplomatic side of the house. Isn't that true?

Q: Yes.

Adm. F.: Well, as I said, that's just about it, I think, on that thing. It ended up in my being surprised and very disappointed. The routine, the pattern, in those days had been that a newly selected flag officer, if he was as fortunate as I, would get one of these hunter/killer groups and do a normal tour, and then some time later come back and take an attack carrier division and so another normal tour. So I had expected to follow that pattern, but no. They decided I'd put my x number of months in the hunter/killer and add it to the y number of months in the attack, add them together and it all totaled up a year and I'd had it. So I was finished as a CarDiv commander.

Q: What was the reason for that? Were there so many people to assign?

Adm. F.: I guess so, and I'd had a full year. There was another reason, I guess. At least, I thought I found out when I got back to Washington.

I was ordered back to Washington, why I didn't know, and for what purpose I didn't know. I was called in to Wu's office, the Vice Chief's office, and Wu sat me down -

Q: Wu Duncan was the Deputy, wasn't he?

Adm. F.: Yes, he was the vice chief - and explained to me that they felt a need to set up a new shop, operational readiness, something that apparently they didn't have. And he said:

"I called you back to organize this." There I was. I found that I had an office, a desk, and a secretary. Then I was asked if I knew a fellow by the name of Bill Irwin, and I said, "No, I don't."

"Well, he's between jobs. He's a ball of fire. You should take him."

I said, "Sure." Bill is a submariner, and I found him a fellow who could really knock down walls. He scrambled all over that Navy Department helping me get the submarine people to talk to the air people, and the air people to talk to the destroyer people, and vice versa, you know. Operational Readiness covered the whole ball of wax.

Q: This was the sort of man you needed, was it not? Because readiness had been in Operations, had it not, except that it was distributed all over?

Adm. F.: Sure.

Q: And you were coordinating it in one -

Adm. F.: This was the job of getting the whole thing together, and then trying to determine which are the most urgent problems to sink our teeth in.

So, all right, the job of getting some more people to help me, help Bill and me, then the job of breaking down all these damned walls that grew up around - in - a big bureaucracy.

Q: Empire!

Adm. F.: Right. And getting people to appreciate other people's thinking, and have some consideration for other people. See, the Navy is the most complex of all the armed services, in that it has a surface fleet, it has an air fleet, it has a sub-surface fleet, and the Marines get awfully angry at me when I say, it has an Army.

Q: And land facilities, installations of all sorts.

Adm. F.: Right. So, when you talk about the problems of the Army, they're quite simple. You talk about the problems of the Air Force, and they're quite simple to those of the Navy. And you can talk about the interservice rivalry between the Army and the Air Force and the Navy, but the worst feature of it is the intersection rivalry, you might say, in the Navy itself. Everybody trying to fly his flag just a little bit higher than the other fellow's flag.

Well, all right, that was one feature of the job. I forget what we zeroed in on as first priority, but I think it was probably air defense.

Q: I suppose your priorities were tied in with planning, too, weren't they?

Adm. F.: Yes. So we organized meetings, and the general idea of getting people to think, pick out a problem and make everybody go to work on it. I guess it worked. I don't know how long I had been in that job, but it was during this time that they reached down and picked Arleigh Burke to be CNO. One day Arleigh called me up to the office and said, "How would you like to be Commander, Sixth Fleet?"

I can't remember whether I fainted at that moment or not but, of course, this was just out of heaven.

Q: Do you think that you had accomplished the thing that you set out to do, which was to set up a readiness - ?

Adm. F.: I hope so.

Q: And it continues to function, does it not?

Adm. F.: Well, the organization of the Navy Department and the CNO's office has changed so many times and somewhat radically that I wouldn't know just where it fits into the thing. But I'm sure it is a function of his staff.

Ralph Ofstie was then the commander of the Sixth Fleet and was due for relief when Arleigh told me I was being appointed to that position. So I tried to prepare myself for it. I drew a conclusion and think it's fair to say this - that the Sixth Fleet did not have the reputation of being an operational fleet. As a matter of fact, in cocktail circuits, it had the reputation of being a social fleet. This was an unfair thing to say and it may be unfair for me to put it on the record, but -

Q: The evidence substantiates that.

Adm. F.: Does it?

Q: Yes.

Adm. F.: Well, I looked over the way they operated from what information I could gather, looked over the composition of the staff, and decided that I needed to pump some different people into the staff. People more knowledgeable with developments coming along, nuclear weapon tactical use, and so on and so forth. And I selected these people and arranged for them to go and get some schooling.

This was going along satisfactorily when all of a sudden Ralph was sent to the hospital, very seriously ill, and it was determined I must go, right now. This upset all the plans Kathryn and I had made, because it had been laid out that we were going to travel by ship, the United States, across the Atlantic, something that we'd never done. We were going to stay in London a few days, make our manners with CinCNelm. Then we were going to Paris to make our manners with the NATO headquarters, and finally work our way down to relieve Ralph. But, as I say, it didn't work out that way.

We took off from Anacostia in an airplane and flew to Nice.

Q: Had you completed your arrangements to have a new staff?

Adm. F.: All my choices were in school but were a month or two or three months away from being ordered in.

On arrival at Nice, I found that the flagship was over in Spain, in Barcelona, and I was met in Nice by the Consul General and Rear Admiral Buddy Yoemans and his wife. Buddy was the Deputy or chief of staff of Commander, Sixth Fleet, NATO staff, with headquarters in an office in Naples. He'd come up to Nice to meet us.

The Consul General had in his hand a couple of tickets to the Grace Kelly wedding and asked if Kathryn and I would attend. I told him I was sorry, I could not attend because I had to go and take over and wouldn't be available, but arranged for Bud and Helen to take Kathryn, which was quite a lovely experience for her.

Anyhow, we went to Barcelona, took over command, and immediately I had a problem on my hands. I asked Kathryn, in thinking about this a couple of days ago, whether it was a real serious morale problem, and she said, no, she didn't think so. But arrangements had been made for this cruiser flagship to go over to Majorca, an island off the Spanish coast, for a three- or four-day holiday. Practically all the wives of the staff were already in Majorca when I arrived in Barcelona.

Q: What was the flagship?

Adm. F.: The <u>Newport News</u>, I believe. I had two of them, and I get mixed up as to which was first.

After taking over, I announced that we would sail for the eastern Mediterranean almost immediately, and there was consternation among the troops!

Q: What was your objective?

Adm. F.: It wasn't an objective. It was an order. The Israeli-Arab thing had gotten very hot. 1956. And I was ordered to take the fleet over to the eastern Mediterranean - just in case.

On the way I stopped in Malta and conferred with the British, feeling very sorry for the British because you remember they had tried to do something about the Arab situation with an attack force, but it was a force that had a speed of advance of about 5 knots, very limited capability, and before they could solve the problem in their own way, it was solved politically by saying "Get the hell out of there."

Q: And the French, too, were involved?

Adm. F.: Were they involved in it?

Q: Yes.

Adm. F.: Well, at this meeting with the British in Malta, the British admiral suggested that we plan and organize a combined command. This thought wasn't new to me because I'd fought this as a planner many times. I said:

"No, I don't approve of this sort of organization." (Just as an aside, I didn't say this to him, but my observation had been that if you agreed to this, it would be an arrangement whereby a United States officer would act as commander-in-chief for a while, then turn it over to the British officer. Rotate the command, with an intermingling of ships. I'd seen some of that intermingling during World War II, but never under British command.) I refused to go along with this, but suggested that if we got into any kind of hassle, it would seem appropriate to me for us to divide up the area in accordance with our relative capabilities. He had some air capability, but not very much, limited compared to ours. Well, he finally accepted that and then there was an interchange, flying back and forth, for subsequent discussion.

Q: This was prior to Washington's stepping into the situation politically?

Adm. F.: No. This was just afterwards, I think.

Well, my problem was, and I sent back to Washington or to CinCNelm and asked the question: if this thing breaks out between the Jews and the Arabs, whose side am I on? And I never got a satisfactory answer to that.

However, we operated around in that area. Everybody knew we were there, of course. Then we kicked around the problem of whether to try to impose a blockade, and we ran into all of what that word means, all the significance of it.

Q: That's an act of war!

Adm. F.: Right. So we decided no, that isn't appropriate to the situation.

Q: Hadn't yet arrived at the use of the word "quarantine"?

Adm. F.: And, believe it or not, we gave birth to the concept of quarantine.

Q: You did?

Adm. F.: Yes.

Q: How interesting!

Adm. F.: Yes, and we had it all set up the way it would be handled in the eastern Mediterranean.

Q: You say "we did," did you give birth to this idea?

Adm. F.: My staff, approved, of course, up the line. I don't remember the details of it but it was a thing where you could control, in and out, the things you wanted to control to either the Arabs or the Jews. Just like they controlled the thing in respect to the Soviets in Cuba.

Well, that finally cooled down. Meanwhile, Kathryn had gone into quarters at Villefranche. She'd taken over a floor of a big house that had been turned into a sort of apartment deal, and learned how to do housekeeping. Villefranche was the home port of the flagship. The only thing home-ported in the Mediterranean was the flagship. There were a few facilities for people there. A little facility to provide baby foods and I believe a liquor store. There was an arrangement with the French to have some beds in a hospital and an organization of wives who tried to take care of each other.

Q: Why only the flagship had a place? Because of the system of rotation?

Adm. F.: Yes, and there wasn't any permanent assignment of ships. It was in and out from the Atlantic to the Sixth Fleet on, possibly, a three-month rotation basis.

Q: That must have been a difficult command, under those circumstances?

Adm. F.: It was. You had a turnover of people all the time, but there was one advantage of it. One of the objectives of the Sixth Fleet, like it was when I was a hunter/killer guy, was to give as many people as you could the experience of operating in those waters.

Q: Did you, as Commander of the Sixth Fleet, have any control over the ships that were assigned to you for that short period?

Adm. F.: Oh, sure. They were mine. I had operational control over it all.

Q: But the selection of them to come into the Mediterranean?

Adm. F.: Oh, no, I had no control over that. I took what they gave me. I had a logistics force and two - I can't remember whether it ever worked up to three carriers or not, but these two carriers, a destroyer squadron, two or three cruisers. It was a good-sized, powerful organization.

My real problem was making them operational. I found out that money and operational funds had a lot to do with this and, of course, restricted what I could do to improve what I saw. But I found out that, for one thing, they would go to sea for an operation lasting maybe five or six days, and at least almost half of that would be taken up in getting out of port and maybe replenishing once, and returning to port. So I said we're going to sea for at least ten days or two weeks at a crack, and really operate. I put this across.

Q: The confining limitations of the Mediterranean Sea itself, was this not a handicap?

Adm. F.: No. There's plenty of room. I found that the flagship itself hardly, if ever, joined up with the task force at sea, to operate as part of the task force. It just went around paying protocol visits. We decided that the flagship would be part of the tactical unit, which caused a little consternation among other ships' skippers. When they saw the flagship coming, they said, "Let's get out of his way because he hasn't had any experience in formation."

I found that Commander, Sixth Fleet, Ralph Ofstie issued every operation order for these five-day operations, and I decided this was ridiculous. I issued what I called a letter of instruction, which set forth the basic concept of operations, and then told the CarDiv commander that he would write the op orders for the task group operations. These were little sticky points along the line, but we made that work.

Then on this rotation business, a system was set up where when a new flag officer was coming in with another bunch of carriers, he would come with part of his staff by air and get indoctrinated before his ships arrived. Red Pirie came over one time with that.

Q: Did the diplomatic aspect of the Sixth Fleet operations suffer because of this emphasis?

Adm. F.: I don't think so, no. We had a doctrine of never allowing a concentration of ships in any one harbor. That was just a pure safety precaution, always conscious of this Soviet threat. So when we did get to port, we dispersed all over the place. There was adequate representation. One of the problems was that, you know, a flag officer on a mission like that has an allowance of money - I've forgotten the terminology for it - to use in official entertainment, and I disbursed these monies to junior officers, captains of destroyers, who had the same kind of job as the Sixth Fleet commander had, going into a port and representing the United States.

Q: Was this completely acceptable to some of the foreign dignitaries?

Adm. F.: Oh, sure.

Q: They usually looked upon the need for the commander-in-chief to be there.

Adm. F.: No, this worked fine. We had always two flag officers in addition to myself in the fleet. We had the carrier division commander and we had the cruiser division commander. Then we had a very senior captain as the destroyer squadron commander. So there was quite adequate representation there.

Incidentally, a problem arose or was there, a festering problem, one that had always bothered people. It bothered Burke when he was a cruiser commander - cruiser division commander - in the Med, as to what kind of responsibilities you can give to these various flag officers, particularly the non-aviator flag officers and the destroyer squadron commander. I held tightly to the concept that when flying is being conducted, the carrier division commander, an aviator, should be in operational control. For replenishment, one of the other officers would take charge. I made the cruiser division commander the air defense expert, to develop air defense concepts and tactics. Missiles were just coming into the thinking. And I made the destroyer man the anti-submarine expert, which partially solved the problem, anyhow.

Those were some of the things that were going on in those days. Just before I left - I don't know how long before I left - we started to develop a concept which was voiced by a young officer on the staff. He was a lieutenant and I turned him over to Cat Brown with very strong recommendations. I did this in front of the whole staff. He came up with the idea of the Haystack concept, which Cat developed and, I believe, operated. That is, dispersing instead of putting your ships at sea in one relatively tight big formation - dispersing them in all this merchant ship mess that's going back and forth through the Mediterranean.

That young officer - Denton is his name - is now a prisoner of war up in North Vietnam.

Q: How strong was the Royal Navy in the Mediterranean when you were there?

Adm. F.: Not very strong.

Q: Had they already begun to pull out?

Adm. F.: I don't know that there was a pull-out visible, it had already happened I guess. As I say, they had one carrier. Whether by reason of boiler power or economy, I don't know, but they were limited to - oh, I don't know, 25-knot speed, and their aircraft had range and altitude limitations. Their concept was quite different than ours in carrier procedures.

By the way, back in the days when I was in the Saratoga - this is World War II - out came to us a British admiral and a couple of his people to observe us operate on and off carriers and determine whether the British should adopt our system. He finally got the hang of it, and when he left said he was going to do so. Well, they did, except for this one exception - I'll come back to the Sixth Fleet in a moment. He finally went away with the understanding that when a signalman put his hands up like this, it meant too high, you're too high, or down like this, you're too low, come up. The British were just 180° out of this. Up like this means come up, down like this -

Q: The reverse?

Adm. F.: Yes. Anyhow, they adopted the same signal business, but one time in operations off Malta, an operation with the British, we were attacking Malta and they were defending. Some guy got fouled up and got lost, a British fellow in a British fighter, and said he was coming aboard. And we said OK. He came round making his approach and, all the way around, he was being given a wave-off because the deck was fouled - our deck was fouled. Somebody'd got hung up in the gear and it wasn't clear. He just came, landed, he thought to hell with that signal. Fortunately the deck got cleared just in time and he was safe and we were safe.

I called him up to the bridge and asked him how come he was having a wave-off all this time, why did he land. And he said:

"In our system, when you get committed to a landing, you make the landing, no matter what."

They had no wave-off concept at all. That's just a little aside on tactics.

I want to go to one other of my problems. The Sixth Fleet, as I think I mentioned, had two hats. One was the NATO hat. I've forgotten the title, but anyhow this was in connection with the defense of Europe and, of course, ourselves in the Mediterranean, and had to do with long-range delivery of weapons, which we were pretty adept at - long-range practice, interjecting ourselves into Europe, all over the place where everything was cleared, making these long-range flights. But our problem was one of jurisdiction, just like in the Korean War. The Air Force gent, ComAirSouth, insisting that as soon as my planes crossed the shore line, they were his, and we insisting uh-huh. So that went on and I turned that one over to Cat.

I think that's about it. There's not much more to say except the normal operating thing. You think of the Mediterranean as always good weather. It isn't. It can be very violent sometimes. It can come up very suddenly. The usual in and out of port. The white hats I've already talked about.

Q: Did your NATO hat require you to go to Paris?

Adm. F.: I only got to Paris once during my tour, to go up and pay my respects to General Gruenther, and that was after I'd gotten back from the eastern Mediterranean. I did that as soon as I could.

It turned out that one morning I got a message from Burke - this was after I'd had the job a little less than four months, having gone prepared to stay a long time. Burke's message opened:

"If when you start to read this message you're standing up, I suggest you sit down," and that message told me I was being ordered back to Washington to be his Vice Chief. Remember now, Wu had stayed on for several months in the position of Vice Chief. That's the story of the Sixth Fleet.

Q: Tell me, what was your relationship with Clare Booth Luce? Wasn't she in Naples at that time as the ambassador?

Adm. F.: I never saw her there. I was only in Naples just very briefly, once during that tour, believe it or not. I made a special effort to go in and be present at the change of command where our naval officer, ComNaval Forces South, was being relieved. She was ambassador there and she lives here now. We've become pretty good friends and discussed those days when she was ambassador, but I never had an opportunity to get to Rome when I was Commander, Sixth Fleet.

Q: In light of the fact that Malta is such a controversial subject at the present time, and when you were there I understand the British fleet was not very numerous. Was it the policy then of the Sixth Fleet to throw things in the direction of the Malta shipyards for minor repairs and that sort of thing?

Adm. F.: No. There was never any occasion to do that. We had our own afloat repair facilities and there was never any casualty of a magnitude to require anything really extensive. The ships weren't worn out yet!

Q: They weren't old enough to vote in that time!

Adm. F.: You mentioned going in to Malta for assistance. If I may I'll go back to the FDR again, the days when Forrest Sherman was Commander, Sixth Fleet. I had the FDR. We were at anchor in Augusta Bay. The whole kit and caboodle were in the harbor. Came the morning to get under way and here I am on the bridge and they're paying the anchor in. There's no foc's'le I can see. Everything's just by voice telephone, and the usual thing, you know, the reports as the anchor comes in, "Anchor up and down, anchors away, Sir. Lost the starboard anchor, Sir."

I said, "Repeat that, please."

And, sure enough, as they hoisted that anchor over the bill board, an old destroyer term, the damn thing broke, right in half, in the shaft. And there they had a little piece of this thing and the anchor plopped down into the bay.

Forrest Sherman sent a message over. I think perhaps his message got there almost as fast as the message from the foc's'le. "Do you want me to recover your anchor for you?"

Well, I sailed out of there with only one anchor, and that's an unpleasant -

Q: An uncertain kind of thing!

Adm. F.: - thing for a skipper to contemplate. So we made an arrangement for a new anchor to be shipped, and it came over eventually. Then we had the job of transferring that anchor from its barge. They put it on a net tender, hooked it up, and brought it aboard ship, and we went in to Malta to do this. The British gave us a lot of assistance.

Q: Now the vignette!

Adm. F.: Oh, I've got two or three more I can think of.

In those days - and perhaps they still do it - part of your exercises to determine how proficient you are were towing exercises. Each type of ship had to participate in some kind of towing exercise. This is <u>FDR</u> again. We were detailed to tow a cruiser. The cruiser went dead in the water, and we had to do all the transferring of lines and a big steel hawser, and we draped that hawser over the stern, up over the flight deck, all the way up to the bow, with men standing on this hawser, and we got that cruiser under way and made about 12 knots before we were finished.

We transferred the original line by helicopter, instead of monkey fist.

Q: Helicopters were of increasing use?

Adm. F.: Yes.

The USO. I found this outfit. I didn't know anything about them, was made an honorary vice president or something. I found them very useful and very helpful. They had a headquarters in the Mediterranean and, as the fleet moved around, they moved with the fleet. If we were in the western and moved to the eastern Mediterranean, they'd move east also.

Q: But they were shore-based?

Adm. F.: Yes - with their staff. In some of these places they didn't have facilities, but they'd arrange for facilities. For instance, in Greece Kathryn and I would always go to one of these places to see what was going on, and it was done beautifully. The food would come from the ships, the music would come from the ships, the USO would hire the hall and they would find the girls. This particular time in Greece, there were a lot of girls there, boys and girls dancing. When the party was over, the girls were put in buses and taken home. No late dates. But what a contrast to when I was there in the FDR. You couldn't meet a girl. Young people couldn't meet girls because they were very closely chaperoned and mama and papa would have no part of a girl having any traffic with a sailorman.

When we got to Istanbul, that's a tough seaport town, the USO did the same sort of job. A big gymnasium sort of thing, and when we arrived they put us at a table right up front and a Turkish belly dancer was entertaining when we arrived. She became very self-conscious, until Kathryn gave her a wink and then she let herself go, and I have a photograph of her.

Now, let's wind up with this one.

This is the change-of-command time. We'd gone to Venice and Cat Brown was to join me in Venice and take over in Venice, just about a three-day stay. The first day I made my manners. There was an American Consul there and I did everything that he suggested I should do, and I thought I'd gotten all that finished.

The second day Cat arrived. No, he arrived the third day. The second day somehow or other I was alerted to the fact that the Number Two Catholic - Number Two authority in the Catholic Church was resident in Venice. I can't remember the title. And that he was a little perturbed that I hadn't made a call. So when I found out about this, naturally I got my boat and found my way to his castle, and made my manners. He was a delightful man. I had a lovely time. He showed me all around the castle, showed me things he'd collected from time to time, and I told him that we were having a change-of-command ceremony the next day and asked him if he would attend.

He said, "No, no, I don't wish to do that, but I do wish to repay your call. I want the people to know that you've called on me and I've returned your call."

I said, "That's fine," and we established a time. All right. Third morning, Cat arrives, and here's the cruiser with its formal protocol area up forward, starboard gangway up forward. My cabin, you go around onto the port side and go into the door into my cabin. Got the picture?

Q: Yes.

Adm. F.: Cat arrives. They give him all the honors, the band and the whole works, and just as I'm taking Cat down the port passageway to take him to my cabin and have a cup of coffee before the change-of-command ceremony starts, back on the fantail, up from the stern on the port side of the ship comes my friend, the Number Two man in the Catholic Church.

Q: He must have been a cardinal?

Adm. F.: Yes. He'd come in his own boat and he'd come aboard the port gangway aft, which was the enlisted men's gangway. Cat was startled. I was surprised, and Cat said, "What do we do?"

I said:

"You go in the cabin. I'll take care of this."

Q: He spoke English, did he?

Adm. F.: Yes. I took this lovely man around to the ceremonial area. The captain was still there. The band had been dispersed. The side boys had been dispersed. I told the Captain to go and get them, bring them all back, stood with this lovely person until it was all set up. Then I took him by the hand and put him out on the top of the gangway. I went back aboard ship and I said:

"All right, let's have the honors." We gave him full honors, and he thanked me and left the ship. That was Pope Paul.

Q: Oh. He was Secretary of State, wasn't he? At that time?

Adm. F.: There was another term. I've forgotten the term. I want to correct that. It was Pope John.

Q: John XXIII?

Adm. F.: Yes. Well, that's the end of that story.

Q: That's a fascinating story.

Felt #4 - 292

Interview No. 4 with Admiral Harry Donald Felt, U.S. Navy
(Retired)

Place: BOQ, Makalapa, Pearl Harbor, Hawaii

Date: Tuesday morning, 7 March 1972

Subject: Biography

By: John T. Mason, Jr.

Q: Admiral, this morning I think you want to resume by adding a few incidents to the account of the Mediterranean tour of duty as Commander of the Sixth Fleet.

Adm. F.: Yes, Doctor, I would like to add a couple of postscripts.

As I recall the recording yesterday, I emphasized perhaps operations more than anything else.

Q: Which was splendid, I must say!

Adm. F.: I'd like to say something about the diplomatic situation. I'm not going to try to cover all of the Mediterranean when I do this, but there are about three things that occurred to me after we broke off yesterday.

First of all, you recall when I talked about my tour over there as captain of the FDR, we cruised and visited North African ports. During this period of time when I was Commander of the Sixth Fleet we made no visits at all to North African ports, except for one visit of a destroyer -

that was finally arranged. But the flagship nor any of the big ships visited, let's say, Arab countries.

Q: This was due to the political situation?

Adm. F.: Yes, and just why this was I can't now be sure, but I remember when I took over and scurried out to the eastern Med there was a situation brewing between the Israelis and the Arabs.

I'd like to recall a little experience we had in Greece. This was at the very beginning of this tour, and Kathryn and I were in Athens on Easter and I asked for an audience with the King and Queen. This was granted, somewhat to my surprise. The King and Queen came in from the country and granted us an audience. It was quite interesting to me. I'd heard a lot about this couple, and had heard particularly that the Queen was the real power -

Q: A strong force!

Adm. F.: The strong member, and, sure enough, she did most of the talking. However, the King would chime in every once in a while and I came away with the definite impression that although she was strong, he was by no means a weak member of that family.

During the course of the conversation the Queen told me that she expected perhaps a riot the next day down in the large public square, down town. She said she couldn't estimate what might come of this, but it might turn sort of anti-America, and made a suggestion that perhaps it would be well if we weren't visible during this time.

I took that as advice and we got under way and left, and then came back the next day.

Q: Did the riot take place?

Adm. F.: It took place, but of course there were none of our American sailors around to be targets, so to speak. We were very conscious in those days of the Cyprus situation and there were some sticky aspects of that insofar as our relationship with the Greek government was concerned.

The other thing that comes to mind is Israel. Two different things.

When I was in Turkey and at a formal affair in the evening, I was sitting on a couch between a couple of ambassadors, and one of them was the Israeli ambassador. After a bit of conversation he asked me, "Why don't you visit Israel?" and I said, "Well, because I've never been invited." That grew into an idea, which Burke picked up. He knew of a Naval Reserve officer, a rear admiral, Naval Reserve, a Jewish rabbi. He sent this Jewish rabbi over to me and I met with him and my cruiser rear admiral, and we decided to send the two rear admirals in a cruiser into Israel. When they arrived, the rabbi went down the gangway and greeted these Israelis in Hebrew, which just flabbergasted those people. They couldn't conceive of an American speaking to them in Hebrew. It was a very successful diplomatic visit.

I think those are the postscripts I had in mind.

Q: This indicates that Admiral Burke kept very close to the political developments in the Mediterranean area?

Adm. F.: That's right.

Q: Were you involved or were you very cognizant during your tour there of this implacable opposition between the Greeks and the Turks?

Adm. F.: Oh yes.

Q: Did it have any manifestations in that time?

Adm. F.: No so far as we in the fleet were personally concerned, but I talked to many people, Americans, who had been involved in this. Tobacco people, for example, who told me tales of the atrocities and the bitter feelings between the Turks and the Greeks. Some of them had evacuated and come over to Athens, to Rhodes, and places like that.

Q: How did you take to the diplomatic role?

Adm. F.: Well, there's no particular problem. First, I

suppose you have to know your manners, be familiar with the customs of protocol, and finally not be overawed by pomp and dignity and rank. After the first ice is broken, you move into a conversational piece, knowing something about the country you're visiting. I suppose the key to the whole thing is to get people to talk about themselves.

Q: What aspect of your training and background was most useful in this area? Was it the National War College or was it the Naval Academy itself, or just what?

Adm. F.: Gee, I don't know. I think it's just a combination of learning, which of course is a very important part of philosophy, to continue no matter what age and experience you have to want to continue to learn.

Q: Would you say that more emphasis on this aspect of a naval officer's career should be emphasized in the Academy, in the curriculum?

Adm. F.: I'm not qualified to say "more emphasis" because I don't know how much emphasis there is now. I know that there have been vast changes and improvements made at the Naval Academy, with all their selectives and all that. All I can do is go back to my own experience and that was a long, long time ago. There wasn't enough emphasis then. But a naval officer, if he's as fortunate as I was, gets a very rounded education in world affairs by reason of not only visiting and having experience in the various oceans of the world and visiting various ports of the world, but also by the schooling that's available.

Q: It's the learning in maturity that counts.

Adm. F.: Yes, sure. There's not much difference in this really, when you look back into naval history to the days when senior naval officers were really the diplomats of the United States with responsibility and lack of communications which relied on those officers to carry out a mission.

Q: Well, that's very interesting. Your tour of duty came to an abrupt close, however, didn't it?

Adm. F.: Yes. So, with your permission, I wanted to add those postscripts before I carried out the orders that I'd received in that telegram from Burke.

Sworn in as Vice Chief, I found that I had been elevated, so to speak. In other words, I'd been made the Vice Chief as a full admiral, now senior to the deputies, who had been senior to me. This posed a problem, of course. Most of the deputies had elected to stay as members of the team when Burke was elevated up to the Chief of Naval Operations.

Q: The choice was in their hands, was it?

Adm. F.: Yes. One I can think of turned in his suit, but most of them elected to stay on.

I asked Burke how I should handle this and he said:

"Well, you can be sure that they're watching every move you make, and if what you do is in the interests of the Navy, that's fine."

Q: He spoke from experience!

Adm. F.: Right. "But, if you slip, you can expect to get it." Well, that was fine.

The other thing that impressed me immediately was the latitude I had, or responsibility I had. There was I believe it was a letter agreement that I had, as the Vice Chief, the full powers of the Chief. I could act as the Chief, even though he were there. In other words, it wasn't quite the same as being the chief of staff.

Q: This meant not within certain categories but the broad spectrum?

Adm. F.: Anything. Therefore, it was essential, with that sort of an arrangement, that the Vice Chief and the Chief - or, rather, put it another way - that the Vice Chief knew and believed in the policies of the Chief.

Q: This had been tested before, hadn't it?

Adm. F.: Yes, I think that had been standard.

Q: I mean in your case in the fact that you'd worked together.

Adm. F.: Oh, yes, that was easy. Well, that was the beginning. And here, as the Vice Chief, I was part of the Joint Chiefs operation, talking the Joint Chiefs' meetings when Burke was not available.

Q: This was often, was it not?

Adm. F.: Quite often. In contrast - and I think I mis-stated this yesterday - in contrast to my association with the Joint Chiefs' organization when I was a planner. At that time, I worked with the Joint Chiefs' planning group. Now I was working with the Joint Chiefs themselves, working with the Secretary of Defense and his deputy, and the Assistant Secretaries, establishing contacts with them, some of which persist to this day. Probably a very important aspect of this, because there is a history or at least experience in the past of lack of let's call it communication between the military part of the Navy Department and the Secretary of Defense's office. You see, the Secretary of the Defense's office isn't really very old, and there was a long period when there were some bumps in the road.

Q: And at that time it wasn't a very large organization, was it?

Adm. F.: No, not nearly as large as it is now, for example.

The other thing that is outstanding in my mind now - another thing - is the relationship established, or confirmed let's say, between the civilian Secretary and his Assistant Secretaries and Deputy and the Chief of Naval Operations and his staff. It was agreed that the civilian side of the house was to take care of the business part of the job, and the Chief of Naval Operations would take care of the military side of the house.

Q: And this was clearly understood?

Adm. F.: This was clearly understood and honored. It was very good.

Now, of course, when you get into budgeting and that sort of thing, your lines all cross and you had to work together on that. Mentioning budgeting brings to mind that there was an area that needed a lot of improvement. It had been a haphazard process in the past, a sort of catch-as-catch-can thing, where each little segment of the Navy came in with their offering or their recommendations, and you packaged the whole thing up and sent it up to the Secretary, and then he had to devise some formula for bringing it back out of the sky down close to earth, at least. And that was an awfully difficult thing for him to do. I remember it going up as far as Charley Wilson one time and his only solution was to say, "Well, 10 percent across the board." That's not a satisfactory way to work out a budget.

Q: It certainly isn't.

Adm. F.: So we decided that we'd put these deputies in this budgeting business. That is, immerse them in it, whereas before they'd just sort of had their toes in the water, and as the Vice Chief I was the head of a committee composed of the deputies, and a great deal of our work all year long was working on the budget, which after all when you stop to think of it the money is what makes the thing go. And the fight for money between all the services is a very hard fight.

We were successful in at least getting a start in doing it the right way. I lost complete track of the organizations, reorganizations, and still other organizations of the Navy Department, but I understand that they do it in much better fashion now.

I'm trying to think of things I tried to do, and this that I'm going to speak about now was very important to me, and I've spoken about this before, as we've sat here. That was breaking down the barriers between the various segments of the Navy, as represented in the Chief of Naval Operations staff. I recall attending a meeting of submariners and the talk was all about submarines destroying shipping, as they had done so successfully in World War II, and trying to anticipate or trying to visualize what the situation might be if war broke out with the Soviet Union, I asked them where is that shipping that you expect to sink. It's there now, of course, but it wasn't in these days. The Soviets didn't have any merchant marine.

Q: No. This is a relatively new development.

Adm. F.: Right. And as a result of all this I managed to change their fundamental concepts around to submarine-fight-submarine.

Q: That was a triumph, wasn't it?

Adm. F.: Well, I thought so because the targets were under the water, instead of on the surface of the water in those days.

Q: That was almost the total effort of the Russian Navy, wasn't it, submarines?

Adm. F.: Well, the Russian submarine Navy was growing fast in those days. To say it in broader terms, what I was trying to do was to bring the staff together as a staff and not each little segment being representative of specific interests. Let's work in the interest of the whole picture.

Q: This was a major attempt, wasn't it?

Adm. F.: I don't know whether it had been tried before. I

Felt #4 - 303

know everybody believed in it, but it didn't exist in practice. Op-05 all they cared about was naval aviation. There was the submarine outfit and that was all they cared about. The surface-ship people - you know.

Q: And there was always Rickover!

Adm. F.: Yes. Yes, these were the days when the Chief of the Bureau of Ships was tearing his hair over the nuclear-submarine problem.

Q: Who was that, Jimmy James?

Adm. F.: He was one of them. Mumma was there. I remember a conference - since you bring up the nuclear-submarine thing, a conference attended by about four people, Rickover, Burke, sombody else, and myself, probably Op-03, Theda Combs, having to do with the cruise of the submarine that went under the north pole. The question on the table was who will take the responsibility for ordering this cruise to be made, and Burke took it. Rickover was very reluctant to sponsor this at all because that submarine was only a single-screw submarine. I hadn't thought of mentioning that but it came to mind when you mentioned Rickover.

Q: And since you are talking about this area, I understood that at one point, and I think it was true then, Rickover was persona non grata in many of the conferences that had to do with nuclear power, and very often wasn't even invited?

Adm. F.: I don't know about that. Of course, I give him credit and I think everybody did, that he was the nuclear-power man. So did the Chief of BuShips. But what irritated a lot of people was that - I don't know whether Rickover himself claimed this but at least he was billed as the Father of the Nuclear Submarine. It was BuShips who designed the submarine and he was the originator and designer, I suppose, of the power plant.

While we're on that subject. The shipbuilding program was always, of course, of perhaps Number One interest to the Chief of Naval Operations, and the question was always hot as to whether we should have more nuclear-powered ships. It was decided yes back in those days, that we should, we should have a nuclear-powered navy, really. And the argument was put forth by Rickover that the cost of nuclear power would go down on a fairly steep curve. Actually, it never worked that way. The cost of nuclear power went up all the time, which has been one of the reasons why this program has been slow.

A decision was made at this time on the Polaris submarine, and people have asked me many times, how come that number of forty-one. Remember this number, Doctor?

Q: Yes, I do.

Adm. F.: And a program was put in and started to build so many each year, or try to build so many each year if we could get authorization and appropriations, and at a meeting in the Secretary of the Navy's office someone asked: "Well, what kind of program do we want? How many do we want?" Burke said, "Forty-one," and, of course, when we walked out of the door together I said, "Where did you get that figure?" He said, "Damned if I know! Just off the top of my head." But that's the figure that has stuck all these years.

Q: A mystical number!

Adm. F.: Yes. Missiles and guns.

Just the word "missile" became very sexy, and there was an interesting part of the organization in those days. The oufit in charge of developing missiles was in Op-05. That's the deputy for air, and Saavy Sides, a non-aviator, was in charge of this. He did a very fine job.

Well, the argument on one side was that the ships that are being built and that ought to be built would be all-missile, no guns. I took a different view on it, but I was on the minority side. This was particularly in respect to building destroyer types. I guess they had started to call them frigates, which I didn't like, but big destroyers.

Q: After the British.

Adm. F.: Yes. And the advocates of the missile won, and the first ones of those ships that came out were all-missile. Now we're talking about the Talos and the other short-range one whose name has escaped me at the moment. Well, I was unhappy with that.

Q: Regulus, was it?

Adm. F.: No. And finally I was able to get people to back down a little bit and, as other ships came out, they came out with missiles and with a gun or two.

I'm sure I was right. It's been proven that I was right in thie Vietnam situation, where our ships have been used to bombard from this Viet Cong installations or groupings ashore. And I suspect that CinCPacFlt has had quite a problem finding guns to do this job. There was a big argument in those days as to whether the carriers should have missiles. Remember I told you that when I was in the operational readiness business one of the important problems was working out and thinking of R and D and the future of devising better air defense. So there were a lot of people who said carriers are not protected well enough, fighters can't do all of it, screens can't do it all, they'll have to protect themselves, therefore they need surface-to-air missiles. I doubt that it's been proven that the cost was worth it. It increased the cost of the carriers quite a bit.

We never developed a surface-to-surface missile for the

Navy and, as I understand it now, we still don't have one that was started from the Research and Development stage and into production. We're converting one of the surface-to-air to have a surface-to-surface -- or have, I guess, converted to have a surface-to-surface capability. Now I'm jumping way ahead and thinking of a lot of criticisms of the Navy, particularly after one of the Soviet boats given to the Egyptians sank an Israeli ship with a surface-to-surface missile.

So the argument is that our ships are sitting ducks. I think that the argument, however, on the other side, that carrier air with its long-range capability in the form of airplane delivery of weapons is far superior to fast-boat, short-range capability.

I'm trying to get back to my two-year tour as Vice Chief. Those are some of the problems -

Q: Did you also wrestle with the suggestion that there be missiles placed on merchant vessels? Was that to the fore at that time?

Adm. F.: I can't remember when that thought first surfaced. I don't think it was while I was Vice Chief. I think it was later. To me it's a very attractive thought, and I believe that George Miller, whom you mentioned yesterday, certainly has this in mind, to disperse our offensive capability at sea and not concentrate it on land and invite the other fellows to wipe us out. So dispersing on merchant ships

Felt #4 - 308

makes a lot of sense. The thought is so simple that apparently it gets laughed out of the room when it's brought up, but it seems to me it's a very sound thought.

Q: Some aspects of the missile as a weapon were under the cognizance of a kind of joint committee, were they not, of what was then BuOrd and AEC?

Adm. F.: I don't remember. I'm sure that there was a big family arrangement. It wasn't only just one service. All services were up to their ears in the missile problem.

Now, what I'm talking about back in those days, 1956-1958, are two things. First, the surface-to-air missile. That seemed to be right up here in the Number One position. The threat from the air. Those missiles we developed and started to put in ships were all surface-to-air. The only what you might call strategic missile we were talking about was the one in the Polaris submarine.

Q: Did this discussion involve you with the Air Force?

Adm. F.: Yes, but the Air Force in these days was all-out for SAC, Strategic Air Command, and the strategic deterrent. At the beginning of this period Lemay was CinCSAC, and then he came in as Vice Chief of the Air Force and we started to work together and managed to come up with an understanding. But your question. The Air Force was thinking in different terms than we were really.

However, getting back to the strategic missile thing, during this period of time Red Raborn was put in charge of developing a submarine missile, the Polaris, and devised a management program which got the attention of industry, the Defense Department, everybody.

Q: It was a remarkable effort, wasn't it?

Adm. F.: He put in a management system - I don't think there was anything new in it perhaps - he just picked up knowledge that was available and put it together, and it became a place to be visited by industry and everybody. He did a remarkable job on developing that missile - a missile which, when ready to fire, fired without -

Q: Mishap!

Adm. F.: There must have been one or two failures, but the record was just fantastic. Quite different than the record of the missiles that were developed for our ships, surface-to-air. They were full of bugs.

Q: According to Freddy Withington, the component in that whole situation was Raborn himself, his drive.

Adm. F.: Right. He did a beautiful job.

I'm trying to remember when this happened. Let me lead up to this.

The relationship between the Chief of Naval Operations and the chief of the materiel bureaus was another interesting point. This was sort of a double-pronged thing. Remember now, there was an understanding that the civilian side of the house would be involved with the business of the Navy, and the materiel bureaus, of course, are involved in that, too. So they had direct lines in to the Secretary and his civilian staff. On the other hand, the materiel bureaus were involved in pure military aspects, too, not only procurement - well, starting with R and D. So it was agreed that they also had a direct line to the Chief, and the Chief had a direct line back to them.

However, there had been unhappiness with this bureau system over a long, long period of years, although studies made from time to time would come up and say, well, the materiel bureau system that the Navy has is better than what the Army and Air Force have. Then it was decided that there would be an amalgamation. I can't remember who was BuOrd at that time. It might have been Freddy, but I don't believe it was. Anyhow, there was a consolidation.

Q: Was it Stroop?

Adm. F.: Stroop, who had been chief of BuAir, became chief of the amalgamation, consolidation, of BuAir and BuOrd.

That made a lot of sense, I thought, because BuOrd was developing weapons and BuAir was using them, and here again there was a moat that one had to cross to get from one to the other.

Q: Why was this? Because of the inevitable tendency toward empire-building?

Adm. F.: I don't know. You can go back to old terms used, you know, the Gun Club and the Fly Boys, I suppose. Well, they didn't care for each other particularly.

This was a good move, I thought, and now you see it's developed later into Naval Materiel Command, which is the same thing the Air Force has had for a long while.

Q: Did you get involved or was this prior to the controversy over conventional carriers versus nuclear carriers?

Adm. F.: Oh, yes, that was part of this whole discussion, debate, on nuclear-powered ships. Cost, naturally, was a great item, and of course the cost of everything had started going up. Inflation has taken us way up in the sky. I was inclined to be on the side of non-nuclear because of the cost element. I knew we had to have ships, and it's all right to think in terms of quality, of course, you have to think in terms of quality, but I think it's wrong to discard the consideration of quantity, particularly with the national responsibilities carried by the United States of America.

Q: And they were growing at that time.

Adm. F.: That's right, spread all over the world. Now, you see, there's some contraction because of the Nixon Doctrine, but they're still spread all over the world. And look what's happened in this Vietnam War. There are a lot of aspects of it that are wrong, a lot of things approached incorrectly and done wrong, and I'm not going to go into all these, but one of the things that has happened to the Navy is that they're fighting a war on a peacetime force levels, resulting in long deployments, short turnarounds, a breakdown of family morale, and all these other things.

So quantity is a factor, and as I tried to look at the future I could see, well, if we won the fight, convinced Congress that we had to go nuclear in our carriers, we'd probably get one every - I don't know - two or three years at best. Our ships were wearing out. On the other hand, if we went for nonnuclear we might get one every year. See what I mean by numbers?

Q: Yes.

Adm. F.: Well, the decision was made to go nuclear, and as a result we got a nuclear carrier, the Enterprise, eventually.

Q: That was later, a little later, wasn't it?

Adm. F.: Yes, that was after I left. However, the decision was made then, I suspect, because she became operational while I was CinCPac.

We got three ships at the beginning, a nuclear-powered cruiser - The Long Beach and one other. I can't remember when the nuclear-powered merchant ship idea, the Savannah, raised its head. In there some place, I suppose.

Well, that about covers the field of problems.

Q: In your roving interests in the department were you interested in the development of the helicopter at that point?

Adm. F.: Oh, yes. Remember I said that when I was hunter/killing was the beginning of this ASW helicopter business.

Q: Based on this experience, did you - ?

Adm. F.: Yes, the helicopter had proven itself to be mose valuable.

It was during this time the concept of the helicopter landing ship or carrier surfaced. This is the one, you know, to participate in amphibious operations. And in our ship-building program I think the first one of those was inserted.

I haven't mentioned the Marines. We had very close relationship, of course, and there was a little Marine office right in the office of the Chief, sort of quick liaison.

Q: Were you interested at all in the development and pushing forward the idea of hydrofoil or anything of that kind?

Adm. F.: There were some beginnings. I think there were some tests being conducted on a first model down in the Miami area, but they were having control problems and nothing significant came out of it at that time.

Charley Wilson was Secretary of Defense for the first year and then he was relieved by McElroy. And Charley Wilson inaugurated something that was carried on, which was to call senior officers from the major commands and from the Navy Department for a conference in Quantico, and at that conference have senior people report on their activities and requirements and developments.

Q: This was a periodic thing?

Adm. F.: Well, he held one of these. He was the first to do something like this, which was very good. As Vice, I only got down there one day, as I remember. Burke was there all the time. That was carried on by McElroy and by Tom Gates. I understand they don't have them any more. McNamara, I believe never had such a thing.

It was interesting to see McElroy come in. I attended a luncheon at which Charley Wilson was greeting McElroy, and McElroy's speech to us was to the effect, now I want you fellows to understand I've been in charge of a big business and when a policy decision is made I expect to have that policy carried out.

Well, this didn't bother us particularly because it was understood by everybody from way back that the civilians at top level make the policy. However, the feature that we thought we saw in between the lines was "don't you guys come up here trying to make policy." That was something we insisted we should have a part of.

As time went on he got into reorganization, of course. That has to always happen when a man comes in. The first thing is to cure all the problems and cure all the ills by reorganizing.

Q: In private life they write a constitution!

Adm. F.: Right! It was quite a turbulent time, really. Here again - I don't know why he did this - but remember I said that I spent time and energy making contact with the civilian members of the Secretary's staff. One day I'd been to church, out at my old church in Woodley Park, on Cathedral Avenue, and decided I'd go by that Sunday morning after church and call on the Secretary and his wife. They were living in that apartment house that was right on the corner of Woodley Road and Connecticut Avenue - it's part of what I call Wardman Park, that big place.

Q: Park Sheraton.

Adm. F.: Yes. This was wonderful. We had a lovely time. I stayed for lunch. I met their daughter and son. You know, I was the first naval officer ever to call on the Secretary!

Q: With their proclivity for making courtesty calls!

Adm. F.: Well, I tried to analyze this. I talked with Secretary McElroy and his wife about this. People apparently had the impression that he didn't want people to call and be friendly. It was quite the reverse, of course.

Well, that started a relationship that turned out to be very nice. I'll jump ahead. He was still Secretary when I became CinCPac, visited me out here. Every once in a while he comes here for a little vacation and we always get together.

On his reorganization business, I don't remember anything really significant, except we got briefings from time to time as to what was in the wind. I think there was a lot of flak in the air, but I didn't come away with any Purple

Hearts, as I remember.

Q: Would you talk about any relationships you had with the White House, as Vice Chief?

Adm. F.: I can't remember accurately, but I think I was over at a meeting in the White House only once.

Q: With Eisenhower?

Adm. F.: Yes. I went to receptions a couple of times there, the first when Truman was President, one of these annual things they give for the uniformed services.

I met Mr. Truman first at the airport. Let me see now. What was the occasion?

CinCPacFlt had been over there - he also has a NATO hat, you know - had his airplane over there in Europe someplace, and our ambassador to Ireland died, and CinCPacFlt was bringing the remains back.

I think this was when I was Operational Readiness. I was a rear admiral, and I was detailed to go to the airport and represent the CNO or the Navy or something, having no idea that President Truman and his entourage would be there. They arrived. I was a little overwhelmed, of course, so I sort of stepped back into the background and all of a sudden the President looked around, saw me there, and he came to me and shook hands and conversed with me a little while. That was my first meeting with President Truman, my first contact with him, and I came away with the thought, gee, what an observant man he is and what a considerate man he is. That's going back.

Your question was about going to the White House. I think only one meeting. The thought that I came away with then is that the Joint Chiefs' system wasn't working as it should, hadn't been working as it should for a long time. This goes back to I suppose it's the charter of the Joint Chiefs. They are what you might call a corporation. When the Joint Chiefs act, they don't act as individuals. They act as a body. In the old, old days it used to be that the chiefs of services had access to the president as advisors. Then came along a series of efforts to establish a single chief of staff. General Eisenhower, when he was chief of staff of the Army, tried this, and others have tried it. That effort was unsuccessful. The Joint Chiefs as a corporate body still are in business, but in fact the chairman is the one who has the voice. This is very clear. It's the chairman who goes to the meetings at the White House.

Why I was there I can't remember. It was an exception of some sort.

Q: He supplanted the former system where the service chiefs - ?

Adm. F.: That's right, and I suppose I went because Burke was out of town. Why Burke as a member of the Joint Chiefs and a chief of service wouldn't be there I can't remember, but the normal procedure is the chairman is there and he's the voice of the Joint Chiefs.

Q: And in this time Radford was the spokesman, wasn't he?

Adm. F.: Yes. And this is true or was true up until the time of Gates, which was after my time as Vice Chief, in respect to communications between the Joint Chiefs and the Secretary of Defense. This means there's great latitude possible in this.

Let's say that the Joint Chiefs have met, they've argued, they've come to a conclusion and made a decision that this course of action should be taken.

Q: This had to be unanimous, didn't it?

Adm. F.: Not necessarily, but let's assume that there has been a difference of opinion but it's finally gotten together and this is the recommendation the Joint Chiefs wish to make to the Secretary of Defense.

Now, the chairman goes to the Secretary, and let's assume that during the course of this argument and debate, he wasn't in favor of this decision, and let's assume that he's absolutely honest. The latitude I'm speaking of is this. He goes to the Secretary and says, "The Joint Chiefs recommend this, but . . ." and I suspect the Secretary is more apt to accept the "but" than the other.

So in some large degree we do have a single chief of staff.

Q: Since there were aides at the White House for the various services, were there occasions in your time as Vice Chief when, say, the naval aide, Pete Aurand, had some direct contact with you in terms of something the President wanted to know?

Adm. F.: I don't recall anything precisely like this. I went over to the White House maybe twice and had lunch with Pete. I think the object of the drill was that he wanted me to meet members of the staff, and what I came out with on that was an impression as to how they worked in preparing speeches for the president. He would come over occasionally and see Burke on I don't know what problems. I didn't happen to be present during these conversations.

Q: Well, very often they were highly specialized things that the President commissioned him to find out.

Adm. F.: I don't know. I can't answer that. Of course, that aide business was changed radically later on. At the time you're speaking of there were aides from each of the services and perhaps a senior aide. And then later on - I don't know whether it was the Kennedy administration -

they washed out this system, or at least changed it so that the seniority of the aides was lowered and eventually I think it developed into just one military aide. I believe that's the way it is now. I'm not quite sure but I think that's the way it is.

Q: Did you have any dealings with Bryce Harlow over at the White House, who was very knowledgeable about military affairs?

Adm. F.: No.

Q: What about your relationshipwith the Joint Chiefs? Tell me about some of your - the occasions when you had to sit in.

Adm. F.: Well, it was perfectly normal. I wasn't the only vice chief who sat in on these meetings, pinch-hitting for the chief, so to speak. Occasionally Curt Lemay would sit in or Willie Palmer of the Army, and when the vice chief sat in it was understood without any question that he was speaking as a member of the Joint Chiefs.

Q: How much preparation would you go into in preparation for a set meeting of the Joint Chiefs?

Adm. F.: Oh, this was quite a problem, and a time-consuming problem, because the papers that came before the Joint Chiefs had been worked over by the joint planning group, the joint logistics group, by the services, and more times than not they'd be split in their opinions. One service disagreeing with another on these things. So you had to know your lessons before you went down there, and it took a long time to get prepared for these meetings.

One of the objections that the Secretary of Defense had, and it was a fairly valid objection, was the length of time it took to process a paper, a decision paper. And the reason for this was because of the interservice rivalries.

Q: Are you thinking in terms of emergency situations?

Adm. F.: No, I'm thinking in terms of just normal business, business having to do with who gets what cut of that pie. That sort of a simple thing.

Q: But in case of an emergency, an international situation, which the Chiefs are going to deal with -

Adm. F.: Oh, well, then it was a different ball game.

Q: It was streamlined?

Adm. F.: Yes. But you see what this led into - and now I'm jumping way ahead to the McNamara days - it led into his decision, having organized his staff with the Whiz Kids, that they could make decisions much faster than the Joint

Chiefs.

Q: And more to his liking, maybe?

Adm. F.: Perhaps! Well, not "perhaps." I think the record shows the answer to that is yes!

Q: Doesn't this pose a problem? I mean the CNO being also the permanent representative on the Joint Chiefs wears two hats, and since the time necessary in preparation for the meetings of the Joint Chiefs is so great, it poses a real problem, doesn't it?

Adm. F.: Yes, it does. For a person like Burke it wasn't an insurmountable problem because his capacity was so great - his capacity and his work schedule. On the other hand, I argued and got no place with it that in view of this unhappiness at the lack of speed with which the Chiefs operated, that each chief of service with his Joint Chiefs' hat should have an office down in the Joint Chiefs' area. Have a little staff down there where they would deal directly with the Joint Planning Group. I thought that would be a step toward unification. That thought never bore fruit. As it was, a paper would appear out of the Joint Planning Group, let's say. In those days they called it a White Paper, I believe.

Q: At various stages it was different colors?

Adm. F.: Yes. Well, this would represent the best that the Joint Planning Group could do. Now, by "Joint" that meant the planning group was composed of officers from all services. This would be the best and perhaps would reflect the split opinions in that paper, too. Then each service would take it and work on it, and it turned out that the Army had a system that worked faster than anybody else's. They had a night shift. Then papers would go from each individual chief on the subject, and gradually it would develop into I guess a Green Paper and the Chiefs would have to meet on it and try to solve these differences of opinion.

Q: This gave a great deal of authority to the Chief of Staff to the Joint Chiefs, didn't it?

Adm. F.: The Director of the Joint Staff, you mean?

Q: Yes.

Adm. F.: There wasn't such a thing as a chief of staff. There was the chairman and the Army, Navy, and the Air Force chiefs and the Marine Commandant. He was always present but he could vote on only certain things. And always present at those meetings would be the Director of the Joint Staff. That's the job that Herb Riley took when he left me.

Q: Is that the job that Count Austin had too when you were there?

Adm. F.: No, Count wasn't there in any capacity like that. While I was there it was an Air Force officer who, incidentally, is retired and living out here now. It was a rotating thing between services.

I might comment on my concept as to how I should work. I got some criticism on this, particularly by the Navy League people. I remember their coming to me one time and saying:

"You're not well known. You should get out and make more speeches."

Q: That's in their interest!

Adm. F.: Yes. My concept was that Burke was the front man. He was Mr. Navy and I was just helping him do his job. In other words, I was a backstop, and thatworked well as far as Burke and I were concerned.

Q: Well, did you in any way succumb to the Navy League's - ?

Adm. F.: Oh, I went out a few times. I remember this first time I said, "Well, where do you want me to speak?"

"New York."

"How much of an audience?"

"Oh, maybe 100 prominent businessmen."

"What impact will that have on the civilian community in New York?"

"Not much. Chicago."

"Do you have any Navy League chapters, if that's the right word, out in the Middle West?"

"Why do you ask that?"

"Because personally I think that the Middle West is the heart of this country."

"Oh, I don't know. I'll look."

Well, I finally went to Kansas City. I went down to Tulsa one time and that was invasion. This was sponsored by the Junior Chamber of Commerce, I think. That was an invasion because the Air Force had captured that part of the country.

Q: Naturally!

Adm. F.: And that turned out real well. That speech was repeated in The Congressional Record. I didn't make many speeches.

Q: With whom were you dealing in the Navy League at that time?

Adm. F.: I was hoping you wouldn't ask that question. Yes, I remember now. It was Bergen. I don't remember his rank at that time in the Reserves -

Q: Rear admiral, probably.

Adm. F.: He was promoted to rear admiral in the Reserves. He was quite active and a hard worker for the Navy League.

We met with the Navy League people in the Navy Department many times. They were trying to get ideas as to how they could do their job better.

Q: A staunch ally of the CNO, weren't they?

Adm. F.: Yes, and, of course, it's interesting to observe the difference between the Navy League and the Army and Air Force Associations. As you probably know, the Navy League is an organization of civilians and an officer on active duty cannot be a member of the Navy League. In contrast to that, the Army and Air Force Associations not only welcome but encourage active-duty officers to belong. The object of all three of them is the same, to promote the interests of their services.

We were talking about public relations, I suppose, and the small part I took in the business by making speeches, and we've mentioned names from time to time as we've gone along. At that Kansas City meeting, it was an evening meeting, who showed up? Bergen? Of course. Jocko Clark and Jimmie Flatley. And, at a social gathering after the dinner and speech, Senator Symington came in. That was the first time I'd met him and I've watched the change of his opinions over the many years to now being apparently in the Fulbright camp.

Q: Quite a fluctuation for the span!

Adm. F.: Yes. Jimmie Flatley was quite a boy and at this time he was at a place there in eastern Kansas, a naval air place, quite close to Kansas City, and had done a really bang-up job in public relations. He was known all over the area. Some time during the evening they got Jimmie and me confused. They didn't know anything about me, apparently, but they knew all about Jimmie, and they started calling me Jimmie. We're both about the same size.

I remember going to another place, Milwaukee I guess it was, and was quite impressed up there with the Navy League. I think the oldest chapter of the Navy League was up in that area.

Q: May I ask, when you went out on speech-making tours of this sort, did you tie in with Chinfo?

Adm. F.: I don't remember, and I can't recall when this happened. Perhaps during my time as Vice Chief. I may be wrong. It might have been later, but came out an edict that our speeches must be submitted all the way up to the Secretary of Defense's office and over to the State Department for perusal and editing. I did this a couple of times and regretted that I did it because they deleted things that were meaningless, really. Subsequently, I made this decision for myself. I would ignore this and if I said something that warranted dismissal, all right, I'd be dismissed. But I thought I knew policy directions well enough to be guided accordingly.

Q: What was the overriding idea back of this?

Adm. F.: I don't know. Sensitiveness, apparently, to officers getting completely out of line. I don't think there was any feeling that we in top military positions weren't free to argue and criticize, but I think very properly an insistence that that be done within the family and not take these serious differences of opinion out to the public.

Q: So there was one policy being expressed from the Defense Department?

Adm. F.: Yes. In other words, fight within the family and solve the problems that you could. I sort of sense that it's different now, particularly after the Pentagon Papers and so forth. All the arguments should be taken to the public as they arise.

Q: Well, the press would have it that way!

Adm. F.: Yes. I vote for the other way around. After all, let's just use a simple analogy of your own personal family. If you have problems with your children, that's where it should be solved not out on the street.

Q: There was an effort at one time within the Eisenhower administration to more or less coordinate the speech-making government-wide. Not only Defense but all the departments, so that there was some kind of -

Adm. F.: I guess this is what I'm talking about, although I wasn't conscious that it was an effort to coordinate.

In regard to speech-making, I'm not a prolific speech-maker but I write my own speeches. I've never been able to accept the product of a speech-writer. I don't say I'm a "yes man." I've never been a "yes man." On the other hand I do realize the bounds of propriety, I guess you might say.

Q: What was the attitude of the naval command at that time in terms of public relations? We'd had the "silent Navy" concept prior to World War II. Then we'd sort of evolved from that. What was it under Admiral Burke?

Adm. F.: Well, the Navy was conscious of the importance of the public image, of course, and they were working as best they knew how then to improve the image, realizing that the Navy had to overcome a handicap in that the Army and Air Force were living in these communities and the Navy, with the exception of shore establishments, mostly on the coast, was at sea.

Q: And wasn't as visible!

Adm. F.: Wasn't as visible.

Let me project on into my days as CinCPac while we're still on this subject. One time a group of civilian gentlemen came over here as the Secretary of the Navy's guests and CinCPacFlt was the man to handle them here. But one morning one of these gentlemen from Texas came up to see me and he said:

"You know, the Navy's doing a very bad job in public relations."

I said, "In what manner?"

"Well, remember," he said, "I come from Texas. I'm thinking in terms of that vast area of the Middle West, and what we hear the Navy say is this: We are the strongest, biggest Navy in the world, but we need your support for shipbuilding, new ships. And it doesn't make any sense to us. In one sentence you say 'We're the biggest and strongest in the world,' and in the other sentence you ask us to help you build. Why do you have to build? You haven't told your story. On the other hand, the Air Force tells their story in terms that we can accept."

Q: In terms of the Middle West, the Navy hadn't plowed its ground.

Adm. F.: Yes, and prepared its soil.

Q: This was an educational effort.

Adm. F.: Yes. The relationship of Chinfo in the Department was interesting. It was never quite clear just what the lines were, except that there was a direct line between Chinfo and the Secretary of the Navy. The line between Chinfo and the CNO was there, but it was a little fuzzy. It wasn't as solid as the line to the Secretary of the Navy.

Q: That was more a civilian line?

Adm. F.: Yes. The fellow who swore me in in Chinfo when I was Vice Chief was Chester Ward. Chester has an interesting background. He was a naval aviator at one time and wears wings, and he's also a lawyer, and he was Chinfo. Burke used him a lot, not as Chinfo, but just to get ideas from him on various aspects of a problem.
    Well, let's move on.

Q: As Vice Chief, what relations did you have with the Bureau of the Budget and the Director of the Budget?

Adm. F.: When you say "the Bureau of the Budget" you're talking of the President's organization?

Q: Yes.

Adm. F.: None. No, that was a relationship between the Secretary of Defense and the President's staff. In the

Navy Department we had our own comptroller's shop, I guess it was called, under the Secretary of the Navy, and of course the military side worked with them. But our budget work was, as I tried to say, to get our own people together so that we could present something reasonable to first Burke and then to our own Secretary, who in turn, took it up to the Secretary of Defense. We'd be present as these things went up the ladder.

Q: What activity did you have that related to the congressional committees?. Appropriations and Military Affairs or whatever it was termed at that time under Carl Vinson?

Adm. F.: Burke was the fellow who went up with his voluminous background papers to make his plea for authorization in the first place and appropriations eventually. He was always in town and ready and prepared to do that.

Q: He liked to do that did he?

Adm. F.: Well, that was his job. The only time I went in these days we're talking about to a congressional committee was to support the provision of ships to foreign countries in connection with our military assistance program. And this was always quite an issue. I believe this was before Mr. Vinson's committee. You know, Mr. Vinson really considered himself as the head of the Navy and, if he didn't consider himself the head of the Navy, he certainly considered that every one of these ships in the Navy, whether in mothballs or where, was his ship! His committee had to appropriate the money for these ships.

There was something in the law that required congressional approval to put one of these ships in the military assistance program. It was always a loan, not an outright grant, and you had to get Mr. Vinson's personal approval of this which was very hard to do!

Then I think I went before another committee in regard to military construction. That is, you know, the building of installations - before a committee headed by a congressman from California. He'd been there for years, but I just can't recall his name - a fellow who'd been in the contracting business before he was elected to Congress and really knew his business. This was always an interesting chore, to go up and try to convince him that you needed a new hospital or a new barracks or something like that. That was another aspect of the planning that I forgot to mention - the shore establishments, military construction.

Q: When you made these appearances before the Congress, did you tie in with JAG for your testimony?

Adm. F.: Yes there was a tie-in.

You know I said that Chester Ward was Chinfo. I wonder if that's true. Maybe he was JAG. That's probably what he was.

Q: As a lawyer, yes.

Adm. F.: Yes.

In connection with this military construction I traveled a little bit to look at various installations and get my own impressions of them, of course, although I didn't travel extensively. Burke was the traveler and I was the housekeeper, homekeeper, really. But I went down to Florida, I remember, one time and visited that place on the coast, a few miles from Jacksonville. We had developed a harbor and some piers with the idea of home-porting ships down there. Up until this time it had all been concentrated in the Norfolk or Newport area, and this was in the interest of increased operational efficiency in that the weather off the Florida coast is quite different than the foggy weather off of the Virginia coast. We were thinking particularly in terms of home-porting a carrier or two down there.

When I looked at it it was completely inadequate, with housing practically non-existent. The piers could take a couple of small ships, so that was a high-priority project for us. That's come about. That's been developed.

I didn't have anything to do, as I recall it, with recommending improvement and enlargement of the facilities at Charleston. Mendel Rivers took care of that all by himself!

Q: Yes! What was your impression of Mendel Rivers?

Adm. F.: Impressions of Mendel have to change over a period of time. The first time I saw him was when I picked him up down there in the Caribbean - remember I told you about that? But while I was Vice Chief Mendel was a problem child in that he liked to travel on these junkets, he insisted on having a naval officer be with him, and that naval officer would come back a mental wreck from trying to take care of Mendel!

I think that's all I need say about that.

Q: Yes. I understand. I knew him when he first came to Congress!

Adm. F.: But as time has gone on, and I haven't had contact with him over years, and as I read - I don't know whether it's Pearson and also Jack Anderson - attempts to destroy Mendel. I checked back and I was told that Mendel had sort of gone up the pole and gone on the wagon, despite the accusations of Pearson and or Anderson. I don't know anything except what I was told.

Oh, since we're on the subject. Now I'm going to jump way ahead to the time I'm retired.

I became associated with the American Security Council and was made a member of what they call their Strategy Committee. One of the projects we undertook was to write a paper on the Navy versus the USSR. We did this at Mendel Rivers' request, submitted it to Mendel, he liked it so much he tore our cover off, put his committee cover on and issued it as a committee report. And that's my last indirect association with Mendel Rivers.

Q: During your time as Vice Chief was there any discussion of the possibility of closing some of the Navy yards as being surplus?

Adm. F.: Yes, oh, yes. That was a live subject from way back, and a subject that was very frustrating because of the political opposition to closings. It's all right for you to close something in his bailiwick, but I'm not going to let anything close in mine!

I think there was some progress made on this during my time there but I can't recall specifics.

Q: Since this was a time when the administration was thinking in terms of cutting down on expenditures, I wondered if it hadn't been to the fore?

Adm. F.: Yes. I can't recall the volume of the military budget in those days. I suspect it was somewhere in the neighborhood of - well, later on in McNamara's time it was around 50 billion dollars, and in my Vice Chief time perhaps in the area of 40 or thereabouts and the Navy had perhaps the

Felt #4 - 338

lowest percentage of that, reflecting our inability to win these fights! No, and reflecting a strategic concept on the part of the President and the Secretary of Defense. As I say, the Strategic Air Command was the first priority, and the Air Force tactical air was a country cousin in those days.

Q: This is all a part of a thesis that George Miller expounds so eloquently.

Adm. F.: Yes, sure. Now let me see, your question was - ?

Q: Navy yards.

Adm. F.: Oh, yes. I'm sure there was some action taken to close down certain installations. Certainly there were some close-downs in the small stations inland. I remember that. There was a big argument about whether or not to continue developing outlying fields for the Air Training Command and, as I recall it, the hottest thing on the fire was Long Beach Navy Yard, which was sinking and they were making efforts to keep it afloat by pumping water under it. Somehow or other it survived and is a very active Navy Yard to this day. But it almost closed its doors, as I recall.

Perhaps the decision was made then about closing Brooklyn Navy Yard. I can't remember when that was done.

Q: What about the National Security Council? Did your shop

Felt #4 - 339

have any relationship with them?

Adm. F.: No, not actively but it was in effect and working in those days and, of course, papers which came out were policy papers which dictated our courses of action.

Q: But you never appeared as a co-opted member of the Security Council?

Adm. F.: No.

Q: What about the subject of the merchant marine?

Adm. F.: Concern about the age of it and the dwindling size of it. Let's see, we had MSTS in those days, didn't we, and that was converted during these days to a - in other words, converted so it had to pay its own way. I've forgotten the size of the MSTS in those days. Of course, that went out of business later on.

Q: Was there any effort being made by the CNO and his office to - ?

Adm. F.: To encourage shipbuilding?

Q: Yes.

Adm. F.: Oh, yes. I can't give you specifics nor can I

assure you that enough emphasis was put on it to alert Congress and the public as to the serious nature of this deterioration.

Q: What was the stumbling block?

Adm. F.: I don't know. Remember I said that I can't assure you that there was enough emphasis on it, because I just don't remember actively that there was enough emphasis on it. If there were, as you say, a stumbling block it was probably a lack of appreciation or lack of vision as to what might happen, what might take place in the future. Remember, when I spoke of talking to the submariners and convincing them that they should get off of this beam of fighting another war against surface shipping. The Russian merchant marine hadn't appeared over the horizon yet.

Q: The memories of World War II were still fresh in mind and the need for merchant shipping was so obvious then?

Adm. F.: Yes, but in those days remember we had a tremendous backup of mothballed ships in various places which still had some life left in them. We also probably relied pretty heavily on being able to commandeer foreign-flag but U.S.-owned ships.

Q: Panamanian and Liberian?

Adm. F.: Yes.

Felt #4 - 341

Q: Was there any liaison in your time as Vice Chief between the Navy, as such, and the Maritime Administration? Was there communication?

Adm. F.: I can't answer that question. I don't remember. I can't even remember the details of the Maritime Administration in those days, except to realize they were in existence, and I suspect my first incomplete understanding of the Maritime Administration was when I was in the Middle East and dealing with the question of evacuation and trying to understand the problem of commandeering foreign-flag ships to assist in evacuation. I'm sure there was an office in the Chief's office that dealt with this, but it wasn't, as I recall it, a hot subject in those days. We're talking about 1956 to 1958. At least, I'm not impressed now that it was a hot subject in those days.

You were asking while the tape was off about shipbuilding and problems associated therewith. I do recall that there was one very serious aspect of this, and the Deputy SecNav was involved in this personally all the time, and that was the question of alterations and changes after a ship had been built. None of us could provide satisfactory answers to him. His desk would be piled high with these extensive changes that BuShips and others said had to go into the ships, and he couldn't understand why this hadn't been designed in the ship in the first place.

I'm probably not describing this accurately but that's

Felt #4 - 342

generally what the problem was, and I suspect it was because of the rapid development of technology during these days. It was an age of ideas coming to full bloom, one right after another.

Q: World War II had given the impetus to this!

Adm. F.: I suppose that's right - and a feeling that, I suppose, you shouldn't sit on these things having a concept "well, maybe it's not the best, maybe we'd better just sit on this and let it develop further before we commit ourselves to it." We'd had the sad experience in World War II of dealing with radars - and before World War II - in this respect. So that accounted for a lot of our budget, putting these new concepts into our ships after they were built.

Oh, and which brings to mind that during the time I was there a system of control was being developed and a mock-up was made. I visited the mock-up. Let's see now if I can remember the name of the system. It relied a lot on computers, particularly in the CICs of the ships, to assist in making decisions aimed primarily in those days to air defense, realizing that the manual system was just too slow for the speeds that we could see coming up, and with the magnitude of the defense job, automating a lot of this. The only influence I had on it was to insist - well, first, to approve and support the idea of this automation but to retain in it a capability to revert back to manual in case the thing broke down.

Q: Dual control, sort of?

Adm. F.: Yes. Well, this was being developed during my time. A mock-up was being made for a new CIC concept in a big ship, and now it's standard in the Navy. All ships have this. It ties everything together.

Q: With the development of these new techniques, it meant intensive preparation of the officers who were going to deal with them, didn't it?

Adm. F.: Oh yes, of course.

Q: What did this entail then?

Adm. F.: I'm not sure what you're driving at, but let's go way back to my early days. An attempt was made to prepare you for duty in the fleet at the Naval Academy, introducing you to the fundamentals of the technologies and engineering practices in vogue in those days, and as the Navy has grown it has meant that officers and men have had to acquire new knowledge. And during this time I'm talking about, when I was Vice Chief, the requirement for this acquisition was just growing by leaps and bounds. We went through a period when we thought that our enlisted men would not be able to acquire the capability to service all of this new development stuff being put in, with the result we had many civilian technicians aboard. However, it worked out beautifully. Our enlisted men were capable of doing this and I believe you find very few technicians in the fleet now. As a matter of fact, this is one of the reasons why the Navy has been relatively unsuccessful in retaining their personnel. In the minds of civilian engineers and technology people I've talked to the enlisted man, second class petty officer, electronics expert, can come out of the Navy and be classed as a junior engineer and the offers he gets are far superior to what he's offered by staying in the Navy.

Q: Admiral, in the time you were there as Vice Chief and certainly during most of the decade of the fifties, the prevailing military attitude centered on the doctrine of massive retaliation. Would you talk about that and how the Navy tied in with this whole strategic policy?

Adm. F.: Yes, it's an interesting thought.

As I said, the Strategic Air Command was given the top priority position insofar as strategic thought and budget support was concerned. At that time in the Navy there was concern about the future of the carriers. In other words, tactical air had been sort of disregarded, the long-range strategic concept was paramount in people's minds - the delivery of these atomic or nuclear weapons - so the Navy decided they'd better compete and develop a capability of their own.

The Polaris we've already mentioned, the Polaris submarine, and also the development of techniques and airplane equipment that was capable of long-range delivery. Many presentations were made all over the place, showing curves and so forth, how the Navy could reach strategic targets. I don't know whether that caused carrier aviation to stay alive but it was a factor and, of course, a subject of great controversy. The Air Force, of course, pooh-poohing the whole idea, and I've already mentioned Curt coming up to the War College and saying in his view the Navy should have zero carriers.

The thought often intrigued me, however, that if Curt LeMay could have gotten carriers transferred to his Strategic Air Command, he would have loved the carriers!

Q: Well, I think of this policy of massive retaliation and what effect it probably had on the thinking of the average citizen in the United States. Did he not feel secure, hiding behind this policy, and was he in approval of it?

Adm. F.: I wouldn't know whether he felt secure, but everything is relative, of course. Let's put it a different way. I don't think he was terribly worried about the future prospect because he did feel, sure, that the United States power was supreme, and probably felt there's be no more wars of the kind which had been fought in the past. If there was ever to be another war it would be this horrible thing, and I think the strategic thinking in those days was, well, if somebody makes a mistake we've got the power to destroy. They haven't got it. We're supreme. And there was sort of a happy atmosphere, I suppose.

Q: Is there any relationship between that attitude and the atmosphere that prevailed and what your Texas friend said to you about the Navy doesn't really put its story across, talking about the need for more and more ships? Did the general public have this idea perhaps because they felt secure and there was no need for a larger and better navy?

Adm. F.: Possibly so. We tried to do something about this. I mentioned this business of the Navy going long-range-delivery-minded, but in addition to that we instigated a program, a public relations program, whereby then-Captain McCain traveled all around the United States with his Navy story, with graphics and all of this, to try to convince the public that there was another side to this, that their security depended in large measure on the Navy's ability to control the seas.

Q: Well, the balloon, so to speak, was pricked at the time of the Suez crisis, when we were confronted as a nation with a situation wherein massive retaliation probably was the answer, and we didn't do it?

Adm. F.: Well now, let's see. When you say the Suez crisis you're talking about 1958, I believe.

Q: Yes.

Adm. F.: That was after I had left the Pentagon and come out here. It resulted in our mustering the Sixth Fleet, augmenting the Sixth Fleet, and putting on an amphibious operation in Lebanon, as I recall. My son, incidentally, was there at that time flying over in those areas. It was squashed quickly by our show of power at that time, our prompt show of power, without, as I understood it, any threat of massive retaliation.

Q: Miller's of the opinion that this was a watershed time and this is what induced the Russians to change their ideas and policy and to go ahead and -

Adm. F.: Develop the navy, you mean?

Q: Yes.

Adm. F.: Might have been. In the days when I was Sixth Fleet commander we had some contacts with the Russians. Every once in a while they'd send a ship into the Mediterranean, not necessarily a cruiser or a destroyer but a ship of some type, and we made it our business to watch that fellow from beginning to end. In other words, from entry to exit.

There was also some thought that the Russians were infiltrating a submarine in there every once in a while. Not through the Bosporus and Dardanelles, but round from the Northern Fleet -

Q: Through Gib?

Adm. F.: Through Gib. So there were indications in those days - this was 1956 - that the Russians were spreading their wings, so to speak, or starting to spread their wings.

Q: Were there fishing trawlers in being at that time?

Adm. F.: Not like off the California coast or off the Atlantic coast, where the trawlers were around gathering information. Incidentally, that goes way back to the days when I was in the Houston. Every time ships would go out for gunnery practice or something like that, there was always a trawler hanging around.

Q: Admiral, you knew well in advance of your being named as CinCPac, that you were destined for that job, I believe? Do you want to tell me about the preliminaries to your appointment?

Adm. F.: Well, the lead-in to my appointment was interesting. Admiral Stump, who had been two-hatted, CinCPacFlt and CinCPac, had been directed by the Joint Chiefs to divest himself of the CinCPacFlt hat and set himself up separately as CinCPac. Admiral Stump had served beyond his sixty-second birthday, which was the retirement age according to law, and the President had extended him.

Arleigh and the Secretary of the Navy decided that they would nominate me as his relief, and there was quite an exchange between Arleigh and Felix as to how this should be done. Stump contending that I should be ordered first to CinCPacFlt so that I'd be familiar with the area and people with whom I'd associate and the Asians would know me. Arleigh and I, on the other hand, held to the view that if the nomination was to be approved the best place to build the foundation was right there in Washington. So we disagreed with Stump on this, and I stayed on as Vice Chief.

Arleigh made the nomination and it went through without any problems at all, catching, I believe, the other Chiefs somewhat short because they weren't prepared to make their own nominations at that time.

Q: Does this imply that there was some idea of rotation among the services?

Adm. F.: Oh, yes, that thought was very much on the front burner.

Felt #4 - 350

Q: Is this something that Burke couldn't accept? I mean the idea of rotation.

Adm. F.: Well, we didn't think it was a logical idea at all. CinCPac out here in the Pacific with ocean responsibilities and the significance of the fleet.

Anyhow, it went through.

Q: Why would the other services presume to think that it would be effective that way?

Adm. F.: They just held to the view that all of these jobs should be rotated. There wasn't any strategic substance to their argument. It was just, "Look, all of these big jobs should be rotated among the services, just like the chairman of the Joint Chiefs is rotated." That rotation, of course, didn't actually take place either. If you look at the history, there are more Army officers having served as chairman than the other services.

Q: Yes, it certainly isn't one, two, three, is it?

Adm. F.: No, it hasn't been that way. However, perhaps after my nomination had been approved - perhaps not - Arleigh said, "How about taking a trip out to the Pacific and the Far East?" which I did.

The first place I went, I believe, after I got out into

the Pacific area was the Philippines where Admiral Stump was conducting what he termed "a weapons demonstration."

Q: This was for SEATO?

Adm. F.: No, not necessarily for SEATO. This was an idea of his own which the State Department enthusiastically endorsed, to invite the senior officers of all of the services of all of the friendly countries, the free countries, out in that area to meet with him in Baguio and become acquainted, And then embark in the carrier and cruise up to Okinawa so that all these fellows could witness the carrier operations and get some appreciation of naval power. Into Okinawa where the Army put on a demonstration and the Marines put on a demonstration and the Air Force put on a demonstration.

I joined him at sea, off the Philippines, and met for the first time some of these senior Asian, Australian, New Zealand, Japanese, Chinese, and so forth officers. I stayed a day and a night and then flew off and went into Taiwan and paid my first call on the President of the Republic of China. In the course of this conversation he asked me about this weapons demonstration and I described it as best I could. I told him, of course, I'd met Tiger Wong there, and described the whole concept to him. He said,

"Why wasn't I invited?"

I said: "Well, Mr. President, yes, you are a five-star generalissimo, but you're also President and I think your presence would have overpowered the exchange of comradeship that takes place between three and four-star guys."

He accepted that.

Q: I would think your answer in that case qualified you eminently for politico-military relationships?

Adm. F.: I don't know, but that started a relationship that went on for years.

I continued on the trip and someplace along the line - I can't remember just where it was - the announcement came out that I had been appointed as CinCPac.

Q: You had prior to that been before the congressional committee, had you?

Adm. F.: No. All this required was Joint Chiefs' approval, SecDef's approval, and the President's approval.

Well, I went back and some time later came out to relieve Admiral Stump.

So that's the build-up to that.

Q: You were not new to this whole area of politico-military dealings, were you?

Adm. F.: I don't know why Admiral Stump felt so strongly that I had to be re-introduced to the Pacific. Maybe, he'd forgotten that I had served a considerable time in the Pacific in various capacities, but of course not in a four-star capacity and not dealing with the Asians' military and diplomatic people.

Q: But you wanted to make that tour on your own anyway, didn't you, just to see the lay of the land?

Adm. F.: Oh, yes, even if I weren't going to be appointed as CinCPac, it was a valuable thing for me as Vice Chief to do, and I suspect Admiral Stump - well, Admiral Stump was revered by his Asian contemporaries out there. There wasn't any question about that. SEATO had been organized -

Q: Almost under his aegis, hadn't it?

Adm. F.: Well, while he had the two hats, yes. CinCPac, you know, carried several hats - members of this, that, and the other thing, all these various arrangements made between the United States and these various countries, among them being the military advisor to SEATO. Perhaps one thing he had in his mind was that CinCPac was charged with administering the Military Assistance Program and, of course that meant dealing with presidents, right on down, as well as military officers.

There was some merit in his thought that I should be known by these people before I relieved him, but I don't believe Admiral Stump ever served in Washington. I don't believe that he understood the importance of the politics in Washington. In other words, nobody's going to be appointed as CinCPac unless he has generated in the Washington scene some feeling of confidence.

Q: And I suppose he has to have the approval of the State Department, doesn't he?

Adm. F.: I don't know whether that was necessary or not. I really don't know. I think it was a military-presidential decision, but you can speculate with some degree of assurance that it was discussed with the State Department because of all the diplomatic aspects of the job.

INDEX

to

VOLUME I of the

Reminiscences of

Admiral H. D. Felt, USN (Ret.)

Adm. H. D. Felt

AURAND, VADM E. P. (Pete): p 320.

BARNABY, Capt. Ralph: p 45-6.

BEARY, VADM Donald B.: President of the Naval War College, p 221-2; p 224.

BOMBING SQUADRON # 2: See entries under USS LEXINGTON: Felt takes over Squadron just after defects are corrected in O2-U - Vought, p 85; state of Squadron personnel, p 85-6; it becomes Hawaiian Detachment, p 87-8; participation in army maneuvers in Louisiana, p 88-90; hurricane forces evacuation, p 90-92; increased preparations for war (1941), p 94-5.

BROWN, Adm. Chas. R. (Cat): Nimitz sends him to the Naval War College as President, p 181-2.

BURKE, Adm. Arleigh: Becomes head of Strategic Plans Division in the Navy Department - Felt is # 2, p 256-8; 262; asks Felt to become VCNO, p 285 (See additional entries under Vice Chief of Naval Operations); Burke and the Joint Chiefs, p 323; p 325; p 349-50.

CAR DIV 3: April 1954 Felt takes command of attack Carrier Division 3, p 266 ff; Felt discourses on tactical operations, p 267-8; a search operation in Gulf of Tonkin, p 268; Felt's tour comes to an end in July, 1954, p 270.

CAR DIV 15: Felt takes command in June, 1953 - an A/S hunter/killer operation in the 7th fleet, p 263 ff; difficulties with helicopters, p 264-5.

CHENANGO - CVE: Felt takes command (Feb. 1945), p 164-5; kamikaze activity off Okinawa, p 166; escape from typhoon

Adm. H. D. Felt

p 167-8; taking aboard former U.S. prisoners of war after Japanese surrender, p 168-9; MAGIC CARPET operations, p 170-1; attitude of crew to demobilizations, p 173.

CHIANG Kai-chek, Generalissimo: Felt's first meeting with him, p 351-2.

CINC PAC: discussions about the appointment of Adm. Felt to succeed Adm. Stump in 1958, p 348-9; Adm. Burke sends Adm. Felt on a tour of the Far East after his nomination had been approved, p 350-4.

CROMMELIN, Capt. John: p 59-60.

DEMOBILIZATION: comments on too rapid demobilization after WW II, p 172-3; p 176.

EASTERN SOLOMONS: Battle of, p 108-111; sinking of Japanese carrier RYUJO, p 111; USS ENTERPRISE damaged in action, p 111; Felt reports on action to Adm. Nimitz and staff, p 112.

USS FARENHOLT: DD p 33-35; Australian cruise (1925), p 36-7; fruits of DD duty, p 38-39.

FELT, Adm. H. D.: Personal data, p 1-4; naval academy entrance, p 7; romance and marriage in Pensacola, p 43-4; family accommodations at San Diego, p 83; accidents in Hawaii, p 92-93.

USS FRANKLYN D. ROOSEVELT - CV: Felt takes command, June, 1948, p 194; previous command and state in which the Captain took over, p 195-6; preparations for Mediterranean duty, p 197;

Adm. H. D. Felt

cruising routine, p 199; characteristics of the FDR and her sister ships, p 203-4; gets her first jet engine squadron when she returns to Norfolk, p 206; lessons in ship handling, p 207; handling VIPs, p 209-210; Adm. Sherman's reaction to the cartoon of FDR on the ship's pick-up truck in Naples, p 214; preparation for shore leave, p 215; Felt and his enlisted personnel, p 216-7; an illustration of skill in towing exercise, p 287-8; p 289.

GUADALCANAL: USS SARATOGA participates in operations off Guadalcanal, p 106-7; Felt involved in maintaining control of air over Guadalcanal at time of U.S. landings, p 106-7 ff; SARATOGA's air group ordered ashore to assist Marines after the carrier was damaged, p 113.

HAWAII: preparations in the islands (1941), p 95-6; relaxation in number of reconnaissance flights, p 98.

HAYWARD, VADM John T.: (Chick) p 208.

HILL, Adm. Harry W.: p 185; p 190; his interest in carrier aviation, p 192-3.

USS HOUSTON: Felt joins her in the Brooklyn Navy Yard as senior aviator, p 67; flying activity in port, p 68-9; FDR joins ship for a fishing expedition in the Caribbean, p 69-70; a second fishing excursion of FDR, p 70-71; Felt's philosophy of keeping the crew informed of operation at hand, p 73-4; aviators come off with honors as watch officers, 74-5; Felt detached in two years and goes to North Island,

Adm. H. D. Felt

p 76; after Japanese surrender in 1945 - the rescue of ouston personnel who had been prisoners of war, p 169.

IRVIN, RADM Wm. D.: second in command to Felt in the new Operational Readiness Office in the Navy Department (July 1954), p 271.

JOHN XXIII - His Holiness: As a Cardinal his visit to flagship of the 6th fleet, p 290-91.

JOINT CHIEFS OF STAFF: Discussion of the system of Joint Chiefs and what was intended when they were set up, p 318-9; the VCNO often represented the CNO, p 321-2; necessity for intensive preparation for the sessions, p 323-4.

KING, Fleet Admiral Ernest J.: skipper of the USS LEXINGTON, (1929-30), p 49; Felt tangles with executive officer over a blanket order, p 50-1; near disaster with the fighters squadron from the LEXINGTON, p 51; at Pensacola, p 52.

LeMAY, Gen. Curtis: speaks at Naval War College, p 219.

USS LEXINGTON: Felt joins Scouting Squadron # 3 on her, p 46-8; formative state of dive bombing p 48-9; p 53-54; practice landings of the Squadron on the LANGLEY, p 57-8; night flying, p 64; record of an accident, p 65; p 97; Felt detached shortly after Pearl Harbor attack - takes the air group in the SARATOGA, p 100; returns to Pearl Harbor on Dec. 13 from Midway mission, p 102.

LUCE, The Hon, Clare Booth: p 286.

MAGIC CARPET: missions of the USS CHENANGO, p 170-171.

Adm. H. D. Felt

MALTA: 6th Fleet did not use Malta for repairs except in emergencies, p 286-7.

McCRARY, Capt. Frank: Commandant, Pensacola, p 56; p 60.

McELROY, The Hon, Neil H.: Secretary of Defense - takes over as SecDef from Wilson, p 314-5; Felt pays a call, p 315-6.

MIDDLE EAST FORCE: Felt in command from March, 1951 to October, 1951, p 233 ff; atmospheric conditions, p 234-5; local customs and visits, p 237-256; visit to Pakistan and India, p 248; American policy in the Middle East and dependency on oil, p 253-4.

USS MINNEAPOLIS: Felt ordered to her in Philadelphia as # 2 aviator - ship in process of commissioning, p 66; Felt reassigned as senior aviator on the USS HOUSTON, p 67.

MISSILES: See entries under VCNO.

USS MISSISSIPPI - BB: Felt's first duty, p 23-6; p 28-32; p 41; p 54; p 203.

NAGASAKI: Rescue operations there immediately after the surrender, p 169.

NATIONAL WAR COLLEGE: p 184-5; p 187; the story of Jacqueline Cochran and the general, p 187; p 189; organization into groups - social activities, p 191-2;

U.S. NAVAL ACADEMY: Plebe summer, 1919, p 7-9; comments on course of study, p 10-15; summer cruises, p 15-16; athletics, p 17-19; regulations, p 19-21.

NAVAL AIDE: Felt's concept of an Aide and his duties, p 60-63.

NAVAL AIR STATION, Daytona Beach: Felt takes command (Jan. 1943)

Adm. H. D. Felt

for training of dive bombing pilots, p 117.

NAVAL AIR STATION - North Island: Felt assigned to engine overhaul, p 78-9; a new engine overhaul plant is built and fitted out, p 78-9; engine manufacturers representatives present, p 80.

NAVAL AIR STATION, Opa-Locka (Miami): Felt takes command (July 1943) - training of various kinds involved, p 118; first time Felt has WAVES under his command - comments on their work, p 118-119; British pilots trained, p 119; problem with training command 'plow unders' (Instructors) as they prepared for combat duty, p 120-121; disciplinary policies, p 122; reserve training program, p 123.

NAVAL AVIATION: p 39-40; Pensacola training, 1928, p 41-44; gliders, p 45-6; Felt goes from Pensacola to the LEXINGTON and Scouting Sqaudron # 3, p 46; back to Pensacola (1931) as an instructor, p 55-57; developments in communications - BuAer asks for ideas, p 58; early precision teams, p 59-60; Felt becomes Executive Officer for a utility squadron based at North Island, p 76; plane ferry trips from coast to coast, p 82; striking power of the aircraft carrier, p 212-213; carrier aviation in the middle 1950s, p 344-5.

U.S. NAVAL MISSION - Moscow: Felt assigned as the Naval Aviator on Moscow Naval Mission staff (March 1944-Feb. 1945), p 124-6; vicissitudes of the journey from Washington, p 126-8; living accommodations in the U.S. Embassy, p 131-2;

Adm. H. D. Felt

visit to the Russian Fleet at Leningrad, p 133-6, p 147-8; special visit to the Crimea, p 136-8; Yalta, p 139-40; visit to U.S. prisoners of war camp, p 141-3; visit to Poltava and destination of U.S. bomber pilots on the Polesti raids, p 145-7; description of Felt's visit to Leningrad as recounted from a letter to his wife, p 149; Adm. Clarence Olsen effects a change in policy as it pertains to inspection trips, p 152-3; a theory about a last stand for the Japanese and suggestions that it influenced the Yalta agreements, p 153; Felt ordered to Pacific after Yalta Conference, returns in airplane of Secretary of State, p 154; Felt sent on temporary duty to relieve our representative at Archangel, p 155-7; another comment on this duty - from Felt's letter to his wife, p 172; illustration of Russian-American cooperation when the Second front became a reality, p 183-4.

U.S. NAVAL WAR COLLEGE: p 180-1; Felt's reaction to the correspondence course, p 182-3; Felt goes there as head of the Intelligence Department (July 1949 - March 1951) - takes charge of the lecture program, p 219 ff; Rickover as a guest p 218-9; LeMay as a guest, p 219; efforts to induce an understanding between services, p 219-30; improvement in the selection process for duty at the Naval War College, p 220-1; task of revising the curriculum, p 223; after retirement of Adm. Beary Felt serves for brief time as

Adm. H. D. Felt

Acting President until Adm. Conolly comes from CincNelm command, p 224; laying the ground work for use of computers, p 225-6; logistics course, p 224; the new course for junior officers, p 226; global strategy conferences, p 227; discussion of feedback to College from the Fleet, p 227-9; foreign students, p 229; use of "murder boards" p 230; classification of information, p 231.

NAVY LEAGUE: p 325-7.

NIMITZ, Fleet Admiral C. W.: orders Felt (Dec. 1941) to take over air group on the SARATOGA; p 100-1; Felt reports to him in person on the action in the Eastern Solomons, p 112; Nimitz and the Naval War College, (1945-6), p 179.

OFSTIE, VADM Ralph: In command of Sixth Fleet (1956) - relieved by Felt, p 273-4; P 280.

OLSEN, RADM Clarence: p 133; p 159-60.

OPERATIONAL READINESS: Felt called to organize the office in July, 1954, p 271-3.

PEARL HARBOR: Japanese attack on, p 96; wargame attack by U.S. Fleet on Pearl Harbor in spring of 1940 (Sunday a.m.) caught everybody off guard, p 97; probably reported by the Japanese Consul, p 97-8.

PENSACOLA: see entries under Naval Aviation.

PERSONNEL WORK - Op.54: Jan. 1946-July 1947, p 173-4; special problem in selecting students for the National War College, p 174-5; problems of officer re-assignment, p 177; illustration of promotional system, p 181-2.

PHILLIPS, VADM Sol: Commander of the First Fleet (1954), p 266; p 268-9.

PIRIE, VADM Robert Burns: p 281.

POLARIS: Adm. Burke's decision on the original number, p 304-5; p 309.

PUBLIC RELATIONS - p 327-8; the Navy and its public image, p 330-1.

RABORN, VADM Wm. F. Jr.: p 309.

RAMSEY, Adm. D. C. (Duke): skipper of the SARATOGA off Guadalcanal, p 107; becomes flag officer and chief of BuAer (1943), p 121.

RICKOVER, Adm Hyman George: speaks at Naval War College, p 218-9; nuclear power, p 303; attitude towards the North Pole expedition of NAUTILUS, p 303.

RIVERS, The Hon, Mendel: p 335-7.

RUSSIA: U.S. Lease-Lend program, p 155; p 159-61.

USS SARATOGA: Felt ordered by Adm. Nimitz to take over air group on the SARATOGA (Dec. 1941) - skipper objects and is overruled, p 100-1; training in the Pacific south of Oahu, (Jan. 1942) torpedoed, p 105; Felt takes part of air group with him to West Coast to assist with a training project, p 105; returns to Hawaii but misses Midway action, p 106; torpedoed off Guadalcanal - taken to Tongatabu for temporary repairs, p 113; Felt ordered to Pearl Harbor to organize a new air group for SARATOGA, p 113-4; SARATOGA and her new

Adm. H. D. Felt

group return to south Pacific with Capt. Bogan in command, p 116-7; see also entry under GUADALCANAL.

SIXTH FLEET: Felt takes over from Ofstie, April 1956, p 275 ff; British Admiral in Malta suggests a combined command, p 276-7; birth of the idea of a "quarantine" instead of a blockade, p 277-8; rotation of fleet units, p 279-81; diplomatic duties, p 281; commander, 6th fleet also has NATO responsibilities, p 284-5; 286; exchange of visits with the Cardinal in Venice, p 289-90; diplomatic affairs, 292-3; Cypress reactions in Greece, p 293; a naval visit to Israel, p 294-5.

SLED-RECOVERY SYSTEM: for retrieving airplanes landing at sea, p 69; p 71.

STALINGRAD: Felt visits city shortly after successful defense by the Russians, p 129.

STETTINIUS, The Hon, Edward R. Jr.: Secretary of State, p 154; p 163-4.

STRATEGIC PLANS SECTION - Op. 30: Adm. Burke as # 1 and Felt as # 2 - Oct. 1951 to June, 1953 - reliance on intelligence reports, p 260; dealing with force levels, p 261.

STUMP, Adm. Felix: His system of handling VIP's as ComAirLant, p 209-10; CincP-cFlt (1954), p 266, 268; he wanted Felt named first as CincPacFlt before becoming CincPac, p 349; conducts a weapons demonstration in the Far East, p 351-3.

TOLLEY, RADM Kemp: p 126, 131.

TRUMAN, The Hon, Harry S.: President of the U.S. - p 317-8.

-10-

Adm. H. D. Felt

USO: Value of the organization to the fleet in the Mediterranean, p 289.

VICE CHIEF OF NAVAL OPERATIONS: Felt named as VCNO to Adm. Burke, p 285; carried the full powers of the Chief, p 298-9; relationship with Joint Chiefs and Sec Def, p 299-300; the budgeting process, p 300-1; efforts to "break down the barriers" between branches of the Navy, p 301-2; ship building program, p 304-5; discussions over missiles vs guns in new construction, p 305-8; relationship of CNO and Chief of Material bureaus, p 310-1; conventional carriers vs nuclear carriers, p 311-3; Felt represents the CNO at Joint Chief meetings, p 321-2; Felt's attitude towards his role, p 325; Public Relations, p 327-8; need for clearance of speeches, p 328-330; Congressional Committee appearances, p 333-4; shore insta lations, p 334-5; problem of closing down certain installations, p 337-8; concern for merchant shipping, p 339-40; plans for use of computors in the CICs of ships and elsewhere, p 342-3; technical training requirements, p 343.

VIP's: The Fleet and VIPs, p 209-212.

WILSON, The Hon, Charles: SecDef - his Quantico Conferences, p 314.

ZONDARAK, RADM Charles J.: accomplies Felt to Moscow to join naval mission - a Russian language student, p 126; p 130-1; p 146-7.

ZUMWALT, Adm Elmo: his efforts to restore morale in the modern navy, p 27-8.

www.ingramcontent.com/pod-product-compliance
Lightning Source LLC
Chambersburg PA
CBHW082149070526
44585CB00020B/2149